Conversations with Czeslaw Milosz

CONVERSATIONS

WITH

CZESLAW
MILOSZ

by
Ewa Czarnecka and
Aleksander Fiut

Translated by Richard Lourie

HARCOURT BRACE JOVANOVICH, PUBLISHERS

SAN DIEGO   NEW YORK   LONDON

HBJ

Rozmowy z Czesławem Miłoszem by Aleksander Fiut copyright ©
1981 by Wydawnictwo Literackie, Kraków.
Podróżny świata: Rozmowy z Czesławem Miłoszem by Ewa Czar-
necka was first published in the Polish language in 1983.
English translation copyright © 1987 by Ewa Czarnecka, Aleksander
Fiut, and Czeslaw Milosz.

Library of Congress Cataloging-in-Publication Data
Conversations with Czeslaw Milosz.
    Translation of: Podróżny świata / Ewa Czarnecka, and Rozmowy z
Czesławem Miłoszem / Aleksander Fiut, with new material.
    1. Miłosz, Czesław—Interviews.   2. Miłosz,
Czesław—Criticism and interpretation.   3. Authors,
Polish—20th century—Interviews.   I. Miłosz, Czesław.
II. Czarnecka, Ewa.   III. Fiut, Aleksander.   IV. Lourie,
Richard, 1940–   .   V. Czarnecka, Ewa, Podróżny
świata. English. 1987.   VI. Fiut, Aleksander.
Rozmowy z Czesławem Miłoszem. English. 1987.
PG7158.M5532A33   1987   891.8'58709   86-33550
ISBN 0-15-122591-5

Designed by Francesca M. Smith
Printed in the United States of America
First United States edition
A B C D E

*Permission acknowledgments appear on page 331, which constitutes a
continuation of the copyright page.*

Contents

Chronology of Czeslaw Milosz's Life and Works

1911 Czeslaw Milosz* is born on June 30 in Szetejnie (or Šeteiniai, in Kėdainiai District, Lithuania), to Weronika née Kunat and Aleksander Milosz, a highway engineer.

1914–1918 Aleksander Milosz is drafted into the tsar's army after the outbreak of World War I. As a combat engineer officer, he builds bridges and fortifications in front-line areas. His wife and son accompany him in his constant travels about Russia. The Milosz family returns to Lithuania in 1918.

1921 Czeslaw Milosz enters the Zygmunt August High School in Wilno (Vilnius [Lithuanian], Vilna [Russian]).

1929 After graduation, Milosz matriculates in the law department of Stefan Batory University in Wilno; he is active in the Polish Studies Literary Club.

1930 Milosz publishes his first poems in *Alma Mater Vilnensis*, a university periodical.

1931 Milosz becomes a co-founder and member of the literary group Żagary. He is also active in the Vagabonds Club and participates in summer travels to Western Europe with

---

*In Polish orthography, Czesław Miłosz. Throughout this book, the diacritics have been omitted in his name because of accepted English usage.—TRANS.

other students. This is his first time in Paris, where he meets his cousin Oskar Milosz, the French poet.

1933   The Polish Studies Club of Stefan Batory University publishes *Poem on Frozen Time*, Milosz's first volume of poetry. With Zbigniew Folejewski, he co-edits *Anthology of Social Poetry*, also published in Wilno.

1934   Milosz receives his Master of Law degree. The Union of Polish Writers gives his poetry the first Philomath Literary Award in Wilno. A grant from the National Cultural Fund allows him to spend a year in France, for which he leaves in the fall.

1935   In Paris, Milosz studies at the Alliance Française and audits lectures on Thomism at L'Institut Catholique. Among other poems, he writes "Hymn" and "Gates of the Arsenal."

1936   After returning from France, Milosz begins work as a literary programmer at Polish Radio in Wilno. The Union of Polish Writers helps him publish his second volume of poetry, *Three Winters*.

1937   After being dismissed from Radio Wilno for his leftist views, Milosz travels to Italy. On his return he takes a job in the planning office of Polish Radio in Warsaw. He publishes poems and articles in literary periodicals.

1938   Oskar Milosz's translation of "A Song" ("Un Chant") appears in the French journal *Cahiers du Sud*, the first translation of a poem by Czeslaw Milosz. His short story "Reckoning" wins a prize in a competition sponsored by the journal *Pion*.

1940   Milosz escapes from Soviet-occupied Wilno to Nazi-occupied Warsaw, where he joins the socialist resistance. In Warsaw he publishes a volume of poetry, "Poems," in mimeograph form under the pen name of Jan Syruć. In 1941 he is given a job as a janitor at the Warsaw University Library.

1942   Milosz's anthology of anti-Nazi poetry, *The Invincible Song*, and his translation of Jacques Maritain's pro—

de Gaulle *À travers le désastre* are published by underground presses in occupied Warsaw.

1943 He writes "The World: A Naïve Poem" and the cycle *The Voices of Poor People*, and translates Shakespeare's *As You Like It* on commission from the Underground Theatre Council. He also takes part in clandestine poetry readings.

1944 After the destruction of Warsaw, he spends a few months in Goszyce, near Cracow, in the family home of his friend Jerzy Turowicz. He writes a number of poems there.

1945 Milosz moves to Cracow. He publishes poems and articles in the literary press. The state publishing house Czytelnik brings out his collected poems in a volume entitled *Rescue*. He leaves for the United States in December to assume a diplomatic post.

1946 Milosz works in the Polish consulate in New York. His poems of this period include "Child of Europe."

1947 Milosz is transferred to Washington as a cultural attaché. He writes *Treatise on Morals*, published the following year in the journal *Twórczość*. He is a correspondent for the literary press in Poland and translates poetry into Polish.

1949 Milosz makes a brief trip to Poland in the summer. He is shocked at the full dimension of the system's totalitarianism.

1950 Milosz is transferred to the post of first secretary of the Polish embassy in Paris. He travels to Warsaw at the end of the year, and his passport is taken away.

1951 The passport is returned. Milosz goes back to Paris, where on February 1 he asks the French government for political asylum. He moves to Maisons-Laffitte and publishes his first article as an émigré. Entitled "No," it appears in the May issue of *Kultura*. He begins work on *The Captive Mind*.

1953 *The Captive Mind* is Milosz's first book published by the Polish-language Instytut Literacki in Paris. There are concurrent translations in English and French. His novel *The*

Seizure of Power (*La Prise du pouvoir*) is awarded the Swiss book guilds' prize, the Prix Littéraire Européen. The Instytut Literacki publishes *The Light of Day,* Milosz's first volume of poetry as an émigré.

1955   Instytut Literacki publishes *The Seizure of Power;* Milosz's second novel, *The Issa Valley,* and his translation of Jeanne Hersch's philosophical essays *Politics and Reality.*

1957   Instytut Literacki publishes *A Treatise on Poetry* in book form. Milosz is awarded *Kultura*'s annual literary prize.

1958   Milosz publishes his autobiography *Native Realm,* a volume of his essays and his translations of poetry, *Continents,* and his translation of Simone Weil's *Selected Writings.* He receives the award of the Union of Polish Émigré Writers.

1960   Milosz moves to the United States to assume the position of lecturer in the department of Slavic languages and literatures at the University of California at Berkeley. Soon thereafter he accepts a professorship and for the next twenty years combines his writing with teaching at the university.

1962   Milosz publishes *King Popiel and Other Poems* and his study of Stanisław Brzozowski, *Man Among Scorpions* (Instytut Literacki).

1965   His seventh volume of poetry, *Bobo's Metamorphosis,* is published by Instytut Literacki. He also publishes poems he has selected and translated into English, *Post-War Polish Poetry: An Anthology.*

1967   Oficyna poetów i Malarzy (The Poets' and Painters' Press) in London publishes an extensive selection of Milosz's poems in a volume entitled *Poems.* He receives the Marian Kister Literary Award in New York.

1968   *Native Realm: A Search for Self-Definition* is published in the United States. Milosz receives the Jurzykowski Award.

1969 His next volume of poetry, *City Without a Name*, and a collection of essays, *Visions from San Francisco Bay*, are published in Polish by Instytut Literacki. His textbook, *The History of Polish Literature*, is published in the United States.

1972 Instytut Literacki publishes *Private Obligations*, a collection of literary essays.

1973 The Seabury Press in New York publishes the first volume of Milosz's poetry in English, *Selected Poems*, reissued in a revised version by The Ecco Press in 1982.

1974 Milosz publishes the volume of poetry *From the Rising of the Sun* (Instytut Literacki). The Polish P.E.N. Club awards him its prize for his translations of Polish poetry into English.

1976 Milosz receives a Guggenheim Fellowship to pursue work on his own poetry and his translations.

1977 The University of Michigan Slavic Publications publishes an extensive selection of his poems in Polish under the title *Utwory poetyckie: Poems*. The University of Michigan at Ann Arbor confers an honorary doctorate on Milosz. Instytut Literacki publishes *The Land of Ulro*. A collection of essays entitled *The Emperor of the Earth: Modes of Eccentric Vision* and Milosz's English translation of Aleksander Wat's *Mediterranean Poems* are published in the United States. *My Century*, Wat's memoirs as taped in conversation with Milosz, is published in London.

1978 Milosz receives the Neustadt International Literary Prize, presented under the auspices of Oklahoma State University. For his literary and academic merits, the University of California presents Milosz with the Berkeley Citation. The second volume of his poetry in English translation, *Bells in Winter*, is published in the United States.

1979 Éditions du Dialogue in Paris publishes Milosz's translation of the Book of Psalms from Hebrew to Polish, for which he receives the Zygmunt Hertz Award. *The Gar-*

den of Knowledge, a collection of essays and translations of foreign poetry into Polish, is published by Instytut Literacki.

1980 Éditions du Dialogue publishes Milosz's translation from Hebrew to Polish of the Book of Job.

Milosz is awarded the Nobel Prize. Books of his poetry are published in Poland for the first time since 1945. Instytut Literacki begins publishing a multivolume edition of Milosz's *Collected Works.*

1981 In June Milosz visits Poland for the first time in thirty years. He receives an honorary doctorate from Lublin Catholic University; he meets with Lech Wałęsa and other Solidarity leaders in Gdańsk. An exhibit devoted to his life and work opens at the Literary Museum in Warsaw. A bilingual, Polish-English edition of the Nobel lecture Milosz delivers to the Swedish Academy in December 1980 is published.

Milosz holds the Eliot Norton chair at Harvard and gives six public lectures on poetry. He is awarded an honorary doctorate by New York University.

1982 Instytut Literacki publishes his tenth volume of poetry, *Hymn to a Pearl.* Éditions du Dialogue publishes his translation of *The Books of Five Megiloth* (that is, Lamentations, Ruth, Esther, Ecclesiastes, and Song of Songs).

1983 Milosz receives an honorary doctorate from Brandeis University. His lectures at Harvard appear under the title *The Witness of Poetry.*

1984 A new volume of translated poems, *The Separate Notebooks,* is published in a bilingual, Polish-English edition. *Unattainable Earth* is published in Polish by Instytut Literacki. Éditions du Dialogue publishes his translations, from the Greek, of the Gospel According to Mark and the Apocalypse.

1985 *Starting with My Streets,* a new volume of essays, is published in Polish by Instytut Literacki.

1986 *Unattainable Earth* is published in English.

Conversations with Czeslaw Milosz

Part One

Part One

Home

FIUT In your Nobel lecture, you pronounced a few blessings, one of which concerned Lithuania. You said: "It is good to be born in a small country where nature is on a human scale, where various languages and religions have coexisted for centuries. I am thinking here of Lithuania, a land of myth and poetry." That's how you saw Lithuania after many years, from the vantage of the Nobel Prize. But what was Lithuania to you when you were a boy? Can you cast your mind back to that period, your early childhood?

MILOSZ It's very difficult to reconstruct the perceptions you had at one age or another. We usually project back from the present. Even our ideas and the books we've read transform reality—our outlook on reality is constantly shaped by literature. Many things in the world are shaped by literature, even where one would least suspect it. The trials and hangings of the witches in Salem resulted from a book about witches by Cotton Mather. The book was widely read, and women under its influence came to believe they were possessed. That's how it started. It all came from a book.

Let's not deceive ourselves: the image of the country where you live is formed by literature in the same way. Very early on I was exposed to literature about Lithuania that had orig-

3

inated in Poland during the romantic period of Polish literature. Since we're talking about literature, I must tell you of
my first encounter with *Pan Tadeusz*.* I had bones to pick
with Mickiewicz, because at the time I had no feel for literature, only for nature. And so I sensed that something was out
of joint. Specifically that nature, to which I wanted to devote
my life, served his poem as an ornament and as a structural
element. Either you can have a totally direct relationship to
nature, or you can have literature. But there was something
wrong about transforming nature for literary purposes. That
was my first complaint. It wasn't put into words, but I sensed
it, I think, the way I'm expressing it now. My second complaint was even stranger. Namely—what landscape was he
in fact describing? It wasn't just like ours! I had an incredibly
strong sense of exclusivity, of local patriotism, as far as landscape, vegetation, and trees were concerned. I considered
sandy pine forests inferior. Real fauna, real vegetation, meant
the wilderness, a mixed forest growing in good soil, like in
my region, by the Niewiaża River.

I said that literature shaped my perception of Lithuania.
There were other elements as well, and I've written about
them often—fierce patriotism, for example. A patriotism of
a sort that might be found in Great Britain. The patriotism of
the Scots, whose language is English but who say: "We are
not English, we are Scotsmen." We had a strong sense of that.
Our antagonism to what were called "Crown Poles" and
"Galicians" was very strong. We were something else, Lithuanians, but not in the accepted twentieth-century sense, which
says that to be a Lithuanian you have to speak Lithuanian.
That aspect certainly had a strong effect, and on that point
the analogies between Scotland and Lithuania could probably not be any closer.

---

* *Pan Tadeusz* by Adam Mickiewicz (1798–1855), a long poem, something between a novel in verse and an epic, written in exile in Paris (1834).
Its place in Polish literature is similar to that of *Don Quixote* in Spanish
literature and *Eugene Onegin* in Russian. —TRANS.

FIUT   So, then, which of your family traditions were connected with Polish history, and which with Lithuanian history?

MILOSZ   Lithuania as a separate state was just in the making then, and this is described in the correspondence between Oskar Milosz and Christian Gauss that I discovered in the Princeton University Library. It shows how Oskar Milosz became a Lithuanian. Before the First World War he belonged to the Society of Polish Artists in Paris, but in 1918, during the Versailles Conference, he suddenly learned that the Poles were against recognizing Lithuania's independence. That made him furious. He said, "In that case, I'm a Lithuanian." He was completely unaware of the existence of a Lithuanian national movement and only learned of it later, after declaring himself. Lithuanians came to him and said, "But there's a whole Lithuanian national movement." It had existed throughout the nineteenth century, constantly growing. But God forbid anyone in our house should know of it—out of the question! On the other hand, there was the history of Poland. My grandmother, ethnically a Lithuanian type—you couldn't imagine anyone more Lithuanian, you could tell by her face she was Lithuanian—was a patriot of Cracow. Because Cracow was the true center, where one could imbibe a pure Polish. And like all the other ladies she brought her daughters to Cracow—that must have been in 1908.

FIUT   Was the anti-Russian Uprising of 1863 still alive in your family tradition?

MILOSZ   On the Milosz side, not the Syruć side. The Kunats couldn't have had any such tradition. My grandfather came from the south—Krasnogruda, their farm, was much farther south—and they didn't seem at all interested in the Uprising there. My mother's family, the Syrućes, was a matriarchy, because, after the death of her husband, who was killed in a railroad accident near Baden-Baden—one of the first railroad accidents—my grandmother assumed control of the farm, beginning a line of resourceful women who ran their own estates. Military matters played no role for them. On the other hand, they did for the Miloszes. During the 1863 Uprising, my grandfather Artur Milosz was Sierakowski's aide-de-camp. Sierakowski was one of the commanding officers in Lithuania, and he was hanged on Łukiszki Square in Wilno. And I used to cross Sierakowski Street, near Łukiszki Square, every day on my way to school. When the Uprising collapsed, my grandfather, my father's father, simply returned to his estate and pretended nothing had ever happened. But the Russians came after him, and a case was brought against him to determine if he had been away from home. Russian colonists, Old Believers, lived in the next village over, and they saved his life by swearing that he had never left home.

FIUT   When did the tradition of the Grand Duchy of Lithuania truly come alive for you?

MILOSZ   You see, to be honest, I think people have an enormous need for mythology. It's a constant need. You know Cracow, you know how many myths are born and cultivated there. Ultimately all patriotism is sustained by mythology. The myth of the trumpeter in Saint Mary's tower, the Wilno myth of the passages beneath the city that led to the castle in Troki—local legends, animosities. I'm not a computer, and it's fantastically difficult to re-create all the elements. All this certainly was the substratum that, when transferred to a greater political area, caused Piłsudski to be so stubborn and contemptuous when he was in Belvedere Palace. A Lithuanian ruling Poles, with their light, breezy temperament. At home they used to say that Poles, those "Crown Poles," were "straw fires," whereas we were substantial, stubborn people. For all I know this might have influenced me not to quit studying law, which I found utterly disgusting. I graduated and received my diploma so as not to be open to the accusation of being like a "Crown Pole."

FIUT   You belong to the social class that still grew up in manor houses and basically belonged to the nineteenth century—the intelligentsia of gentry origin.

MILOSZ   It's not true that my origins are in the nineteenth century; they're in the seventeenth. I was in Salem recently looking at the seventeenth-century houses. And I said to myself, That's where I belong. That's no more exotic than restoring a manor house in Szetejnie and showing it to tourists. It would be exactly the same thing. There were various wooden implements, farm tools—for combing flax or churning butter, for example. Everything exactly the same as in Lithuania. I was amazed by a bedspread whose design was absolutely Lithuanian. The loom there was exactly like the one in Szetejnie. And so, of course, it's in that sense that my origins are in the seventeenth century. Things changed very slowly in past centuries. It's today that we're subjected to acceleration. . . .

   In the coach house in Szetejnie there were various vehicles that were never used: carriages, the most bizarre vehicles, made of leather, wood. Sometimes I would crawl in there, sit on the seats, and play. Naturally, they were all from the eighteenth century—not even the nineteenth. On the other hand, as far as the various workshops go, that's something I wouldn't be able to describe accurately, because I only heard about them. Szetejnie, too, had been touched by the Organic Work Movement* sometime toward the end of the nineteenth century. There was a plan to begin producing wool. Speaking of wool, there were weaving workshops, old ones, where wool was made. But I remember a large weaving workshop, and I re-

---

*A movement that arose after 1863, calling for economic and cultural development as a solution to Poland's problems—chief among them the loss of political independence in the late eighteenth century. The movement was influential throughout the nineteenth century, during which Poland attempted twice, in 1830 and 1863, to regain its independence through uprisings. These were unsuccessful; Poland did not become a sovereign state again until 1918. —TRANS.

member the board used for fulling the cloth. When I was a child there were no businesses in the area, but I do know that the peasants from the vicinity brought in their hand-made homespun cloth, for fulling.

FIUT   Did your grandparents deal with their farm personally, or did they have tenants? What was the economy of Szetejnie?

MILOSZ   My grandfather and grandmother can't be said to have worked. My grandmother didn't do anything. She was a dreamer; she'd lock herself up in the room with her prie-dieu and her holy pictures, which were quite beautiful and represented various Catholic saints. That was her own world, her own life. It's hard to know what she thought about. She was charming, in a world of her own. My grandfather dealt with the farm, but what did that mean? It meant the work was done by the farm hands who lived in rows of small houses that may not have been as good as the usual houses in Lithuania, which were large and very comfortable. The farm hands' quarters were the size of the houses on the flats in Berkeley. The farm hands worked on the manor. In exchange they were given a little house and were paid in kind, in farm products. Most likely they got some money, too, but not a lot. Payment in kind, meaning grain and potatoes, was the mainstay of their existence. Those farm hands were the basis of the estate. There were also a few servants and plowboys who didn't have homes or families and lived on the estate. There was a large servants' hall where they went for their meals. It was a separate building that contained the stable, the carriage house, and at one end the steward Sypniewski's lodgings. The servants' hall was Paulina's domain. The flies were so thick there that you couldn't see the walls, because the servants' hall was connected to the dairy, where butter was churned and sour cream was made. The walls weren't white but black, one solid mass of flies. That was where the people who ate at the servants'-hall table went. There weren't that many of them—a few more at harvest time.

FIUT   Would you be able to describe your memory of the manor house in Szetejnie, which doesn't exist any longer?

MILOSZ   I think those buildings were built in the eighteenth century. For a long time manor houses were built of wood; then that was replaced by stone and plaster. My grandfather's house was made of wood and brick. So unfortunately constructed that it was damp and very cold inside.

FIUT   How was the manor laid out? How would you describe entering it from the main entrance?

MILOSZ   First you entered the porch through the little columns. It was warm on the porch; in summer and fall a great many seeds, mainly flower seeds, were set there to dry. When the nasturtiums, for example, were mature, all the seeds were shaken onto cloth sheets. The porch was covered. Then you entered the house, actually the hallway. To the right was the parlor, actually two of them. They had parquet floors, always clean and waxed. There was a piano, and the furniture was covered with slipcovers. I would get the chills when I ventured in there. I could sense the ghosts. A main parlor and a small parlor, probably in Empire style. Everything there was as clean as could be, untouched. No one ever used them. When you entered the hallway you faced what we called the "chimney"—the toilet—which was used only in the winter: a wooden seat over an abyss. A red brick floor. It was very stately, and the stink was subdued because it was rarely used even in the winter. The dining room was to the left. The couch covered in oilcloth that I described in *The Issa Valley* was in that room. The couch on which I was initiated into Sienkiewicz's *Trilogy*. In 1918, my cousin Marysia Pawlikowska came to Szetejnie. A tall girl, very *fin de siècle*, with a black ribbon around her neck, she read me Sienkiewicz on that couch. The dining room was impossible to use in the winter and was kept locked. It wasn't used very much, though I do remember having dinner served there and entertaining guests there before the First World War, when I was three years old. That was when I fell in love with Ela. I was three years old at the time. My first *passion d'amour*. Farther on, past the dining room, was what was supposed to be a guest room, but no guests ever stayed there, because it was damp and terribly cold. Then came the library, with shelves built into the wall, incredible stacks of books, vellum, illustrations. It was there that I first laid eyes on color illustrations from the first half of the nineteenth century, 1840 and so on. All sorts of fashion magazines, pictures of blacks and Brazil and other such things. There must have been a set of Mickiewicz's works there as well.

FIUT   Didn't you transpose some aspects of that manor house to "The World" as well as to *The Issa Valley*?

MILOSZ   I should say so. I was talking about the dining room. Right off the dining room was the door to the corridor that led to the kitchen—just like a Dutch painting! Szetejnie is straight from a Dutch painting. If you take the light, the way the room looked, even the paintings on the wall—some landscapes, as far as I remember—it was all seventeenth-century Holland.

FIUT   And was that also where the copper pans were hung?

MILOSZ   Yes. Absolutely! And then there was the most magical place of all in Szetejnie—the apothecary. Good God! Now that apothecary seems the source of all my poetry. Its walls were lined with drawers. And in a certain place, on a sort of counter on top of the drawers, there was a mousetrap composed of an incline and a water tank. When a mouse took the bait, some bacon, a trap door opened and it fell into the water. There were various brass pots, the wonderful gold color of vermillion, on the shelves, and various ingredients and scents in the drawers—ginger and so on. Those vermillion-colored pots along with those scents—it's pure Chardin! Chardin and Dutch painting. That's the key to my fondness for Dutch still lifes and Chardin.

FIUT   What was life in the manor like?

MILOSZ   Excuse me, but I am not the product of the manor, and I suppose that my class position, a very indefinite one, was the result of my never having really experienced gentry culture. Not like the other students in my gymnasium, as it was called then, who were the pure products of gentry manors. My father was no longer a landowner but a highway engineer, and so our connections with manor life were quite marginal. There were my grandparents, of course. But my grandparents had no manorial tradition. In Lithuania, especially in our part, there were a great many so-called eccentrics, meaning people who lived as they saw fit and paid absolutely no attention to any of the conventions. My grandfather paid them no attention, and neither did my grandmother.

FIUT   Does that mean that no gentry traditions were observed in the manor in Szetejnie?

MILOSZ   A very interesting question. There were no gentry traditions, since my grandparents were ill-disposed to all that, for reasons of a rather personal nature. My grandmother, that dreamer, could not bear guests; moreover, she couldn't abide regular meals. I've described all that in *The Issa Valley*. And so there was no socializing, or very little. Naturally, that was something that had changed over the course of time. It was probably different when my mother and my aunt were young. In any case, it's worth mentioning that in the Niewiaża valley—a very beautiful valley—there were manors and parks terraced down to the river. A manor had been built every mile or so. On both sides of the river. But my grandfather was a graduate of the Main School, quite Positivistic in his outlook, and he definitely took all those gentry traditions with a grain of salt. Besides, as far as Szetejnie is concerned, there was, as I've said, a tradition of matriarchy, and no place for male traditions. My grandfather, a gentle man, had no great liking for them. There was more of that on my father's side of the family.

FIUT   I'm interested in the manor's agricultural and liturgical year. Do you remember the holidays? Which traditions were maintained, Lithuanian or Polish?

MILOSZ   Naturally, we celebrated Christmas and Easter at home, not only in the country, but when we lived in Wilno as well. All the ritual preparations for the Christmas dinner, the traditional dishes, the Easter dishes hallowed by tradition, we children picking the raisins out of the Easter cake, we did all that regularly. What else? Rolling eggs.

FIUT   What was that, rolling eggs?

MILOSZ   It's a very common thing. I don't understand why I have to explain what rolling eggs means. First the eggs are painted different colors, usually with onion skins, to shade the eggs brown. Sometimes people would buy dyes. Rolling eggs is . . . Take this rug; it's very good for rolling eggs. You make a slope to roll the egg down. I roll mine down; then the other player rolls his down so that it makes the right sort of turn and hits my egg. If he hits my egg, he takes it. The trick is to calculate the angle of the slope and the special features of each egg so that it rolls and hits the other one.

FIUT   How about Palm Sunday? Did people bring palm leaves to church?

MILOSZ   Of course they did! You should be aware that making so-called palm leaves was a whole folk industry. The architecture of those palm leaves was very complex. They were made from various plants, and flowers that were colored and dried. Wilno palm leaves.

FIUT   Do you recall any other local customs?

MILOSZ   You astound me. To me it all seems so close. . . .
In America they have Halloween, the night of the witches. Pumpkins are hollowed out and lighted candles placed inside.

I did the same thing when I was little. The fact that this custom exists in America, the identical custom, after all those years, all those centuries, is a very curious thing. Probably, it came to America from England. It's part of Europe's pagan past.

FIUT   Was that custom connected with All Saints' Day?

MILOSZ   All Souls' Day and All Saints' Day were, after all, introduced by the Church to more or less coincide with the time when the pagans celebrated the day of the dead, so as not to deprive the pagans of their customs entirely. It was the same in England—those are remnants of the cult of the dead, of ancestor worship.

FIUT   Could you try to sketch a sociological map of the region of Lithuania that has Szetejnie at its center? You said that social visits were somewhat rare, but you must have known how people in the area socialized, didn't you?

MILOSZ   I'll try to be as accurate as possible. The point is that, as I remember, what was called visiting, what was called socializing, was an extremely rare exception in Szetejnie. People avoided the manor in Szetejnie, bypassed it, because eccentrics lived there. In fact, I had no access to regular Polish manor life. So, if Szetejnie could be said to have had any influence on my life, it was because it gave me the feeling of growing up in a forester's cottage.

FIUT   People spoke Polish and observed Polish traditions in Szetejnie. Was the population in the surrounding area Lithuanian or Lithuanian-Bielorussian?

MILOSZ   There was no question of any Bielorussian element in that world. Kiejdany is the heart of Lithuania, and there were never any Bielorussians there. The question of the Bielorussians and the Bielorussian language in Lithuania requires special comment. Historical circumstances were such that—in the Wilno area, for example—Lithuanian villages would often have Bielorussian villages next to them. Around Wilno there was some contact and connection with the Bielorussian element, which extended east all the way to Polotsk and Vitebsk, but Wilno was its westernmost outpost. The usual situation was that there'd be a Lithuanian village here and a Bielorussian one across from it. People came into contact, they intermarried. Gradually, over decades or perhaps centuries, a Lithuanian village would become a Bielorussian-speaking village. Bielorussian was more practical, in that it was a Slavic language, whereas Lithuanian was incredibly isolating, cut off from everything. Since the Bielorussian villages spoke a Slavic language, they were open to Polonization. A well-known phenomenon. I'm not saying anything new or different here. None of it's any secret to Lithuanian historians: the retreat of the Lithuanian element and the Polonization of the countryside, not directly but first through a Bielorussian phase, and then going from the Bielorussian language to Polish. And that's the reason for the Polish-speaking villages ringing Wilno. Over the course of several generations, the population there had gone through a series of phases—its culture changing from Lithuanian to Bielorussian to Polish.

FIUT   In what period did that process occur?

MILOSZ   Over the course of a few centuries. But it should be remembered that the Baltic-language element stretched very far east. Marija Gimbutas, a colleague of mine from the University of California at Los Angeles who specializes in Indo-European archeology, has shown that areas as far as Moscow were once occupied by Balts, as can be seen from the names of various rivers and so forth. The Lithuanian element retreated, gradually ousted by the Slavs. My region, the Kiejdany district was, for the most part, never affected by the Bielorussian element. The language of the educated class is a different matter. As you're no doubt aware, Old Bielorussian was the official language of the Grand Duchy of Lithuania.

My family documents—those from the sixteenth century, for example—are in two alphabets and two languages. On the other hand, what language my ancestors used for everyday purposes in the sixteenth century is a complete mystery to me. Was it Lithuanian, or Polish, or Old Bielorussian, the language those documents are in? I can't answer that question, but I tend to think it was Polish.

FIUT   So, then, what language was spoken in the Lithuanian cities and towns?

MILOSZ   In Kiejdany, the population was more or less 50 percent, maybe 60 percent, Jewish—it's hard to figure exactly. The local workers and the middle class spoke Polish rather than Lithuanian. And that was true throughout Lithuania. But Wilno . . . It's natural to make analogies between cities like Wilno, Wrocław, and the cities in today's Czechoslovakia. Wrocław was German in culture, the city was German. The people living on the outskirts of the city may have spoken Polish for a long time, and Polish was spoken in the countryside even longer. But Wilno represents a variation on that theme, because it was unquestionably a Polish-Jewish city. The populace and the intelligentsia spoke Polish. The workers, the tradesmen, the people who lived in the little wooden houses that covered the hillsides around the city all spoke Polish. And there was the Jewish population, who spoke Yiddish among themselves. During the nineteenth century, a significant portion of the intelligentsia switched to Russian. If we compare this with the Czechs, for example . . . An old friend of ours, Hannah Benzion, whom we met in Paris, was from a Jewish family that lived in a small town in Czechoslovakia—Reichberg, I think it was. She used to say, "Czech? The servants spoke Czech!" German was the language of culture, the servants spoke Czech. There's a certain difference here. In Wilno, and in Lithuania in general, Polish was not only the language of the upper classes but the language of the common people as well. That means that the urban population in Wilno and Kaunas and Kiejdany spoke Polish. Or, if they were Jewish, they spoke Yiddish. Yiddish in the lower classes, Russian on the top—that was the influence of the occupation. As opposed to the Jews in Galicia, where Polish was spoken by those on top. This was peculiar to Lithuania, and it strikes me as very important.

FIUT   I'd be curious to know what influence that Tower of Babel had on your own experience of language.

MILOSZ   I did not grow up in a milieu where Polish was spoken exclusively. Only Polish was spoken at home, but there was quite a strong influx of Russian, because my father and the people who visited us in Wilno were fond of switching to Russian when the subject was humorous, something Poles are known to do. Besides, my father had gone to a *Realschule* in Wilno, where he studied Russia's great literature. He had read Saltykov-Shchedrin, Gogol. Those things leave their mark.

The Polish spoken by the lower classes of Wilno was a very peculiar Polish. It wasn't the Polish spoken in Warsaw or in Cracow. Completely different! Very funny, the "local Polish" that was satirized countless times and parodied even in Wilno. It had various borrowings from Bielorussian and Lithuanian. Take gender, for example—nearly everything was feminine. Poland was quite an enigma to me, because it had such an enormous number of people who spoke Polish. And they spoke such fine Polish, which was the height of elegance and beauty for us in Lithuania.

FIUT   What sort of Polish was spoken in your home? I assume it was good Polish.

MILOSZ   Probably better than in so-called Central Poland. Definitely better. Except that we used a lot of expressions which, when I started going to school and used them there, would come back underlined in red ink with exclamation points beside them. Because words that seemed completely normal to me could at best considered local, regional curiosities.

FIUT   You mentioned that your father had a good knowledge of Russian and was well read in Russian literature. Didn't your knowledge of Russian and Russian literature start at home? How did you discover Russian culture?

MILOSZ   I must have been about two years old when I went to Russia for the first time, in 1913, when we traveled to Siberia. My father had gotten his first position as an engineer, in Krasnoyarsk. My mother, my nurse, and I traveled on the Trans-Siberian Railroad with a stop in Saint Petersburg. And I almost seem to remember what happened there. Namely— that I saw my first automobile. I fell madly, passionately in love with it. I put one foot on the running board. There was a uniformed chauffeur. I can almost remember all those things. Then came Siberia, Krasnoyarsk. That was the first trip. It's hard to say how much Russian filtered into me at that time. But we weren't there very long, maybe a year. The next trip took place after the outbreak of the First World War: a trip by horse-drawn coach in the summer of 1914. I was under the sway of the Russian language until the spring of 1918. I was bilingual. I didn't have much of an idea why I spoke one language to some people and the other one to other people. It's very difficult to re-create that process. I know theoretically that that's how it was. Later on, after the First World War, when Poland regained its independence, I used to play with two children, Yashka and Sonka, who lived in our courtyard in Wilno. They were from a Jewish family that spoke Russian rather than Yiddish. Playing with then gave me some practice in Russian. And besides, Russian was used very often at home, in humorous situations. I never studied either Russian or Russian literature. I taught myself the alphabet and read on my own.

FIUT   Over time the contacts between the many peoples and cultures in Lithuania led to conflicts. When did those conflicts become particularly acute?

MILOSZ   Ethnic conflicts—where?

FIUT   You're right. I forgot that the situation was different in each region. What was it like where you came from?

MILOSZ   I have a photograph of the school my mother ran in the spirit of Positivism and Organic Work even though by then it was the beginning of the twentieth century—an elementary school where my mother taught Lithuanian children to read and write. But what language did she teach them to read and write? Polish, of course! It never entered anyone's mind to do otherwise. You speak Lithuanian but you write in Polish. It's a little like Ireland. Irish children study English but speak Gaelic at home. There were no conflicts in that area before the First World War. The conflicts began during the First World War.

FIUT   Did that stem from the increase in national awareness?

MILOSZ   We have to go back to the beginning of Lithuanian national consciousness, which was formed during the nineteenth century and expanded at the turn of the twentieth. As an independent nation, Lithuania was born out of a very passionate patriotism, nationalism, whatever it should be called. And it must be said that not many people understand the problem of nationalism in Lithuania. That nationalism was based solely on the peasants. There was practically no Lithuanian gentry—all the gentry had been Polonized. Only a few gentry still spoke Lithuanian, in the very north of Lithuania, near the Latvian border. A few, a very small number. The peasants spoke Lithuanian, and for a while the only intelligentsia were the priests, who were of peasant stock. Sons of peasants would go to the seminary, attend the seminary under the Russian aegis, and become nationalists, the first wave of the Lithuanian intelligentsia. And so for a long time the poets came from the Catholic clergy—the "fanatic Lithuanian" priests, as they were known to the Poles, who were hostile to them.

High School

FIUT   Your life, like that of your father, seems to support the view that the Polish intelligentsia had its origins in the gentry. The pattern is the same: first the child is brought up in the manor, where he receives his first schooling, and then he departs for the city, high school, the university.

MILOSZ   You exaggerate. Actually, I was educated by constant travel. Fortunately or unfortunately, I received no manor-house upbringing at all. I am no product of the manor. If you compare me with Gombrowicz, who was well brought up, who had a bourgeois manor-house upbringing, I had none. I was brought up on endless travel.

FIUT   What was your high school like? I assume that the linguistic and ethnic mosaic of Lithuania you've presented here was reflected in the makeup of your class.

MILOSZ   Not at all, because Wilno's high schools were differentiated by language. That means that young people who spoke Russian—for example, young Jews who spoke Russian—went to Russian high schools; Jews who spoke Yiddish went to Yiddish high schools. There was one Lithuanian high school, Witold the Great High School, and for a time there was a Bielorussian high school. In other words, everyone went to his own high school. Now, as far as the makeup of my class goes, I can more or less count all those who departed from the norm during all the time I was in high school. For the most part, the norm in our high school was provided by so-called good gentry names from the Grand Duchy of Lithuania. Names that sound like a chronicle from the sixteenth or seventeenth century, the same names over and over: Bołbot, Żagiel, Wojna, and so on. Even when I joined the boy scouts, my first troop leader had what at the time struck me as a strange name. Now I know that this name is famous in the annals of Polish knighthood. And the others? There was a tiny percent of Lithuanian Tartars, whose social status was equal to the gentry's; there were a few, one, maybe two, Karaites—not Jews but Karaites—and a very few Jews, because the Jews went to Russian schools and not to Polish ones if they were of the intelligentsia. Sometimes a Turk, the son of a Turkish baker in Wilno, would attend our school. I think that's it. Of course there were the children of officials from Galicia who had come to work in Wilno. One of the striking memories of my school days was my abiding hatred for the twin Kampf brothers.

FIUT   Could you describe the teaching staff?

MILOSZ   You know, I have great admiration for that high school. Poland created some wonderful things in a very short span of time, in those two decades: A first-rate railroad system whose trains were on time to the minute—a great achievement. Poland created a system of primary schools and high schools throughout the country that ran extremely well and were on a high level—an enormous achievement. I consider my high school a very good school. And if I was later able to succeed as a university professor, more thanks are due to my high school than to my university. In *Native Realm* I described two of my spiritual antagonists, Father Chomski and my Latin teacher Adolf Rożek. I recently received a letter from Adolf Rożek in Germany. He's living in Konstanz and must be eighty or ninety. He had read *Native Realm* for the

first time in a German translation and was delighted to learn
that someone had appreciated his method of teaching Latin
poetry. Rożek came from Galicia; quite a few teachers were
imported from other parts of Poland, though they obviously
met with great hostility in Wilno. I remember hearing terrible
grumbling as a child, hatred for the Galicians, people saying
that we were being invaded by Galicians. That was very pronounced. But the Galicians played a certain role. There was
a schoolmate of mine, Leon Szreder, a poet, a member of
Żagary, who died a tragic death. He was deported to Russia
in '39 or '41 then ended up in Persia in Anders's Polish army.
He committed suicide because he was being tormented by his
sergeant. There couldn't be a more Galician name than Szreder.
His father was a railroad official who had gotten a position
in Wilno. Of course, there were also native-born teachers,
like Kołaszewski, the history teacher.

FIUT   What was student life like? Were there any organizations? You mentioned the boy scouts.

MILOSZ   I belonged to the boy scouts, of course. My experience of scouting was bizarre, because I joined the scouts
when I was still a little boy and so I had no idea what was
going on. That preyed on my mind. I knew you were supposed to act one way and not another. But why this way and
not some other? There were some precepts, some oaths. . . .
It was all so damned unclear! I know that we had to go on
hikes and demonstrate proficiency in tying knots, all those
things. Now, in reconstructing all that, I can more or less
understand the state of mind of Catholics who believe without understanding what they believe. Knowing it was necessary, I was still constantly oppressed by a feeling of "why?"
But I put that question aside and submitted.

   I took it all terribly to heart. Those were matters of passion! For example, what you went through the night before
the test in tying knots to win the gold badge—and I did win
the gold badge—a night like that matters in a person's life,
doesn't it? We may be touching on something important here.

Because for me high school is no laughing matter. I mean, it's both serious and laughable, but to the same exact degree as the university and what came after. When you're in high school, when you're in school, you're in a great revolt against the system you're subjected to. Actually, your state of rage varies with your standing in the class. When I was in my first year of high school, the first year of an eight-year high school, in 1921, I immediately became the top student because I was extremely well read compared with others my age. I simply had the vocabulary, the ability to express myself, and I was the pet of my Polish teacher, Miss Kaczanowska. Over time in high school I kept gradually dropping lower and lower. I went to second in the class, then third, then fourth, then lower and lower, almost to the very bottom, with terrible marks for conduct. I hit bottom in the sixth or seventh year—it must have been the sixth—in both grades and conduct. Terrible: "A troublemaker who is rowdy in the hallways and the classroom." We set papers on fire, we gave the teachers an awful time! Then I gradually began going back up. By the time the graduation exams were coming, the seventh or eighth year, I was getting good grades again in my subjects—and for conduct, too.

Naturally there are different attitudes toward high school. I went through a period of rebellion and hatred for the people in charge, out of a hatred for all authority. The same thing Berkeley students were going through in '68, when I was a professor.

FIUT   Can you tell me any more about the teaching staff in your high school? Didn't you mention your biology teacher in *From the Rising of the Sun*?

MILOSZ   The teachers kept changing. Since Wilno was a university town, some people coupled teaching in high school with their duties at the university. Stefan Bagiński was an assistant professor at the university, a specialist in cytology, and he also taught biology in our school. Stanisław Cywiński was an assistant professor at Stefan Batory University. He gave some classes in Polish literature at our high school, but as it happened I think I only had him for a year. As I recall, that was his course in the basics of philosophy. In my opinion, the most important part of my education were the religion classes. In the lower grades, religion classes began with so-called sacred history, then gradually moved to a higher level—I think Church history was the next step. We used Archutowski's textbook. A gold mine! It had everything! It was actually a history of Europe, a history of European civilization. The history of heresy, the history of the Church, the history of the struggle against heresy. A tremendous number of different things. Then came dogmatics, apologetics, and so on. That was our principal humanistic education. Along with, let's say, Latin, and perhaps French.

FIUT   In your opinion, did the high school try to create a definite ideal for the new state of Poland? In other words, what was the teaching staff's political orientation?

MILOSZ   It seems to me there was a certain balance there. As far as our teaching staff goes, various shades of political thought were represented; you could feel the tension among the various viewpoints. I can't say that this high school educated the students in a strict, definite ideology. For example, the National Democrat ideology wasn't propagated, even though maybe the majority, or anyway half, of the teachers were inclined toward it. But there was a fair amount of basic tolerance there. And as for the National Democrats, they are precisely that, not a part of the fascist wing. And so I couldn't say that our education had a specific orientation. For example, if we take Polish which is usually key in such matters— our Polish teacher was not, to the best of my knowledge, very nationalistically inclined, but was, rather, a skeptic. I think Rożek was a crypto-atheist. In any case, I received a letter from him in which he was still caught up in his obsession, which he pursued like a nineteenth-century Protestant critic of religion. He had a theory that Pilate was a noble figure; he referred to certain Coptic sources that speak of a Saint Pilate as having in fact saved Jesus, who lived in Alexandria after his supposed death. In the period before he began to preach, Jesus had also supposedly lived in Alexandria, where he had been quite taken with the teachings of the Greek philosophers. There you have Rożek in a nutshell! All in one letter.

FIUT   Then how would you define the Church's influence on your high school, the curriculum, and the students' attitude?

MILOSZ   There's no question that because of the concordat between the Vatican and Poland, the Church had a large influence on the way young people were educated. That's certain. Classes in religion were part of the curriculum, and the great majority of the students attended these classes. There were exceptions. When it was time for our hour of religion — and we had these classes a few times a week, I don't remember how many, it must have been two or three — those who weren't Catholic did not have to attend. Those were the Protestants, the Jews, the Mohammedans, but in any case there were very few of them.

FIUT   It would be very interesting if you could describe a typical school day. Has any one in particular stuck in your memory?

MILOSZ   I can, of course, try to reconstruct one. All right, then, since I lived on Podgórna Street, I took Portowa Street and then went up a street called Boufałł Hill. I'd usually see pretty much the same people on Portowa Street in the morning. That was before eight o'clock. The Rymkiewicz brothers would be usually out in front of me as I came out of a side street. One of them, who may have been a year ahead of me in school, was killed while serving as a pilot in England during the war, and the other one, who was a year or two behind me, was Aleksander Rymkiewicz, who became a poet later on. You'd be panting by the time you walked up Boufałł Hill, rushing not to be late. The janitor closed the door

at eight on the dot. And if you were half a minute late, you'd
have to beg like crazy for him to let you in. First there was
an all-school assembly, and we'd sing "At Break of Day" in
chorus. Then we'd all go off to our classrooms. And then—
it depends which year it was. I remember some of my school
years as nothing but sluggish horrible boredom. My third year
of high school, for example. I have no memories of anything
but horrible, yawning, excruciating boredom. Those fall days
when they turned on the lights in school for the early part of
the school day. Morning came late in Wilno, the day started
late, and it grew dark very early during the winter. And so it
was dark when school started and dark when it ended. Those
dismal, rainy autumn days, the darkness, students stammer-
ing out their lessons, and me, totally immersed in a world
that had nothing to do with the reality around me. Math class,
for example. I have to say that school was a torture for me
when I had to do things like calculate the amount of water
draining from a pool or filling a pool. Terrible! I was never
able to do it. It was a nightmare for me. That was in the lower
grades. A class would be in session and there I'd be, madly
drawing away in my notebook—imaginary lands, countries,
plants. In a world all my own. And that's more or less how
the day would end. If not, there was gym class, a total nightmare for me, a true horror, because you had to undress and
then go down to that cold gymnasium, where they had wall-
bars and horses and God knows what else! I couldn't do any
of that. Not because I was physically inept; it's just that it
somehow threw me, intimidated me. If not for that, I might
have been quite good at it. And so I was at the bottom of the
class, with a complex about being clumsy. I wasn't big, and
some of the boys were well developed physically.

A typical day in high school was a sort of mishmash, a
blur, what I would call an unconscious day.

FIUT   What's your memory of the graduation exams? Which
subjects were you tested on? Do you remember any of the
questions?

MILOSZ   The hardest part of the graduation exams was, of course, the written test, which didn't frighten me in the humanities but did in mathematics and physics. I knew absolutely no math, and I copied from a classmate who was kind enough to let me. We'd agreed on it in advance. On the other hand, with Polish . . . You could be tested on Polish or on history. I chose Polish. I wrote an essay on the river of time. The chairman of the examination committee was one of our teachers, Mr. Massonius, a well-known name in the history of Polish philosophy. I received an A.

FIUT   What was the essay about?

MILOSZ   About Heraclitus's river, time, the flow of time. And so I did well in the humanities. What else can I say? Well, I was frightened. Dreams about those exams haunted me for years.

FIUT   Let's speak of something more pleasant. Do you remember the first time you went to a theatre or the movies? The movies had started becoming very popular then, hadn't they?

MILOSZ   The movies have a history all their own in Wilno. There were many movie theatres, but high-school students were not allowed to go to them. You could get caught. And if that came to your teacher's attention, there'd be trouble. The problem was the uniforms, which went through various phases. Uniforms weren't worn when I entered school, but later on they were gradually introduced, and were changed several times. For a while I wore what was called a "kettle" to high school. That was a hat more or less like the kind French policemen wear. It gradually underwent modification, because the cardboard would wear through and there'd only be something like a skullcap left. Needless to say, the more nondescript a skullcap was, the harder it was to tell someone was a student. Those stiff kettle hats were awful. For a time we wore uniforms designed by our drawing teacher, Stanisław Jarocki, a painter, one of Wilno's more colorful characters. He had an aquiline nose and a gray walrus mustache, and he wore a cape and a hat with a feather in it; he was the leading pederast in Wilno, and a scout master. He designed steel-gray uniforms with lapels: pants that went to the knees, knickers, high socks. I don't think that lasted very long.

In any case, as I said, going to the movies could land you in trouble. But I was quite passionate about the movies, from the time I was young and in school. They showed American films, of course. All the latest stars, Chaplin, all the stars of the twenties. I adored Sylvia Sidney in the thirties; recently, to my amazement, I found myself listed near her in a supplement to *The Dictionary of American Biography*. So my film education was pretty much the same as for a child growing up in America or in France. We saw the same films. We also had the municipal movie theatre, which had been set up to show more suitable films. There'd be total pandemonium, because all the students from Wilno's high schools would come en masse. Gigantic crowds. The movies were still silent then. A man would play the piano behind a screen near the movie screen. The audience would hiss, "Come on, baldie, play!"

FIUT   Did you have your favorite movie stars?

MILOSZ   I had a favorite movie actress. Naturally, for a long time I thought that Greta Garbo was the most beautiful woman in the world. It was a tremendous thrill to see a Garbo movie. She was my erotic ideal for a very long time.

University

FIUT   In the light of what you've said so far, your life could have taken various directions. You could have inherited a substantial farm, Podkomorzynek, let's say, or Szetejnie, become a country squire, entertained your neighbors, and whiled away the hours catching flies, as you put it in one passage in *From the Rising of the Sun*. You could also have devoted yourself to studying nature, which was your passion. By virtue of your interest in literature, you could have become a specialist in Polish literature, as you were to do much later in America. In that context, what you chose to study is completely baffling. Why law?

MILOSZ   First, I want to straighten something out—I could not have become a country squire, because my father was no longer a squire by then, and the entire class structure had been overturned. There was still some land from my ancestors on my mother's side, but it didn't amount to much; the Lithuanian land reform was already in effect, and so in fact being a squire became less possible all the time. It seems to me that when those typical changes occur, when the son of a gentry family becomes an engineer—besides, my grandmother had run the estate into debt, so that my father had no land whatsoever—once the gentry start becoming déclassé, it's very difficult to reverse that process. As for a career in the

28

natural sciences, I of course took this very seriously, and I
have to tell you that the natural-sciences building at the university in Wilno, near Zakret, where frogs were dissected,
was a holy place for me for quite a long time. I became very
friendly with one of the other students, a boy by the name of
Bujalski, who was always tops in the natural sciences. But by
my last years in high school, I was somehow spoiled, lost to
that love for the natural sciences. And now we come to the
reason I didn't study Polish literature.

FIUT How were you spoiled? I don't understand.

MILOSZ That's a very interesting question, you know, but
it's a separate question and a very difficult one to answer.
Why did I, who was crazy about the natural sciences, suddenly convert to literature, switch to literature? If you study
my work, you'll find that the sense of guilt is central to me,
and to all my poetry. I also feel guilty for not having become
a naturalist. I had decided to devote my life to studying nature, and that's what I should have done. But I didn't. Very
bad. That might be the reason nature has shown me its cruel
side. In fact, my entire life and all my creative work are against
nature, against so-called Mother Nature—an attempt to liberate myself from its demonic embrace. I can't, and I never
could, but I tried. . . .
  Now the question arises why I didn't become a specialist
in Polish literature. But before I speak about that, I must say
a few words about our university. As you're well aware, Stefan Batory University—Wilno University—ceased to exist for
many decades. It was re-established by Piłsudski in 1919
and, in fact, should have been called Piłsudski University.
There is a certain connection between Wilno University in the
years between the wars and the tomb in Rossa Cemetery containing Piłsudski's heart. I fully support all the attempts by
Lithuanians to demonstrate that this is the same university it
always was: the same university that was founded in 1578 as
the Jesuit Academy, then underwent various mutations and
is today Vilnius University. Nevertheless, I have to say that

the university that came into being in 1919 was a thing unto itself. It was established helter-skelter, on the run, in a display of enormous organizational ability, creation from nothing: they founded a university unquestionably different from the other Polish ones. I don't have much basis for comparison— I can't compare it with the Jagellonian University in Cracow, which I never attended. The Jagellonian had really gone almost untouched by all the great historical upheavals and had known great continuity. But I can compare Wilno University with Warsaw University, which had also been created from nothing, and where professors were appointed quite haphazardly, even more haphazardly than at Wilno, as far as I can judge. In any case, comparing what I can compare—Warsaw and Wilno Universities—I'd grant a certain superiority to Wilno University.

FIUT   Why?

MILOSZ   I may not be at all fair here. The comparisons will emerge when I begin speaking of my classes. I enrolled in the Polish department of Stefan Batory University in the fall of 1929 and began attending lectures. I think what quickly drove me away from the Polish department was somehow connected with my machismo, my sense of myself as a male. The Polish department was known as the "matrimonial department": 95 percent of the students were young ladies. And they were very nice, too. Most of them had thick curls or bobbed hair under their caps. We had special caps at Stefan Batory University, with wolves' teeth, the symbol of our university, on the emblem. That was one thing: the department didn't give the impression of being very serious. In any case, I was a little frightened by that department and the prospects it offered. Why did people study Polish literature? To become high-school teachers. Any other career was out of the question. Now that's changed. Today Polish literature is studied widely, and not only by future high-school teachers; it opens up various other opportunities as well. That wasn't so when I entered the university.

FIUT   You weren't attracted by a career as a scholar?

MILOSZ   Not in the least. Studying literature was probably the last thing that could have attracted me. I was fresh out of high school and full of the devil, full of mockery for our teachers, and the thought of becoming one of them was absolutely unbearable, because I had boundless ambitions. That's the way you are at that age—I was eighteen years old in 1929—you have a marshal's baton inside your knapsack. You just don't know what kind of marshal you want to be, or in which army. After two weeks, I switched to law. Why law? Law was the department for people who didn't know what to do with themselves. Now, in America, for example, we see that what once came under the general heading of law has been broken down into various disciplines. Economics, anthropology, and sociology are separate disciplines now, but they weren't back then in Poland. Those fields were still in the rudimentary stage. Moreover, law was macho: there were relatively few women in law, and those who were, were very intelligent, nothing to sneeze at. Another advantage of law was that it was not such a strictly defined field in terms of a career. Comparing the law department in Wilno with the one in Warsaw—which I can do because I spent a year at Warsaw University—I can say that Wilno had a number of very interesting personalities.

FIUT   What do you remember of your professors?

MILOSZ   The most ominous figure in my first year was Professor Bossowski, who came from Galicia. It's very interesting that the professors were partly local people who represented the traditions of the Grand Duchy of Lithuania and were attached to those traditions, and partly people from other regions, like Galicia. Bossowski had been a hussar, in Franz Josef's army, I think. He was a puzzle to me. On the other hand, he was a caricature of the nineteenth-century professor: his bald head, his mustache, the stiff collar on which he rested his chin, qualified him for the caricature of the absent-minded professor. On the other hand, there was something violent and incredibly rigid in the way he held himself (it was only later on that I learned he'd been a hussar). He was a combination of those two traits. He lectured on Roman law. We had to know all the precepts of Roman law by heart. I can still remember some of them. That was the most difficult part. And the other professors? Ehrenkreutz taught Polish law. Since there were no microphones then, it was actually impossible to attend the lectures on law, too crowded. A large auditorium, a large crowd, and the professors, especially Ehrenkreutz, would mumble. The first two or three rows could hear, but absolutely no chance after that. In other words, attending lectures was a fiction. Everything, all your preparation for exams, was based on mimeographed lecture notes. I bought those lecture notes and studied them, but I flunked Bossowski's exam and had to take it over. Though I crammed for the exam over the summer, I also did so much swimming that I got sharp chest pains and some heart murmurs. That was a time of great, unprecedented athletic feats for me. I was always at it, in good weather and bad. And I was swimming because of bad luck in love. When you expend your energy on sports . . .

FIUT   That's a very curious view of sports. . . .

MILOSZ   I passed Bossowski's makeup test in the fall and then began my second year of law. If I'm not mistaken, an intriguing personality that year was Zawadzki, a professor of economics who came from a famous Wilno family of printers. A purely local figure, from the family who had printed Mickiewicz's books. He would come to school with a bad hangover in the morning, pull out a little mirror, examine his tongue. . . . But there's no question that the most interesting character in the university was Professor Bronisław Wróblewski, who lectured on criminal law. Not just criminal law and penology; what Professor Wróblewski taught wouldn't be taught in a law department today but in sociology, anthropology, or philosophy. He was a graduate of Petersburg University, though he did not have the title of "doctor," because

"Candidate" was the degree they granted there. This created a certain odd sense of disproportion: all the people from Galicia were doctors, even though their degrees had required lower achievements and less effort than those of the candidates who'd studied at Russian universities. Wróblewski revealed a sort of new dimension of society to me, but he wasn't the first. During my first year I had attended the seminar given by Assistant Professor Ejnik, herself an admirer of the famous St. Petersburg professor Petrażycki. As to Wróblewski, he was researching the sources of criminal law in society, which I found interesting and stimulating. I'd put up with the less interesting aspects of his lectures: you had to memorize the Polish criminal code, which I did. I loved that professor and his books about penology, the history of penal institutions in various societies. I learned a great deal from them.

There was Professor Wilamowski, a professor of canon law. He was a priest but not quite entirely priestly. He was fat, a little on the oily side, and all his movements were sensuous— a big cat of a man. I think he led an elegant, sybaritic life. I mean, there was a certain air of ease, good wine, and women about him. You sensed a life that was humming nicely along. I would say the air of a Voltairean *abbé*. I don't know whether he belonged to one of the Masonic lodges in our city, but that would have been in character for him.

There was a Professor Panejko, a Ukrainian. A very elegant man, he was rumored to have his own court of young people, a sort of academy founded on the highest Greek ideals, what today, in America, you'd call a "gay academy."

But looking back, I'd say the university gave me a great deal. It gave me a certain general orientation toward what was happening in the social sciences. I don't know if I'd have been able to do all I've done if I'd studied Polish literature. I don't think so.

One year I lived in a dormitory on Boufałł Hill. Generally speaking, I have never needed much in the way of creature comforts, and the dormitory was ideal for me. It was a new dorm. I had a tiny room, a bed, a little table—absolutely everything you need to be happy. There was a shower in the hall, a good shower. Parquet floors, polished, fragrant. What more do you need? My friend Pranas Ancevičius lived close by on the same floor. Endless discussions, studying for exams, and so on. Just around the corner of the street was a good-natured widow who provided meals for the students. Pranas may have been giving her a tumble in bed, but it was all in good fun. During this period Pranas, the independent socialist, the revolutionary, had a very great influence on me. Because I lived there, I was aware of all the propaganda directed against him—that he was an agent of the Polish police, or God only knows what else, Polish intelligence. But he had no money! He supported himself by writing articles for the Lithuanian atheist press in America. They'd send him a few dollars, but what was just a few cents in America, when translated into Wilno terms, where a meal cost fifty groszy . . . Sometimes they wouldn't send him anything and he'd be completely broke. He was a thoroughly ideological person and he made some fundamental errors. I don't want to go into his life story, which was tragic.

FIUT   I'd like to talk a little about the status of students, which, as we know, was different before the war from what it is now. What did the idea of the university's independence or autonomy mean to you then?

MILOSZ   I'm very sorry to say it, but the principal confrontation that occurred during my years at the university was not connected with any lofty, noble goals of free expression, but, rather, with Jewish cadavers. The disturbances at our university were caused by the nationalists protesting that the anatomy laboratories were furnished solely with Christian cadavers. Wilno University could not have been less sensitive to the entire National Democrat movement in Poland. At other universities the young people were, as they said then, "nationally" oriented. For various complex reasons, Wilno was an exception. But then in '33 there was that uproar over the cadavers in the anatomy labs. The so-called national youth

used the fact that only non-Jewish cadavers were being supplied to the anatomy labs as a pretext for a general attack.
The point here was not only that a large percentage of medical students were Jews; it was more than that—Jews were
only dissecting the bodies of Christians.

FIUT   Here we touch on the very difficult and sensitive issue
of the anti-Semitism displayed at that time in Polish universities.

MILOSZ   You know, I was at the university before the time
of the "ghetto seats," the isolated section for Jews. That began after I'd graduated, and I never witnessed it. On the other
hand, I did witness various incidents and I spoke out, surrounded by a menacing mob of young people armed with
clubs. When I tried to appeal to their humanitarian feelings,
they said, "Go tell it to your grandmother." I remember that
type of incident. I should say here that the business with the
cadavers was one reason some people became communists.
One example is Sztachelski, who was later to become the
minister of health; he was a medical student then and came
to the university in his scoutmaster's uniform. Those incidents pushed him to the left. Evidently he came to the conclusion that, apart from communism, there was no solution to
those basic conflicts, which recall the conflict between the Arabs and the Jews. The incident began over the cadavers and
then spread to the city, where a mob of students began de-
molishing Jewish stores and breaking windows, until they encountered resistance in the Jewish quarter from the porters,
who were strong and prepared. The two sides started throwing stones at each other. A student by the name of Wa-
cławski was hit in the head by a stone and killed. Then
pandemonium broke out. Mobs of students began streaming
through the streets of the city, and the atmosphere was truly
pogromlike. The stores were bolted shut, and so on.

FIUT   What was student life like in Wilno?

MILOSZ   You see, student life in Wilno was in an in-between stage. What do I mean by that? In the second half of the nineteenth century, student life was definitely under the influence of the fraternities, the German pattern of student life. I don't know what the situation was in Warsaw or Cracow; I'm speaking of the Grand Duchy of Lithuania and that area. The students, who were primarily men, organized fraternities that were nothing but German *Burschenschaften* with Polish names. Those student organizations—and incidentally they were filled with young people of gentry origin, because who else studied in universities then?—those organizations were in a certain sense patriotic but were muted: political action wasn't possible. The important things were dueling, honor, jolly drinking bouts, ceremonies. The fraternities that were active in Wilno during my youth had originated in Riga and Dorpat, big centers of fraternities. The most traditional and distinguished fraternities were Welecja, Arkonia, and Polonia. If I'm not mistaken, I was invited to join by all of them, and there was a special effort to get me to join Polonia because—supposedly—a Milosz had been one of its founders in Dorpat, in the nineteenth century.

The fraternity men were distinguishable from the other students by their caps, which had little visors of various colors, indicating standing. The lowest, the "greenhorns," wore a fox tail attached to their caps. My outlook was extremely antinationalistic when I entered the university, and so I had a very negative attitude toward the fraternities; they couldn't tempt me. Had I joined one, I would have taken part in those beer-drinking bouts. I don't know what they talked about there, maybe their families, heraldry. . . . Those were the last outposts for the young gentry. The fraternities were old, very strong, and in the forefront of university life.

There was also another element in my revolt against them. The main role here was played by the Vagabonds, our student club, which stood for a completely different set of values. We made fun of all those sacred cows and were in favor of sports, hiking. There was one group, NOWS—Not One Wasted Sunday. A wasted Sunday meant a Sunday without a hike or a canoe trip. No fraternity caps, no duels, no sashes, just berets with colored tassels. There was a certain hierarchy there, too: the tassels could be red, yellow, gold, and so on. When I arrived in Warsaw in June 1981, I threw my arms around Dr. Wacław Korabiewicz, one of the outstanding Vagabonds, who was known as "Kilometer" because he was two meters tall. It was very strange—after all those years—to be back in the Vagabonds. The Vagabonds weren't the only source of opposition to the fraternities, of course. The Student Puppet Theatre poked fun at the fraternities and was also attacked by the fraternities. And so there were those two worlds.

There's no question that the fraternities were the mainstay of the right wing at the university. Maybe I'm not being fair, because some fraternity men took a different political stance. But in general they were a mainstay either of the conservatives or of the nationalist right.

FIUT   In *Native Realm* you wrote about the great expeditions the Vagabonds made. So now could you describe the workings of the club, how people moved up in rank?

MILOSZ   It would be difficult to call our club organized. It seems to me that what united the members was, rather, a certain sense of being in the community of the opposition, a group of young people sticking their tongues out at the world, predecessors of the hippies in America, in a way.

FIUT   I must say I find that a surprising comparison. Aren't athletics, hiking, the cult of physical vigor the opposite of the hippies' style and ideals?

MILOSZ   We didn't have any cult of vigor. There was none of that! Everything was done purely for practical reasons. No one in our group played sports. We even viewed skiing solely as a means of transportation. Skiing around Wilno was more a way of exploring than anything else. It was very functional, and wasn't done to achieve results or for the sake of vigor. The Vagabonds always made fun of athletes, sports types, and sports regarded as feats or training for a perfect body.

FIUT   What were the trips like?

MILOSZ   Mostly camaraderie, friendship, fun, and adventure. I could compare them to something I saw recently in Cambridge, Massachusetts. A large procession of young people, students, playing the most bizarre instruments, dressed as bizarrely as possible, wearing hats painted various colors, and with their faces painted, too. They were carrying a large banner: "Celebrating Being." It was beautiful. I think that, unlike the serious fraternities, the Vagabonds just celebrated being.

FIUT   Can you give me a cross-section of the student world?

MILOSZ   Even now, many years after studying at that university, I can still remember my classmates' names, and when I see them in something I'm reading I realize what illustrious names they were. My classmates were mainly descendants of the gentry of the Grand Duchy of Lithuania, with a certain mixture not only of local people but of Tartars as well; you'd run into people with Tartar names in Wilno. But there were also the local people. Boys who grew up on estates or on small farms, in little out-of-the-way places. Financially, they were either well to do or barely scraping by. There were a great many Jewish young people from the little towns in the area—Lida, Oszmiana, Zdzięcioł, Miadzioł. Naturally, Jewish merchant families from little towns like those would make every effort to see that their sons were educated. There wasn't much opportunity to earn any money in Wilno outside the university.

I forgot to say that the basic difference between Wilno University and Warsaw University was that Wilno University was a great center of city life, at any rate of Polish life in Wilno— I'd be hard-pressed to answer the question of what role it played for Yiddish-speaking people—whereas Warsaw University was peripheral to Warsaw life. There the students came to the university out of the jungle of the big city, then disappeared back into it. Life, earning a living, all that took place outside the university. Compared with the multitude of things happening in Warsaw, all the ways to make money, all the levels of income, Warsaw University was just the icing on the cake. You could make an analogy between Columbia University's place in New York and Warsaw University's in Warsaw before the war. Columbia University is not central to New York; people return to the jungle of the big city at the end of the day. On the other hand, in the case of Cambridge and Harvard University, Harvard is certainly central to the city of Cambridge.

FIUT   How do you explain the radicalization of the youth, that movement to the left which included you as well?

MILOSZ   Radicalization came in the early thirties. This is very interesting if viewed from an American perspective, because that was a period of radicalization in America, linked to the Depression and widespread unemployment. In New York at that time, a writer was ostracized if he wasn't a Marxist. There was a great wave of Marxism, which broke up into Stalinists, Trotskyists, and so on. In other words, the same process took place in New York, Wilno, and Warsaw. The components of that strange political or philosophical osmosis should be studied and analyzed. Anyway, in the early thirties there were similar movements in many countries, polarizations. Those were, after all, the years when Hitler came to power in Germany, and fascist movements sprang up in various Western and Eastern European countries. The Iron Guard in Rumania, the National Radical Camp in Poland, and so on.

FIUT   Could you say something about your own "leftist leanings"? At one point you mentioned your sense of a split between the public and the personal—what's done for show, so to speak, and what is intimate and not for sale.

MILOSZ   That seems to have been very strong in me, that division between the private and the public. Where did that come from? It was with me very early, but I've unveiled a little of it in *The Land of Ulro*. In any case, I didn't think I had to go running around and shouting what I knew. There's a secret zone, a closed zone, where a person lives his life. Incidentally, I recently found the same idea in Goethe—that a person should not reveal what he knows and should be superficial when relating to others. I think this can lead to very immoral situations. Before the war I found a solution that was used by a great many people after the war: I made jokes. During one of our drinking bouts in Wilno in the spring of 1940, Światopełk Karpiński said that Hitler didn't take any of it seriously; after doing his show for the German people, he'd go someplace where he could change into an English flannel suit and drink whiskey. But, you know, I think I was so alert to the things that started happening after the war because I had some previous knowledge of them.

Wilno

FIUT   Understandably, Wilno is a constant refrain in your memories. It's high time to talk about Wilno more extensively, especially since your previous remarks on the subject were made only in passing. Of course, it's very difficult to speak of Wilno as something closed and unchanging. You must have known several Wilnos: the Wilno of your childhood, the Wilno of your youth, and Wilno in 1940. How did Wilno change?

MILOSZ   It's very difficult to point to changes in any city if the changes occurring within us are projected onto what that city was. I find your question extremely moving when I think of the area around the Place de l'Opéra in Paris, where nothing changed for decades. And here you are asking me about those few years. Half the period between the wars, ten years, what is that? What could have changed? Naturally, things did change, to the extent that Wilno entered the period between the wars as a former Russian garrison town, but then it got its university and a large student population. The city fathers made great efforts to modernize the city. In a sense, I was a witness to that modernization of Wilno. What I mean is that in my childhood the city was mostly one of cobblestone streets and wooden sidewalks. I can remember when Wilno's streets were first paved, at least many of them, and when it started using buses with very thick tires that ran smoothly and quietly. The droshkies that had clattered along the cobblestone streets when I was a child now had automobile tires for wheels. The number of taxis increased.

FIUT   Did that make it look like a twentieth-century city?

MILOSZ   Toward the end of the thirties, Wilno was a neat and trim little city. I don't say that it was especially twentieth-century, even though—as I wrote in my essay "A Dictionary of Wilno's Streets" in *Beginning with My Streets*—the same phenomena were occurring there as those Bruno Schulz describes in Drohobycz. Namely, one or two streets were totally American: twentieth-century capitalism, signs, neon. In Wilno that was Grand Street and parts of the Jewish quarter, on German Street. A very odd mix. No question, it was a truly exotic city. Wilno was visited by various famous writers, like Chesterton, who traveled there in the twenties and was completely delighted by it. Because it was somewhat Oriental, a bit the way I imagine the cities of Asia Minor, but with a touch of Europe, the Baroque, the Gothic. The Baroque is the basic and dominant element in Wilno, and that makes it unusual. Besides, it's a city surrounded by greenery. That's very important. In a way, Cracow is also a city set among hills, but this is more pronounced in Wilno, because its hills are higher and the city has two rivers, the Wilia and the Wilenka, that join there. There's also a third river, a legendary underground river—I've never seen it, no one's ever seen it. It flows under the city, under the cathedral, and empties into the Wilia at some point. So nature was present. Not to mention that in the wintertime children went sledding and skiing down the steep streets.

The natural setting had a large influence on student life. There was a great deal of hiking and canoeing. There weren't many canoes in Wilno, but there were some, and they were a special favorite of the Vagabonds. You canoed upstream, of course. The Wilia has a swift current. You'd set off from the University Sports Association's dock and you had to lean into the current to paddle against it. We'd go to Werki, a few miles upriver. There's a palace there in very picturesque wooded surroundings, and today—I saw a photograph of it recently—I think it's been turned into the Academy of Sciences, or something like that. There were excursion boats to Werki, but the people of the city would row out to it bravely on Sunday, with a bottle of vodka and a jar of pickles. They were mostly shoemakers and tailors, the tradesmen of the city of Wilno.

FIUT   Did they have their own boats?

MILOSZ   They did. The boats in Wilno were very handsome and had stripes painted on them. While we're talking about the people of Wilno, we shouldn't forget that Wilno still had the institution of the public steam bath. That's where my fondness for saunas originates. Steam baths are a perfectly common institution in the north of Europe. My father and I went to the sauna in Wilno every week as a matter of course. The people of Wilno adored taking steam. Fortunately, they were an ecumenical institution, meaning that everyone, Jews and Catholics, went there together.

FIUT   I asked the question about the different images of Wilno because that thread runs through *Beginning with My Streets* and reappears in your dialogue with Tomas Venclova, the Lithuanian poet. Venclova said there isn't just one Wilno but a variety of Wilnos, depending on the observer's social status or the period in which he saw the city.

MILOSZ   Naturally, in my case there's a definite distortion, because, to a large extent, a child grows up in one place, in one specific world, in one definite atmosphere, and has little contact with other aspects of the city. We could say that my horizon was bounded by the Zygmunt August High School and the Tomasz Zan Library. Quite an absorbing area. It contained a few Polish high schools, and I was aware of what was going on in them. I'm speaking of one Wilno, but the

Jewish streets of Wilno were right beside it. A Yiddish-speaking Wilno, different schools, another Wilno. Yet another—and one that I recall from my trips to Werki—was the Wilno of the working class. They were the most durable local element, one that still exists there to a large extent. Not the Wilno of the intelligentsia, the Wilno of schools and the university, but the Wilno of tradesmen and workers. Jewish Wilno was also very varied: there was a Wilno of well-to-do or highly Russianized Jews who sent their children to the Russian high school, and there were the great masses of the Jewish proletariat. Let's not forget that the Bund movement started in Wilno and was based on that very Yiddish-speaking element, or that the YIVO Institute for Jewish Research in New York is a product of that same tradition. As far as I can tell, that doesn't necessarily mean that YIVO is an offshoot of the Bund, but that the Bund arose from the same need to address the common people, who spoke Yiddish and who had a very rich Jewish folklore, as opposed to educated people, who thought the choice was between Russian and Hebrew and who had Zionist leanings. The Bund was definitely non-Zionist: as we know, it was socialist, meaning that it was counting on a transformation of the system and a place for Yiddish-speaking people in the new system.

There was also the Wilno of the civil servants, largely immigrants from Galicia. There was the Wilno of the landowners who kept apartments in the city; they constituted a certain subgroup. There was also the Wilno of the small Lithuanian colony, which lived a life of its own, completely à part, a separate world.

And there was the Bielorussian population. As we know, it's always a problem to classify the Bielorussians. But there were Bielorussian students. They lived a life of their own and did not communicate with anyone. There was no discrimination or persecution, but each street and each ethnic group lived a life unto itself. It was out of the question that Catholics would actually know anything about Jews!

FIUT   Didn't they shop in their stores?

MILOSZ   Of course they did. The slogans of Dmowski* and
the National Radical Camp—to boycott the Jews, to isolate
them—which were so powerful in Poland in the thirties, had
no real influence in Wilno. After all, in the nineteenth century
the Jews had emerged as an urban element in Poland—that
is, competition: "Why do *they* control business, and not
Poles?" The same thing happened in Hungary, and was not
even especially racist and anti-Semitic in nature. It's more or
less like Indonesia, where the Chinese were in control of business. A movement arose against the Chinese because of their
monopoly. Jobs had to be found for the Indonesian villagers
from Java or Sumatra. The anti-Semitic rows caused by the
rightist students may have been fundamentally different from
those in Central Poland. The various Wilnos were rather isolated zones, and I was one of the few people who attempted
to cross the borders.

FIUT   Could you say some more about it?

MILOSZ   I had Jewish classmates at the university. We studied for exams together. They were mainly from the small Jewish towns in the area around Wilno. That's one aspect. And,
of course, studying for the exams was tremendous fun, lots
of drama. All those things created certain bonds. At the university I was against the nationalists, against the National
Democrats, and, as I recall, I made efforts to speak out against
the anti-Semitic excesses.

   As for my friend Pranas, he did a lot in bringing me to view
Wilno and Europe from a completely different perspective.
That's something of key significance—to have a friend who's
not Polish at an age when you're open and impressionable,
just beginning to take form, a friend you spend hours talking
with. Needless to say, Pranas's point of view wasn't Polish in
the least. He couldn't speak much Polish when he arrived in
Wilno. His opinions about the university, Poland, and the

---

*Roman Dmowski (1864–1939), founder of the right-wing National
Democratic Party, one of whose principal goals was an ethnically homogeneous Poland. —TRANS.

world situation shaped and influenced me a great deal. Pranas
was definitely a dramatic person. I've written about him. Very
early on, when he was a young man and still in high school,
he took part in the socialist coup d'état in Lithuania and he
was thrown out of the country as an émigré. And he was a
political émigré from then on, for the rest of his life. That
was a very hard life for a person with political ambitions. He
truly was predestined to be a statesman, a member of Parlia-
ment or at least an influential journalist; he had great jour-
nalistic flair. At that time it was very odd to have a close
friend who was extremely well versed in Marxism, European
revolutionary affairs, and so on, and who at the same time
was not a communist—Pranas was a revolutionary Marxist.
He had spent some time in Vienna, in the Karl Marx Workers' Housing Projects, under the tutelage of the Viennese
Marxists; his basic orientation was toward Viennese Marxism. What a mentor! Naturally, he was not concerned with
all those ethnic conflicts; he was an internationalist by calling. Through him I came to know a great many other students and young people: Lithuanians, Bielorussians, Jews. We'd
go for lunch, for dinner. . . . A whole other world! And of
course he and I would also go to the Jewish quarter if we
happened to have any money. Very modest sums. But Wilno
was a very cheap city. The restaurants, the Jewish food in
those narrow little alleyways . . . Jewish cooking was famous in Poland before the war. Cold vodka and Jewish ap-
petizers—absolutely superb!

Wilno and Paris are very similar. The narrow little streets
of the Latin Quarter look like Wilno. The rue des Rosiers
could easily be in Wilno. And the good Jewish restaurants,
like Goldenberg's on the rue des Rosiers—straight out of
Wilno. All this, of course, gave me a perspective which was
different from that of my classmates in Wilno, and especially
in Warsaw; they hadn't received that type of training.

I don't want to create a false image, though: Warsaw provided others of my generation with a different initiation, since
to a large extent Warsaw was a city of the Jewish intelligentsia. That was an initiation with an entirely different basis. But

what counted for me was discovering that new dimension. As for the Bielorussians, my contact with them was rather scanty, because they weren't much of a presence in Wilno. And perhaps that was mostly because the Bielorussians were persecuted by the Polish authorities. The emancipated Bielorussian youth of peasant origin automatically took their orientation from Minsk, where Bielorussian culture was important. They became communists right away, and so the Polish authorities persecuted them. The Bielorussian high school was always being shut down. It would be reopened and then it would be shut down again. Actually, their one enduring institution was the Bielorussian choir; as we're well aware, folklore, or folk music, is the last bastion of the ethnic. These things don't lend themselves to neat classification. The division I spoke of are approximations. The boundaries between the various Wilnos were fluid.

FIUT   That has to be important, since it's bound up with your tolerance toward other nationalities, cultures, and languages.

MILOSZ   I don't know. I experienced a great variety of influences at home, some fostering tolerance and others intolerance. Yes, there was a mix at home. And there were also the matter of the fundamental deviation I made in life, something I cannot treat fully in conversation. It would be very difficult to trace its causes, but in high school I felt very different from my classmates. A great deal of my behavior stemmed from orneriness. I was sticking out my tongue at the world.

FIUT   You said that you moved primarily in Polish Wilno and that Wilno was a Polish city—at least half the people who lived there were Polish. What was the symbolic center of Wilno then?

MILOSZ   Let's start with the simplest things. If you go to the Wilno cemetery, the Rossa Cemetery, you'll find the whole genealogy of Wilno, generation upon generation. Even when we buried Światopełk Karpiński, we chose a place for him on what's called Literary Hill, where the poet Syrokomla and

the fabulist Gliński are buried. That's not a very long genealogy, of course, because they lived in the nineteenth century.
But going further back—to Wilno's churches and the tombs
in them—everything attests to many, many centuries and many
generations of people who spoke Polish in everyday life. That's
very important. All the centuries are there in the churches,
the tombs in the churches, the cemeteries. And all the traditions, too. For example, in Wilno there's a place called
Bekiesz Hill. Bekiesz was a nobleman, a Protestant of the Ar-
ian—Antitrinitarian–demonination. The name Bekiesz would
indicate Hungarian origins, but Bekiesz spoke Polish, of course.
Not only that—if we take the university, it clearly was entirely Polish, and I'm not speaking of the Romantic period. If
we go even further back, the Jesuit Academy was a force for
Polonization, as some Bielorussians recently remarked to me
in reproach. Those were powerful things. And then there were
the uprisings, which lived on in tradition: the Uprising of 1863,
when Muravyov had a gallows erected on Łukiszki Square
and where my grandfather's commanding officer, Sierakowski, was hanged; the Uprising of 1830 and, even further
back, Kościuszko's insurrection of 1794, and so on. Centuries of tradition.

Wilno was Polish because it unquestionably gravitated
toward Poland and was sharply opposed to Russianization.
As soon as options existed—Russia, Lithuania, Poland—it
was obvious that Wilno gravitated toward Poland. I've spoken elsewhere of the role of Catholicism in all this. Wilno was
Catholic and was attached to Catholicism; Poland, however,
was the only large Catholic conglomerate nearby. Lithuania
was small. And, as I've already mentioned, the hierarchy of
culture also played its role. Poland was culture, and Lithuania was *klausiuki*. *Klausiuki* means people who wear wooden
shoes, peasants. As you know, all Polish culture is gentry to
its marrow.

FIUT   And how did the Jews and Bielorussians who lived in
Wilno define themselves?

MILOSZ   There were scarcely any Bielorussians; there were more Tartars than Bielorussians. The Jews are another matter entirely, a completely separate matter. By the way, I have to say that, from the vantage of my American experience, my view on the Jewish population of Wilno is probably completely different from that of Poles or of people who have lived in Wilno but have had no experience of America. There are innumerable ties between America and the diaspora of Central Europe. A great many of my colleagues and friends in America have their roots in Wilno, Grodno, those regions. And so, in the faces that I can remember, the Jewish faces of Wilno, I can see the fathers, the hypothetical fathers and grandfathers of my colleagues here in America. Very interesting. Polishness was of course not an issue for the Jews: the Jews of Wilno had only the faintest sense of things Polish, as I've said. But when Poland was partitioned, the rabbis of Wilno condemned the act very pointedly and mourned for the death of the Republic. Later on, though, there was a certain assimilation to Russian culture. Just as there was a certain degree of assimilation to German culture in Lwów. We shouldn't forget that Yiddish was the basic language spoken by Wilno's Jews. But let's take the Haskala movement, a movement to enlighten the Jews that arose at the beginning of the nineteenth century. The case of Klaczko, which I've described elsewhere, was very typical. I think Klaczko was in the first wave of the enlightenment and could speak Hebrew, even write it. Ultimately, Hebrew had been the language of Jewish religious literature for centuries, but I think that also played a certain emancipating role in the Haskala movement. I'm not sure about this, I'm guessing here, but the Haskala seems to have contained some proto-Zionist elements, the rebirth of Hebrew and so forth. Later on, Klaczko very quickly shifted to German as the language of emancipation, and then to Polish and French after that; in France he wrote articles in French. In any case, the Haskala was active in Wilno at the beginning of the nineteenth century. Of course, it was logical that the Haskala led young people to the Polish language, as it had in

Klaczko's case. But that process was shattered by the partitions. For ambitious people who wanted to leave the ghetto behind and acquire a general education, the choice was either to emigrate to Germany, as, let's say, Mendelssohn did, or to assimilate to Russian culture, which, as we know, is very attractive. During the nineteenth century, we see assimilation to Russian culture. One element that existed in Warsaw was entirely absent from Wilno. Cylkow, the rabbi of the Warsaw synagogue—I wrote about him in my introduction to my translations from the Bible—preached his sermons in Polish. This was shortly after the Uprising of 1863. That would have been unthinkable in Wilno!

FIUT   It's interesting that there's a certain divergence between what you say and what Polish historiography says. For example, it claims that Piłsudski's federalist platform was increasingly abandoned in favor of the National Democrats' centralist concept the farther Piłsudski moved from the helm. But what you say suggests that in Wilno there was a chance for pluralism—if not political, then at least cultural.

MILOSZ   I'll try to answer that question, which I think is very important. It seems to me that nothing about twentieth-century Polish history can be understood if one overlooks the fact that there were two basic camps, which were constantly clashing. One was the ND camp, the National Democrats, which, in the late thirties increasingly became fascist in its ideology, with a strong tendency to abandon the democratic and parliamentary forms. The other camp is very difficult to define, because it includes people with socialist and liberal sympathies. And the picture was further complicated by the large number of so-called minorities in Poland. That division reaches back to the end of the nineteenth century, when the National League on the one hand, and the Polish Socialist Party on the other, were founded. Narutowicz, independent Poland's first president, was elected by the votes of the socialists, the liberals, and the minorities. He was assassinated by a right-wing fanatic. The clashes and struggle between the two camps continued throughout the period between the wars; sometimes one camp was on top, sometimes the other. In his memoirs, *My Century*, Aleksander Wat mentions that the two camps came to terms of a sort in the twenties, meaning that the political parties active at the time divided up the ministries. "You get education"—for example, the NDs got education—"and we"—for example, the socialists—"will take social welfare." Piłsudski, of course, had a restraining effect on the NDs' impulses. And here I have to say that, were it not for the so-called minorities, Poland would probably have been a thoroughly ND country, because the Church was inclined to the so-called national ideology. The Church was a very powerful representative of that ideology. Of course, the Polish Socialist Party had a strong influence and tradition, but it was not enough to outweigh the Church's influence. Still, a certain balance was maintained, because there were so many minorities and because of Piłsudski. It was only later, in the thirties—just as I was fleeing Wilno, at the end of 1936— and after Piłsudski's death that the OZN, the Camp of National Unification, began heading full-speed to the right, toward a monolithic Polish state. Bociański, who was then the governor of Wilno Province and politically somewhere between the Sanacja * and the Piłsudskyites, launched a campaign of oppression and persecution against the Lithuanians and Bielorussians. The pacification of the Ukrainian villages, the destruction of Ukrainian churches, and so forth at the end of the thirties was the same sort of thing. That is, the different periods assumed different forms, but that basic division was a constant. I attach great significance to that division, because, looking back to the eighteenth century, we see a similar division into Reformists and obscurantists.

FIUT   Going back to Wilno's geographic and political situation, I'd like to ask whether the proximity of the Soviet Union was felt in the city.

---

* Sanacja ("Recovery") was the name given to Marshal Piłsudski's regime and his followers after his coup in 1926. —TRANS.

MILOSZ   There was no sense whatsoever of a Soviet presence. It was, rather, its absence that was felt, because the border was just about closed. We grew up close to that border, knowing relatively little about the U.S.S.R. Unquestionably, there was quite a strong Russian presence in Wilno, but it was tsarist Russian. Ultimately, Wilno was a city of so-called Litvaks, meaning Russian-speaking Jews, the upper levels of society. Poland imposed no discrimination against the Russian language, though that was not the case with the Bielorussians, as I've mentioned. Let's not forget that in some way Wilno's situation was bound up with Piłsudski's vision of a federation. I don't know what would have happened in practice if Piłsudski had gotten the whole of Bielorussia. But, in any case, the NDs torpedoed Piłsudski's plans in the Treaty of Riga in 1920, because Moscow had been ready to cede the whole of Bielorussia. I don't know the details of those negotiations; you'd have to go into the history of the period for that. We don't know how the Ukrainian issue would have been resolved if there had been no NDs, but at least it can be said that, if Piłsudski had achieved his goal, all of Bielorussia, including Minsk, would have been in Poland's orbit, and some sort of federation would have come into being.

FIUT   I wonder if that sort of federation would have been possible in those times, given the increased tendency toward self-determination and the extreme nationalism among the various ethnic groups. Wasn't the federation basically a nineteenth-century concept, an echo of gentry thinking about the old Republic?

MILOSZ   It certainly was. I've said somewhere that Piłsudski's vision came either too early or too late. The Treaty of Riga was a defeat for Piłsudski, and he was aware of that. And Wilno, as a city in an area that was actually more Bielorussian than Lithuanian, paid a heavy price for the incomplete solution to the problem. That was the cause of the constant trials of communists in Wilno, principally Bielorussians, and all the political action against the Bielorussians.

Still, I have to add that this final attempt to restore the Grand
Duchy of Lithuania was part of Piłsudski's struggle with the
NDs, who had a completely different idea. They saw the nation as a body that had to absorb and denationalize the other
elements; Bielorussians and Ukrainians on Polish territory had
to be denationalized, made into Poles. Piłsudski did not want
that at all; that was not his intention. On the contrary. And
that's why there still exists a very clear-cut conflict between
those who are, or would like to be, the heirs to Piłsudski's
ideas, and those who are the heirs of Dmowski's *Thoughts of
a Modern Pole*. Those are two completely different concepts
of patriotism and nationality. Personally, I think of myself as
belonging to the Grand Duchy of Lithuania; I would be glad
to define myself the way a professor of mine, Sukiennicki,
once defined himself—as a Polish-speaking Lithuanian. That's
difficult to do today—the very concept really doesn't exist
any more—but we should be aware that many people in
Wilno, including professors of mine, advocated the idea of a
federation when I was a young man in Wilno.

FIUT   Don't both of those models for patriotism strike you
as utopian in some way, because of their extremism?

MILOSZ   Don't forget that defeat is always followed by reap-
praisal. And, then, certain things seem to have been impossible. Still, a slightly different historical configuration would
have produced different solutions to problems, and some things
would have turned out to be possible. Obviously, both solutions were utopian. Why? For a very simple reason: around
the turn of the eighteenth century, Poland lost its historical
bet with Russia. That rendered the federalist solution somewhat utopian, but Dmowski's solution also assumed utopian
hues, as we can see from the history of the last few decades.
Because the Poland of today is the fulfillment of Dmowski's
plan. Yes, it is! A Poland without minorities, ethnically homogeneous, and back within the boundaries Poland had a
thousand years ago. But that also turned out to be a trap, the
patriotism of policemen. Isn't that so?

FIUT   It is. What I had in mind earlier, when I was speaking of the various Wilnos, was not only a cross-section of one given time but also the city's historical changes. For example, did you see any changes in Wilno when you came back from Paris?

MILOSZ   Of course I did. Those weren't changes in Wilno but changes in my point of view. I returned to Wilno on a number of occasions. Once after the end of the academic year in Warsaw, and then once after Paris. Very strange experiences.

It was during the summer. I arrived in a city that seemed very quiet after Paris, with an unlikely architecture of clouds above the city, Baroque clouds. Very strange. Warsaw, which somehow managed to intrude itself between Wilno and Paris in my life, undoubtedly counted for less. In fact, to a large extent, Wilno and Paris were my cities when I was a young man. As for the intuitions I had back then in the thirties, Wilno seemed to be offering me a chance at happiness. A chance at the happiness that, for various reasons, did not come to pass in my personal life or in the life, the history, of the city as a whole. A great chance at happiness, maybe precisely because of that mix of city and nature.

I returned to Wilno at various times before 1939. One time — this was in 1938 or perhaps even at the beginning of 1939 — I arrived from Warsaw, and Wilno struck me as a backwater. I had very romantic sentiments at that time — suddenly I return, the passage of time, the melancholy of transience. I thought I had already lived a full life and was returning to a city that held memories for me. That's how I saw it at the time. If I'd known then what lay in store for me! It was all very personal and subjective.

FIUT   You mentioned some of the streets you knew well when you were in high school. How about later on?

MILOSZ   For me probably the most important street in Wilno was Harbor Street, which was not even a street because of the relatively small number of houses on it; the rest of it was green corn and cliffs that came right up to the street. For many years I took Harbor Street to school, and then I'd turn onto Boufłł Hill. Either I'd turn onto Boufałł Hill or I'd take a different route: instead of continuing along Harbor, at the intersection of Harbor and Sierakowski I'd climb up the almost vertical hillside. Loose clay, grass, and a path up the hill. And when I was at the top, I'd take the path down the other side to Boufałł Street. Instead of going up Boufałł Street, I'd have done some steep climbing, and then I'd go down the slope, which just about landed me at my high school. That street was very important to me for various other reasons as well. Very important emotionally, because of people who lived there. But later on an important role would be played by those small, narrow, medieval lanes and alleyways, which are one of Wilno's special charms: Literary Lane, Skopówka, Bernadine Lane, and so on.

FIUT   Did Wilno feel like home to you?

MILOSZ   I'm worried about sentimentalizing here. Let's not forget that that Wilno still retained some features of a Russian garrison town, though not in an aggressive way. If I can understand the atmosphere in Dostoevsky's Russian cities, it's because there was a lot of that in Wilno. First the officers and students would go drinking, and then they'd go wenching. There was an amazing number of brothels in Wilno, as there usually are in religious cities. . . .

FIUT   How did the city's garrison qualities manifest themselves?

MILOSZ   A little in the fact that the people who set the tone were the young people, the officers and students. That doesn't mean there was any love lost between them. In fact, they had no contact with each other. But there were some fraternities that made for a sort of middle ground between them—the fraternity men who wore colored caps and who donned sashes and swords for parades. The fraternity men and the young officers had a similar mentality.

FIUT   What else do you see as being typical of Wilno?

MILOSZ   What set the city's tone? There was a great deal of poverty, no question of that. Economically, the city was at an impasse. The cheapness of things in that city—you could buy a dinner for fifty groszy, a dinner with meat. That really was very cheap, even for the Poland of that time.

FIUT   Why was the city at an "impasse"?

MILOSZ   Because it was locked up! The border with Lithuania was closed, the border with Russia was practically closed; there was no economic exchange, no industrialization. A few tanneries, some saw mills, and that was it.

FIUT   So, then, what was the basis of Wilno's economy?

MILOSZ   That's a very good question. What was its economic basis? Little stores, craftsmen, a very few large stores, civil servants living on their salaries, storekeepers, a very small working class, an influx of maids and prostitutes from the countryside—two professions that often merged into one. The city simply had no healthy economic base. The Lithuanians advanced various arguments for why Wilno had to be Lithuanian—"*Mes be Vilniaus nenurimsim*" ("We can't live without Wilno," "We won't give up Wilno")—because it was the capital of the Grand Duchy of Lithuania, the traditions of the grand dukes, and so forth. But their ethnic views were very ambiguous. They claimed that the people of Wilno were all Polonized Lithuanians, but the fact of the matter was that very few people spoke Lithuanian in Wilno. And of course there were also economic arguments: as part of Poland, Wilno was only a provincial city and doomed to economic stagnation, but if it were the capital of a country, that would be a different matter entirely, it would thrive.

FIUT   Does that mean that the city was half dead or that Lithuanian propaganda was on the increase?

MILOSZ   No, the city wasn't dead. From what I've said it should be clear that the city was very alive and interesting. The city showed none of the symptoms observable in the south of France, for instance, where entire small towns die out because the young people leave for the cities. There was none of that at all. People stayed in their little Bielorussian or Polish or Lithuanian villages because there was nothing else they could do. And as for migrating to the city because of the economic opportunity there, that was out of the question! There were no opportunities in the city. The entire countryside was frozen in place. It was an extremely settled way of life. The famous little manor houses in Antokol—Antokol was a district of Wilno on the banks of the Wilia—the famous little manor houses in Antokol that were written about in the eighteenth century had not changed one bit. The same old women and old men, the same people living in retirement as in the eighteenth century. Behaving the same way, going to the same churches.

FIUT   Was the depression of the thirties reflected in Wilno?

MILOSZ   I don't seem to remember Wilno having anything but a depression. I assume that in comparison with Europe's large industrial centers, which were hit hard by the depression, it didn't make much of a difference for Wilno, with its economy that could barely creep along anyway.

Work and Travel

FIUT   You said that two cities, Wilno and Paris, played the key role in your life before the war, that your youth was a mix of Wilno and Paris. Now that you've described Wilno, we should devote our attention to your ties with prewar Paris. What was the city you saw in '34 like?

MILOSZ   When I went there in the fall of '34 on a scholarship, it was not my first time in Paris: I'd been there a few years earlier with my friends "Robespierre" Jędrychowski and "Elephant" Zagórski during the first Colonial Exposition. Of course, I had not the slightest doubt that I was in the capital of the world. My sense of Paris—which I've described in my poem "Bypassing Rue Descartes"—was different then. That year in Paris was unusually important for me, and not necessarily the way people might imagine. I had enormous energy but it was all bottled up. As a young person I was filled with inhibitions, bashful, frustrated at every turn. The same was true of my poetry: I could not say what I wanted. What I mean is that the poems I wrote in Paris, such as "Gates of the Arsenal," are poems laden with imagery and to a large extent written out of enormous pressure from the unconscious, at great effort. I couldn't write. I was blocked. Too much pent-up energy. In retrospect, I can see that I was endowed with demonic vitality but completely pent up.

To be in such a state in a city like Paris generated tension. But the picture changed depending on where I was living in Paris. First I lived on rue Lamandé, in a sort of hotel that I think is still there. It was for people with scholarships, and its most notable feature was the constant fumes: they were always killing bedbugs there because they could never exterminate them entirely. My earliest impressions of Paris are: smoky autumn days, the tartness of Parisian mornings, coffee and croissants. That was the Batignolles quarter, Clichy, and so forth. I knew practically no French people in that period. The only entrée to French life I had was through my cousin Oskar Milosz. Every once in a while he would take me to lunch with some French writers, usually near the Opéra. There was a Polish world in Paris. For a while I attended the Sunday tours of the Louvre, a small group led by the distinguished Polish painter Pankiewicz.

That was the Lamandé phase. I lived there a few months and then moved to rue Valette, right near the Panthéon. Rue Valette runs down to rue des Écoles. I lived in a *pension* owned by Madame Valmorin, a mulatto from Martinique. And there I got a taste of the atmosphere of those Parisian *pensions* so often described in French novels. I would say that people on the lowest social level lived there: pencil pushers, post-office clerks, students. It was cheap. The food was portioned out meticulously, with nothing fancy about the cuisine; you didn't get much on your plate, because they had to keep within their budget. This period was an interesting one, because I met Antoni Potocki, who was also living in that *pension*. Antoni Potocki was quite well known in the Young Poland period at the turn of the century. He wrote *Contemporary Polish Literature,* an eccentric book—both the style and the odd ideas seemed out of control. He did not come from the famous Potocki family. I don't know what his background was, but in any case his name was Potocki. He had a big bushy mustache and was a devoted citizen of Paris. He had a little something to do with the Polish embassy, where he organized exhibits that provided him with a bit of income, but apart from that it would be hard to say what he lived on. He did some writing. A paltry existence. He was old and lonely. A young woman painter, who also lived in that *pension,* looked after him. She was a Russian, from a Russian émigré family, the Khodaseviches—though I'm not sure that's a pure Russian name, it's more Polish. The family had emigrated to Poland. She graduated from the Academy of Fine Arts in Warsaw and married a Polish painter by the name of Grabowski. And so she was Nadya Khodasevich-Grabowska. She took care of old Potocki, and in that respect she was a good, kind person. She and I used to talk. She was a rabid communist and had brothers in Russia. She was living with a young French painter, and the two of them drew and painted in the same style. In other words, her personality was so powerful that she had imposed her vision and her method of drawing and painting on him. Fernand Léger's way of painting was her ideal at that time. Today, Nadya, formerly Khodasevich-Grabowska, is Fernand Léger's widow and the heir to his entire fortune; she lives in Provence. Those things happen. Back then she hadn't even met Léger.

And so that *pension* marks one period. Then I moved to a small hotel nearby where my friend Bochwic, a postgraduate student in chemistry from Poland, lived. It was a beautiful little hotel. The street was supposed to be torn down, because the medieval buildings were in danger of collapsing. The street is still there and so are the buildings on it, and the corner where the hotel was is still the same except that the hotel is gone now. It was called Hôtel Laplace, and it was just across from the École Polytechnique. At that point it was spring and I was going to the Alliance Française and taking the *cours supérieur* in French. I passed the exams, wrote the essays, and got my diploma. Well, that was a relatively more relaxed period: I had been completely depressed by various personal complications in the fall.

Among the events that spring I could mention my encounters with some young Germans. There was one named Günther Eten who espoused the National Socialist ideology. There were lots of young Germans traveling at that time—Europe was full of them. I don't rule out the possibility that many of them were simply spying. Günther was a poet. Like Stefan George, he dreamed of returning to the age of knighthood, to medieval Germany. His racism was very dubious, because he had friends who had fled Nazism, Jews and people who were half Jewish. His romantic conception of knighthood had a definite homosexual tinge; the two things went together, of course. In Eten I saw something I already knew from my first trip to Europe, which was before the advent of Nazism. At that time, young Germans known as *Wandervögeln*—"birds of passage"—had wandered through Germany singing of a return to the blood and the land, with strong elements of male friendship. It was quite curious to observe that young man. He and I weren't friends but we did have friends and acquaintances in common.

I also remember the Congress in Defense of Culture that took place in Paris in the Mutualité Hall in the spring of 1935. I was in the audience, of course, not on the stage. The speakers included Ehrenburg, Pasternak (who had come to Paris), and a whole series of French writers—André Gide, I think, I don't remember who else. Malraux must have been there—it would be easy to check. It was a congress in defense of culture, an antifascist event, to mobilize opinion against fascism. A very noble enterprise, but personally I was skeptical: it was all somehow too obviously orchestrated and devoid of spontaneity. That spring there was also a soccer match between France and Germany, which I describe in *Native Realm*. Busloads of fans came in from Germany and filled half the stands, roaring savagely in cadence. It made a truly sinister impression. That was my first sense of this sinister quality and the danger it posed, and I began writing poems about Nazism and the approaching danger. No, I wrote a poem along those lines on January 1, 1935, and dedicated it to Zagórski, which means I had felt this earlier. My conversations with Oskar Milosz certainly inclined me toward the apocalyptic, because he predicted correctly the year when the war would break out and even that it would begin in Gdynia—

"Gdynia" is an anagram of *gniady,* referring to the red horse of the Apocalypse. And so all that made for a mounting sense of danger.

I openly admit that I vacillated when summer came, but I had to go back to Poland because my scholarship had run out. After that taste of a cosmopolitan atmosphere, and after realizing that there'd be a war soon—Germany, Russia, and so on—I might have stayed if someone had given me the chance to. But life was tough, I told myself. Actually, I didn't seriously contemplate staying, because I would have had nothing to do there. And, after my year in France, I realized that there were forces at work that would prevent the French from repeating the burst of heroism they had displayed during the First World War. I no longer had faith in France. That's one difference between me and my peers. The myth of France was so basic in Poland that the French defeat in 1940 came as a terrible shock; people in Poland really felt it was the end of the world.

It's difficult to define everything that I learned there. In any case, apart from the literature I came to know, we shouldn't forget that at the time it was very hard for a young person in Poland to gain any knowledge of painting. What was there to see in Wilno? And so for me the Louvre and the art galleries of Paris were my entrée into the world of painting. And music . . . I went to the concerts at Châtelet, which had primarily visual meaning for me; I usually sat on the top balcony, "with the gods." The orchestra was far down below. A wonderful vision of an orchestra as a system of rhythmical movements. Of course, when I was in France then, I only knew Paris and the area right around the city—Fontainebleau—but I didn't know the rest of France. I had no money to travel. I got to know those other parts of France later on. I had no way of getting around, no car. It may sound strange today to say that you stayed in Paris and never went outside the surrounding area, but that was what happened.

FIUT   There are mythical cities like Paris or Rome to which people bring a certain pre-existing vision and then compare it to the reality. What was your image of Paris, and how did it compare?

MILOSZ   We might discuss that in connection with my first trip to Paris, rather than my second. Naturally, I had an image of Paris from literature. But it's difficult to say how the two compared. There was something quite bizarre about my experience of Paris as a young man. Besides, you can't separate Paris from my first contact with the West. I had never been to the West, after all; I was completely Eastern European. Warsaw was supposedly an outpost of the West. But in fact I got my first feel of the West when I was at a national exhibition in Poznań, while I was still in school. Warsaw was not a Western European city, but Poznań was. During my first trip, in 1931, Olomouc in Czechoslovakia was the first Western city I saw. And so there were various gradations, the West becoming increasingly real to me. France was a special mutation of the West. I wrote something about the first time I arrived in France. In 1931 we hiked over the mountains of the Black Forest and entered Basel on foot. We crossed over to the French side at Saint-Louis and went into the first café we could find. It was a working-class district. I'll never forget it! We were exotic to them, hairy, wearing shorts, outlandish—*quels types.* We stood out like sore thumbs. We opened the door and found ourselves in the middle of a hubbub and din, glasses clinking, people talking, music playing; naturally they were playing "Java," a popular dance tune then. A huge room packed with people—workers with their girls on their laps, hugging and kissing and drinking wine—we were in wonderland! I had never seen anything like it before in terms of freedom, *joie de vivre,* cheerful boisterousness. I felt dazed and humiliated: "What am I doing in these short pants? . . ." That was how I arrived in France. By the way, as I've written elsewhere, there was great unemployment in France at that time, there were masses of unemployed Polish workers. For me, then, Paris was mostly the streets near the Saint-Paul métro station. Later on I was often to live in that district. Saint-Paul is no longer the Polish district; it's around the rue des Rosiers now. And so there were various gradations. And, naturally, Paris was a continuation of the entrance we had made in that café in Saint-Louis.

FIUT   What you said about your experience of Paris was interesting, but you didn't put any finer point on the image of the city you brought there with you.

MILOSZ   I think it's a bit much to elevate this to too high a level. There were a number of pictures of Paris in the French textbook we used in high school. And I suppose that the images of Paris one acquires in childhood or in school do color the mind a good deal. So I assume that that nineteenth-century Paris was very present somewhere in the back of my mind. It was more or less what I expected.

FIUT   What places or buildings in Paris were the most important to you? What did you want to see as soon as you arrived?

MILOSZ   The Seine, the axis of the Seine around which Paris rotates is at the center of my mental map. And the Tuileries at daybreak, with that immense view of the Arc de Triomphe and the Champs-Élysées. My sense of the city was more or less from the Seine and the Latin Quarter. As for literature, my information about Paris—from novels, for example—was very scanty back then in 1931. I was late in starting to read Balzac, who's the main writer for all that. I don't remember—maybe I had read a few of Balzac's novels by then—but basically I did my reading of Balzac during the German occupation. Everyone was reading Balzac then; I don't know why he held up so well then and didn't pale in comparison with the reality of the Occupation. I read Balzac and Baudelaire's essays on Parisian art exhibitions, his excellent essay "Constantin Guys, le peintre de la vie moderne," which I seem to remember having translated into Polish. I also read Caillois, who wrote about the mythical aspects of Paris, the wilderness at the heart of the city: for me all this was something of a delayed digestion of earlier experience. Or, rather, a confirmation of my intuitive experience of Paris. Because one really does seek a city's mythical center.

Of course, Paris was a bit different then. I say "a bit" because that city displays astonishing continuity and stability, which gives one pause—especially us, people from our part of Europe. The balance of districts shifts. . . . The Paris of the thirties, if we mean the attractions of "gay Paris," the whores, and so on, was still Pigalle, Clichy, Montmartre. In 1931 I went to La Coupole and La Rotonde—Montparnasse in its final glory. That's a chapter in itself. It was staggering! When I would walk by, half the sidewalk would be covered with tables in front of La Coupole and La Rotonde, and to me, a young barbarian at that time, the people sitting there seemed like gods on Parnassus, forever beyond reach. And in fact all those hundreds or thousands of people sitting there were part of a Parnasuss of a sort, though only the dregs of it by then. Dramatic incidents involving refugees from Germany were played out there. But that was the twilight of the cafés, the twilight of Montparnasse. As you must know, a short while later the literary scene shifted to the Boulevard Saint-Germain, to the Deux Magots, the Flore, and so on. Montparnasse was shunted aside. I don't know how it is that certain districts continue to live—I mean, how the fame of certain districts lives on after the fact and continues to pull in the tourists—but it's my impression that a great change occurred. Maybe some people still go looking for women in Pigalle and Clichy, but that's probably not what they're looking for there now.

FIUT   What was the mythological center of Paris?

MILOSZ   In the morning I would hear little bells—a shepherd driving a herd of goats past the Panthéon. Something like that was still possible then. . . . But let's not be too idyllic about it. I simply assume that he had quite a few customers for goat's milk and he would come in with his goats, which he grazed by the forts and escarpments. Paris's mythological center was in Clichy, Pigalle, because that's where the women were. The brothel-café was an institution in the Paris of the thirties. You went in for a beer and there'd be naked girls performing, dancing with each other and so on. The wilderness of Paris, the mythical image of Paris, was always connected with a vision of debauchery or something of the sort.

FIUT   Did the image of the city change for you after your next trip?

MILOSZ   I've spent so much of my life in Paris that I can't separate those two images. It's very difficult. What I said about the goats is probably from my first trip to Paris, in 1931. But the mythical image of Paris I spoke of is, rather, from the second. During my first stay in Paris I was interested in the Colonial Exhibition, which must have lodged very deeply in my memory and my imagination. That was the last exhibition put on by the French empire. Very curious. Another thing was that for a while we stayed at the Salvation Army on rue de la Glacière, where you had to sing hymns for your dinner. Of course all the *clochards* who came there treated that as normal. That Salvation Army hostel on rue de la Glacière was called the Palais du Peuple. Since we were young, penniless, and not fussy, it was fine for us—you got dinner and a place to sleep.

FIUT   Why were you so impressed by that exhibition?

MILOSZ   Probably because the animals and Asian or African natives were displayed in the same way. There were tiger cages side by side with Vietnamese and Annamese huts where daily life was led just as it is in the wild.

FIUT   You said that your encounter with Paris was an encounter with one mutation of the West. What did that mean to you at the time?

MILOSZ   Primarily that the streets were not cobblestone but paved, covered with asphalt. And next, as I said in *Native Realm*, I was impressed by the order, the daily routine, the smoothness of civilized life. When we arrived in Prague in the summer of 1931, we had an absolute sense that we'd left the East and arrived in the West. Besides, I'd experienced something similar when my father worked as an engineer in Suwałki and would sometimes take me across the border to East Prussia. You'd cross the border and find yourself in a different world. The moment you crossed the border, there'd be asphalt roads, inns and roadhouses, nothing like what we had in Poland. The customers were country people, farmers, but all well fed, very well dressed, smoking cigars, drinking cognac. In other words, you'd have to conclude that a higher level of civilization automatically leads man toward the spiritual, in other words that the West's spiritual, creative, and artistic superiority was absolute.

FIUT   That wasn't so in Germany.

MILOSZ   Excuse me, but you missed the humor here. This aspect of cultural level was very prominent if we're talking about the differences between Poland and Czechoslovakia, between Poland and Germany. When I was in Prague in 1931, it was summer and the city's atmosphere was athletic, outdoorsy, democratic. I'm referring to the crowds of people, young workers and students taking their girls outside the city on Sundays. There weren't any motorcycles yet, and so people hiked out or paddled along the Vltava. But the crowds! A democratic mass that would have been very difficult to find in Poland because of the large gap between the proletariat and the upper classes in Warsaw. Of course, Warsaw was evolving before the war—that had changed—but I was still struck by Prague in 1931. Besides, I really didn't know Warsaw well yet when I went to Prague. These comparisons are also a bit skewed by the fact that I knew Wilno, where we— the group of young students I belonged to—we did the same thing, represented the same thing. But how many of us were there in Wilno? Very few, but here were the people of Prague, out in droves, enjoying their Sunday. And the atmosphere was wildly erotic. There's something enchanting about Prague. And so I wasn't surprised when I saw Milan Kundera say in an interview that when he left Prague for the West, he was surprised to discover that Western life wasn't so very erotic at all. He said, "Yes, yes, I know, sexual liberation and so on. The West has all that, of course, but that's not the point."

FIUT   It's difficult to speak of the Paris you visited as a young man without mentioning your meetings with Oskar Milosz. After all, they did have far-reaching consequences for your life and your work. Of course, you judge them from a different vantage now, but what did they mean to you at the time?

MILOSZ   You know, I've written about him so many times, and I wouldn't want to repeat myself here. I've tried various ways of capturing my relationship with him, him as a person and his philosophy. That's not easy. I was full of respect and admiration for him when we first met, not that I understood all his mystical pursuits and prophetic writings at the time. I knew French fairly well in 1931 but just wasn't up to reading that sort of thing. I didn't understand much of it. In any case, I've been reading his works for decades now, and I've translated some of them into English, and I still have questions that I can't answer. An extremely hard nut to crack. But I had an intuitive sense that he was a person of high caliber. In fact, he was the first person I considered to be of a higher caliber than anyone I'd encountered in Poland. Because none of my professors, and none of my older literary colleagues, radiated such strength and depth of mind. If we leave aside a young man's possibly snobbish pleasure in having a relative like him, one with the same last name, all that made an enormous impression on me. I've always had a strong need to admire; to my mind, this has been a constant feature of my nature, and one that, I think, speaks more in my favor than against it.

My relationship with Oskar Milosz was based on my desire to pay genuine homage to someone, to encounter someone superior to me. Not necessarily because of his poetry,
which, incidentally, in 1931 was also a hard nut for me to
crack. I had not yet read the novel *L'Amoureuse Initiation*,
because it's written in difficult French. It's a poetic novel and
not at all easy to follow. I only read it later on. But I had an
intuitive sense of the power and charm of his personality.

Why do some of us intuitively place people in hierarchies,
put them on various levels, while others don't? I suppose I
had an especially strong need to place people in a hierarchy.
I was very critical in my judgments, which is, of course, very
dangerous if not tempered with tolerance for people's flaws.
Later on, only much later on, did I learn to accept people
despite their ridiculous aspects and shortcomings. As for the
signs of madness that supposedly surface in Oskar Milosz's
writing, there was not the slightest trace of it in the way he
lived and acted. And this made him all the more enigmatic, a
quality he shared with Emanuel Swedenborg, who was a model
citizen all his life, a member of the Royal Mining Commission, a witty man, popular in society. He showed no symptoms of what the twentieth century calls schizophrenia, though
even Jaspers detects it in Swedenborg. His life showed no
sign of any discord between him and other people, any break
in communication. It was the same with Oskar Milosz:
there was none of that at all. We're dealing with special cases
here.

FIUT   It's known that Oskar Milosz played an important role
in forming your world view, and perhaps your poetry as well.

MILOSZ   Some of Oskar Milosz's influence can even be found
in the volume *From the Rising of the Sun*. That may seem
very paradoxical, but it's true. Which brings us to the concept
of the two truths: one for yourself, the other for the *pro-
fanum vulgus*. You maintain a certain esoteric way of thinking for yourself but do not reveal it; revealing it would be
unnecessary, dangerous, and would lead nowhere. So, to a

large extent, my poetry was nourished by secretive reflection.
I think that the central problem here was my conflict with the
priest who taught catechism, with Catholicism in school, the
Catholicism of the "better people." And then suddenly in
Oskar Milosz I had encountered a person who threw a completely different light on metaphysical and religious questions: his philosophy did not depart from the teachings of the
Church, but at the same time it represented a system of thought
that had nothing whatsoever in common with Polish Catholicism. A whole new dimension opened within me! Besides, it
didn't take me long to understand his basic struggle against
the mechanistic, materialistic world view, Newtonian physics. His concept of space and time was opposed to an infinite,
existing space, a sort of reservoir for worlds, and to time viewed
as a line extending forward and backward into infinity; he
conceived of time, space, matter, and movement as being created simultaneously. Where there's no matter, there's no space
or time; where there's no movement, there's no matter, space,
or time—everything comes at once. He saw the creation of
the world as a transformation—as he put it—of incorporeal,
nonphysical light into physical light, energy, electricity. All
that led the young man I was into a realm that was, on the
one hand, absolutely alien to Polish Catholicism and, on the
other, opposed to the entire radical, left intelligentsia for whom,
in general, religion did not exist. That was a solitary stance
to take in Poland, very much the exception, but one that I
think was very fruitful and which—despite my apparent political affiliations—defined where I stood.

FIUT   I had something of an ulterior motive in asking that
question. What's striking is that after that stay in Paris your
interests and the tone of your articles seem to change: they
go from very radical and leftist to religious with a moral cast.

MILOSZ   The change you refer to is not one I'm really happy
about. I think I was a lost soul in the years between returning
from Paris and the outbreak of the war. So lost that, in fact,
if it hadn't been for the outbreak of war, I don't know whether

I would have ever extricated myself from all those snarls, that impasse. I also have the impression that it was getting worse. Even when I was in Wilno in 1935 and 1936, after returning from Paris, things weren't so good. I wrote the poem "Slow River" in 1936, and it shows that by then the crisis was quite severe. I find the course it ran very curious. This is connected with various personal matters of which I cannot speak here; I do understand the connections, more or less. Besides, some of the events of my personal life in the late thirties even strike me as exceedingly strange; I can't answer a number of questions I ask myself about that period. In any case, I can see that I fell into an impasse of some sort at around the time I moved to Warsaw in '37. And I don't derive any pleasure from the fact that those articles and essays were so knotted and, as you put it, moralistic in nature.

FIUT You worked for Radio Wilno before you moved to Warsaw. Your life takes surprising turns, as it did when your chose your field of study.

MILOSZ After graduating, I even filed an application for an apprenticeship in law and tried to pull various strings so that I'd be taken on. I think I was accepted somewhere—whether in the court system or a law office, I don't recall. But I never pursued that any further. When was this? I don't remember—it must have been after I returned from Paris. I was just trying to get a toehold. It wasn't easy to find work of any sort in Wilno. A friend of mine named Byrski happened to work for the local station of Polish Radio and got me in there.

FIUT And what effect did the Wilno radio station have on the city and the surrounding area?

MILOSZ That will forever remain the listeners' own sweet secret.

FIUT I'm curious to know whether Radio Wilno had any definite political slant.

MILOSZ   Radio Wilno did have some political orientation, but it was extremely limited. You couldn't even really say there were any regular shows or commentators. Naturally, there were certain programs that the authorities wanted on the air. These included programs essentially beamed to Lithuania, quite brutal anti-Lithuanian propaganda, against the Lithuanian government in Kaunas. Those programs were a form of "servitude," imposed on the Radio by the local provincial authorities, not by Warsaw. Of course, times were no longer so good when I went to work there; OZN—the National Unity Party—had just begun then. My main enemy and Byrski's was Father Maksymilian Kolbe's *Maƚy Dziennik,* which wrote nasty things about us. That's just what the local authorities wanted—denunciations in the press, in *Maƚy Dziennik.* Later on those press clippings made their way to the provincial authorities, and so a certain atmosphere was created. . . .

FIUT   And that led to your being dismissed from work?

MILOSZ   Yes. First I was dismissed, then Byrski.

FIUT   And then you got a job with Radio Warsaw?

MILOSZ   I went to Italy in the interim, between finishing work in Wilno and starting work in Warsaw, at the end of 1937. An educational trip, you might say.

FIUT   Seeking the mythological center of culture?

MILOSZ   You see, that trip to Italy lasted about a month, not very long. Naturally, it left me with many things that are sense memories more than anything usable in rational discourse or for constructing a framework. At one point I said that people didn't have then what we have now—meaning a general familiarity with painting and music through reproductions, albums, records; there was incomparably less of that then. And it was rare for a young person from Poland to have seen the art of Italy. The upper classes were familiar with Italian art, it was the wealthy families who would bring their sons and daughters to Rome, Florence, and so forth. At that time I represented a sort of middle position; later on it was all to become common knowledge. Needless to say, I have many memories of my trip to Italy. I still remember a girl I saw on the Lido, I think it was, wearing a very beautiful green bathing suit, shiny, silky. A German girl in the company of some tall blond men. They were speaking German. And for a long time after, for years, I wondered what sort of Nazi Egeria she was during the years of the "great leader." Still, she might have turned out to be from Austria and I may have been unfair to her. But why do I remember her? Because I was in absolute ecstasy over that woman's beauty!

FIUT   What are your other memories of Italy?

MILOSZ   They don't lend themselves to conversation. Generally speaking, conversation is not a good way to retrieve visual experiences or any other sense impressions, because such experiences can only be approached through extremely precise description, rather inadvisable in conversation.

FIUT   I'm interested in your experience of Italian art.

MILOSZ   Snobbism always plays a role in any experience of Italian art. It's difficult to separate the snobbish aspect from what we genuinely like. Groups of tourists going around viewing works of art make asses of themselves. It's rare that anyone overcomes all that, arrives at a completely independent opinion and says that all that art bores him to death. "Leave me alone! I just want to sit in a café and drink wine and not look at any sculpture or painting." That aside, it's a mystery. Some things we took a quick glance at to pay tribute to foolish fashion come back to us years later, some detail or form becoming a genuine part of our experience. But, as I say, the authenticity of our experience of works of art is in some way sabotaged by our knowledge that they're beautiful, that this is a famous period in painting, and so forth. Making a trip like this one or, later, going to the Louvre, you pick up various turns of phrase, expressions of praise. You learn that communing with the so-called works of art of the past is a part of your indoctrination, a part of belonging to the world of culture, and so on.

FIUT   That surprises me a little. The thirties weren't a period of the sort of mass tourism we have now.

MILOSZ   The very idea of traveling through Italy and viewing the schools of Renaissance painting implies that you've done some reading and know which painter was influenced by which, the genealogy of art, and so forth. This is educational travel, whose purpose is to acquire the language of snobbism so you can communicate with others who move in those circles.

FIUT   Does that mean that it's the people you met in Italy that you remember best?

MILOSZ   No. I was traveling, after all. That's a certain type of excuse, a bit like hunting as a reason for being out in nature since you can't be out in nature without a pretext. It's the same with traveling. Naturally, you go to Orvieto, you see the cathedral in the grass there, you see Signorelli's frescoes, which made an enormous impression on me, and a lasting one. A trip has its own structure. But there are also the completely accidental glances, touches, contacts with people. By the way, Italian Fascism was in full bloom in 1937—the black shirts, and an atmosphere that you felt on your skin rather than consciously, that vile totalitarian atmosphere. Aside from the fact that I had no political business, I made no contact with any revolutionaries. And then there was the great sports arena in Rome, surrounded by marble statues of athletes. The accoutrements of totalitarianism—the uniforms, the blackshirts, the almost imperceptible fear—that was the undercurrent in tourist Italy. In any case, I've written about that.

FIUT   You went from Italy to Warsaw. . . .

MILOSZ   I started working in Warsaw, which seemed like Babylon to me in comparison with Wilno. A feverish anthill. Not to mention what the streets around the radio station were like. First I worked on Zielna Street, sharing an office with a few other people. My job was to sort through the international wires—I was terrified! But the streets around there, like Zielna and Złota, were completely different from Wilno, and in a way exotic. Exotic in their rapacity! There was certainly a great deal of poverty in Wilno, but I never thought of Wilno as a rapacious city. In Warsaw you had a very keen awareness of the struggle for existence. All Warsaw seemed tense to me. A fast, cunning city. Unlike Wilno, with its slow speech and slow tempo, Warsaw was a fast and merciless place. Regardless of how bored I was by my job at the Radio, I didn't dare quit: I saw no other way to make a living. Radio Warsaw was very important for many people in Warsaw, because they either wrote for it, helped with the programs, gave lectures, or worked at the station itself. The people who worked at the station were better off. For example, there was a group of people known as "radio supervisors" who were given radios and whose only job was to listen to programs and write reports on their quality. In-house criticism. Those were low-paying jobs, but much sought after by people from the literary world.

FIUT   What was your relationship to the Warsaw literary world at that time?

MILOSZ   I have to say that I took practically no part in Warsaw literary life at that time. I wasn't very sociable and I simply didn't have the time. There were various personal complications, and my job at the Radio was really so exhausting that I had very little time for any activity. Besides, I didn't care much for that world and was never overly tempted by it. I suffered because I was harnessed to my job, and I dreamed of being free of it. I didn't have enough courage just to walk in one day and say, "I've had it." Because where would I go, what would I do, how could I earn a living? Money was tight. Maybe I could have started living a bohemian life, but I had seen that life with my own eyes, and it was wretched. When you're a young man, elegantly dressed, very refined, and used to a certain standard of living, earning more and more all the time because, though your superiors drive you hard, they also promote you—well, there's no way out of that. It took the war to free me from that.

Poland Between the Wars

MILOSZ Poland between the wars: what it was like then? There is no doubt that the birth of an independent Poland in 1918 was such a miraculous event, such a historical rarity, that it created a heady atmosphere and gave people some basic faith. It vindicated all the madmen who throughout the nineteenth century had thought that one day Poland would again be independent. And so we should realize that Poland had been given a new injection of optimism, a confirmation of Poland's faith in the victory of good on earth. Inevitably that had its effect during this entire period, but it gradually became scattered and blurred, and lost the nobility of mind it had kept into the twenties. Later it lost all its freshness and color. It faded. Especially after Piłsudski's death in 1935, when a dread of what the future held became the dominant motif. At the time it was really almost the end of the world for some people. They were like children whose father had suddenly died and who were thrown into the cruel world. And the atmosphere that came later, at the end of the thirties, was often difficult to bear. It's like the joke about the man in the hotel room who throws one boot on the floor. After a while someone knocks on his door and yells, "Goddamnit, take the other one off." The atmosphere became increasingly ominous. We should bear in mind that this was a time of constant war. While I was at the university, Japan conquered Manchuria, there was war in the Far East, war in Abyssinia, war in Spain, Hitler came to power.

What was Poland like between the two wars? There are two points of view on the subject. One is the feeling that people had after it was all over, after disaster had swept the whole thing away like a house of cards because it was all so defenseless, powerless, and impractical in comparison with the great totalitarian systems on either side of it. That is, people were enraged, furious at the weakness of that creation, the Poland that had emerged from World War I by a miracle and through the prayers of the prophets. The other point of view is also viable: if it hadn't been for the disaster of war, Poland would have solved its problems one way or another. In the end, Poland was an incomparably more humane country than its big-power neighbors, though it was backward in comparison with Czechoslovakia, which was a modern industrial country by then. That was a Poland of immense economic inequalities, where manufactured goods were very expensive and food products were very cheap. As one smuggler said when bringing food into Warsaw during the war, "I've been waiting twenty years for this!" Still, Poland solved many of its problems in that very short span of time. Some of its problems were almost insoluble—the huge percentage of minorities in the country, especially the Ukrainian population. People are right to accuse Poles of anti-Semitism: it was a profoundly anti-Semitic country. But perhaps they forget that conflicts between ethnic groups—like the conflict between Jews and Arabs in Palestine—lead to mutual hatreds. In Poland there were three million Jews, who for the most part spoke another language, practiced different professions, and felt they were a different nationality. Then the Ukrainians made for a terribly difficult problem! And the German population was quite large, and there was the whole problem of Gdańsk, and Silesia, too. In other words, Poland assumed its independence burdened with countless problems.

And what was it like? I'm very much against idealizing it. Today there may be an understandable need to idealize it to some extent, because it was unquestionably a completely independent country. It's not easy to imagine how much Poland was of and for itself. If Poland solved its problems, it solved them itself, and if it didn't, it didn't—everything was up to the Poles and no one else. No one dictated anything to Poland. I think the first signs that Poland was starting to reckon with its neighbors were the hunting trips that German officials made in Poland. In other words, Poland was sucking up to a powerful neighbor. But that didn't last long, and it turns out not to have had any practical results, because at the decisive moment the Polish government sensed the mood of the populace and had no choice but to resist Hitler's demands.

Judging Poland from the point of view of literature, art, culture, and, of course, the universities and all that, I would say that the basic institutions were good. But that point needs some fleshing out, since high schools were not very accessible because of the costs involved and because of the poverty in the countryside, where the majority of Poles lived. There were decent functioning universities and institutions, like the Mianowski Foundation and the National Endowment for Culture. Naturally, it was a meager life, and the life I knew in Warsaw—say, around the State Institute of Theatrical Art, the Academy of Fine Arts, that was my world—was composed of groups that were relatively small compared with the country as a whole. But—how to put this—I think that my relatively poor knowledge of Poland between the wars is one of my great shortcomings. Because I didn't know Poland. No, I didn't. I had not lived in Poland itself before 1937; Wilno and the so-called Borderland regions provided no insight into the real Poland. I had the few years between 1937 and 1939 in Warsaw, and that was all. And Paris didn't provide any insight into Poland, except perhaps through contrast. So I'm not a good source of information here; better ones can be found.

FIUT   What did this period mean to you in terms of your own life and work?

MILOSZ   That was my youth, after all! I was twenty-eight years old in 1939. The period from your birth until you're twenty-eight or twenty-nine always seems to be important. I've often wondered what the difference would be between growing up between the wars and growing up in People's Poland. I assume that there are some important differences. Both Gombrowicz and I are typical products of the Poland between the wars. That means we became conscious adults in an independent country, and we had time during that period to finish school, graduate from the university, and begin our literary careers. By the time the war broke out, our personalities had already crystallized, as opposed to the generation of the young Warsaw poets who were still adolescents when the war broke out. And that explains a great deal.

FIUT   Would you care to characterize your generation's mentality? I mean the essential constituents of that mentality.

MILOSZ   These are all very short periods of time. I sometimes think that the generation slightly older than mine, which could remember the good days before the First World War, must in a certain sense have been surprised by the establishment of an independent Poland. Though I'm not sure, I must have heard some of their conversations, and this filtered into my mind. But in general I think that the stabilized society in which I lived had an influence: the trains ran on time, the schools functioned, the courts functioned, a real society; no matter what the economic situation was (and it was very meager in Wilno), everything was under control, a well-ordered world. But not all that well ordered, either: when I was a child I was always reading newspaper articles and hearing talk about battles and gangs. We shouldn't forget that the so-called Borderlands—including stretches of Bielorussia—was an area of what we'd call guerrilla actions today. The distinction between guerrillas and bandits had been erased; they would cross over into Poland from the Russian side, pillage and plunder, and then go back across the border. Later on all that gradually disappeared. As I've written elsewhere, all those martyrologies, the reckless exploits of nineteenth-century Polish history, the uprisings, Romantic literature—all that was part of the past for us, gone for good. Our school made a field trip to the First National Exhibition in Poznań—in 1928, I think—and it was so beautiful! We had no sense of proportion; we didn't know what mortal danger Poland was in. Perhaps if we had read the German newspapers, which spoke about a *Saisonstaat,* we might have had some idea. But it was just the other way around—there was a feeling of being completely safe in our own home, faith in the Polish army and our excellent defenses, a faith that lasted right up until September '39. The disintegration of that state came as a terrible shock and crisis to everyone. In his memoirs, Aleksander Wat mentions that it was only after September '39 that the intellectuals woke up and understood that they'd been living in a house of cards.

The Occupation

CZARNECKA   At one point you wrote—in *Native Realm,* I think it was—that you were glad to hear the news that war had broken out because that freed you from the obligation of working for Radio Warsaw. But didn't what happened afterward somewhat exceed your expectations?

MILOSZ   To say the least. I have to say that the experience of those years was so traumatic for the entire country—Poland was in the very eye of the cyclone, the lowest depths of the German occupation in Europe. To a large extent my later work is an attempt to deal with that experience. Not only mine as an individual, but the entire collective's experience. And for that reason it would probably be impossible to speak of this in our conversations. If adequate means can't be found for it in writing, how can they be found in conversation?

CZARNECKA   All the same, I'd like to clear up a few issues, a few myths about you personally that appear quite often in the Western literary press. The first is that you were a so-called freedom fighter. That's a tag that American journalists are quick to apply. Is that how you think of yourself?

MILOSZ   That strikes me as romantic embellishment, but it may be inevitable. When you see all those endless films about *la résistance* in France on television, you understand where all those hero myths and the romanticization come from. In Poland, everyone was a freedom fighter—the entire population. It would be difficult to imagine another country so united in its opposition to Nazism and the occupying force. And for that reason it's missing the point to speak here of individuals as freedom fighters. Of course, there were genuine heroes in the resistance movement, and I certainly do not count myself among them. Apart from my initial adventures during the German campaign in September 1939, I spent most of the war in Warsaw as one of the writers, who were all more or less active in the opposition movement against the Nazis.

CZARNECKA   But, in other words, not in armed struggle.

MILOSZ   No, I don't pretend to have seen action. If publishing anti-Nazi works ought to be included in the fight for freedom, then that, of course, was something I did do. It's a question of interpretation.

CZARNECKA   We've been speaking about the German occupation, but there was a double occupation in Poland then. Some of the territory that had belonged to Poland before the war was under Soviet occupation, and the rest was held by the Germans.

MILOSZ   Of course. World War II broke out as a result of the Molotov-Ribbentrop pact, which contained a clause stating that the Polish state would be divided between Hitler and Stalin. The Soviet Union's occupation of eastern Poland resulted in mass deporations to the depths of Soviet Asia and in incredible suffering. The Soviet system yields little to the German in terms of cruelty. Those who are surprised by Polish hostility toward the Soviet Union fail to consider that every second family in Poland had someone who was deported to Soviet camps and prisons.

CZARNECKA   The guilt of the survivor constantly appears in your work, especially right after the war. This has been pointed out by Western critics. How should that theme in your poetry be interpreted?

MILOSZ That's no question of anyone surviving that period in Poland with a clear conscience. There had to be many occasions in which not turning away would have meant heroically choosing to die.

CZARNECKA But, on the other hand, there were also many cases in which you made miraculous narrow escapes, as you wrote in *The Separate Notebooks*.

MILOSZ Yes, but even surviving by a miracle left you with an uncomfortable feeling: "Why me and not someone else?"

CZARNECKA What was an ordinary day like in, say, 1942?

MILOSZ I devoted myself to literary work but not entirely, because a person did have to make a living, too. It would be extremely difficult to say how people made their living in occupied Warsaw. In any case, for a while the work I did was not necessarily for money: I was paid with a bowl of soup for lunch and a few meaningless banknotes. I worked at the University Library in Warsaw, which was closed to the public. The only work done there was internal, putting things in order. I worked there as a janitor, mainly to have access to books. I was like a mouse who found himself inside a huge cheese. I knew French and Russian, and this was when I started studying English. I had those luxurious stacks of books. To a great extent I owe my intellectual education to the huge amount of reading I did then.

CZARNECKA How long did you work there?

MILOSZ I don't remember. I think I worked there from 1941 to 1943.

CZARNECKA You also worked with the Underground Theatre Council. When did that start?

MILOSZ   That started quite early, toward the beginning of the German occupation. Before the war I was quite close to the world of the theatre. The underground organization of actors and directors was one of the wonders Poland performed. As you know, the theatres weren't operating, because the Nazis thought that subhumans did not deserve entertainment. Toward the end of the occupation, they permitted light, frivolous plays, but most actors boycotted the stage. The entire life of the theatre was concentrated in the underground. I took part in planning a reform of the theatre that was supposed to go into effect after the war. Plays were performed in private apartments and translations of foreign plays were commissioned for the future, after the war.

CZARNECKA   The actors worked in cafés?

MILOSZ   Yes, mainly in cafés as waiters and waitresses. Poland's underground theatre is a huge subject and I can't even begin to touch on it here, but one of my greatest experiences of the theatre, as a spectator, is connected with those performances.

CZARNECKA   There were also underground literary readings that you're known to have participated in.

MILOSZ   Of course. One of the people who ran the actors' underground was my friend Edmund Wierciński, the distinguished director. And his wife organized a great many clandestine poetry readings—around a hundred and fifty, I think. I read a number of times. It was very interesting.

CZARNECKA   How large was the audience?

MILOSZ   For technical reasons there couldn't be more than fifty or sixty people at any performance or reading. Otherwise, it would have attracted the Germans' attention. If a performance was given a number of times at various locations that changed frequently, several hundred people might see it.

CZARNECKA   You were also involved with publishing. During the occupation you created a modest operation that was the equivalent of today's samizdat. When did you start on that?

MILOSZ   Very early. A volume of my poetry, run off on a duplicating machine, was the first underground volume of poetry published in occupied Warsaw.

CZARNECKA   What was the danger for a person who published books on his own?

MILOSZ   I don't know, I just tried not to be caught. I don't think it was more dangerous than distributing clandestine newspapers—in other words, the concentration camp. In 1942 I published *The Invincible Song,* an anthology of resistance poetry. But I shouldn't get any credit for the printing—that was done by the printers. The book was beautifully set, predated, and sold under the counter.

CZARNECKA   Who did the printing?

MILOSZ   I don't know the printers' names. I didn't know them. The person who dealt with them was Zenon Skierski, a writer and the founder of a clandestine institution called the Polish Printing House.

CZARNECKA   So you dealt with the literary aspect of the anthology?

MILOSZ   I supplied the material that had been collected from the writers. Some poems, like Tuwim's, were sent in by letter via Portugal; others were already circulating in the underground. The authors of many poems are anonymous or unknown, because I had gotten their work from duplicator copies.

CZARNECKA   And the other books?

MILOSZ   I think the third volume came out the same year as *The Invincible Song*. That was Jacques Maritain's book *À travers le désastre,* which I translated. It's a short book that Maritain wrote after the fall of France; it was against collaborationism, against Pétain, and declared itself for the Free French movement and de Gaulle. I think that book appeared in Canada, but a French copy made its way to us via the Dutch resistance. I provided an introduction that was very friendly to France. It was a small, slender book. As for my poetry and other later works, like *The Voices of Poor People,* they were published in small editions.

CZARNECKA   Like "The World: a Naïve Poem." I've seen a photostat of a copy made by hand where the author signed himself "B. B. Kózka." Very carefully copied, almost calligraphically . . .

MILOSZ   I may even have been the one who did the copying.

CZARNECKA   That's rather unlikely. The handwriting's too careful.

MILOSZ   Could be . . . In any case, *The Voices of Poor People* went into circulation. Many years after the war, I heard a touching story from a man who was a young boy during the occupation. He would visit his friend in the suburbs of Cracow, and the two of them would go up to the friend's attic, where they were secretly assembling a motorcycle. His friend's father worked for the railroad, and one day they both noticed an old suitcase in the attic. The father had found it in an empty train at the station in Cracow after a big roundup when all the passengers on that train had been taken away and shipped to Auschwitz. That suitcase was left behind. When the two boys opened it, they saw that it contained a traveling magician's cape and top hat, posters for "Captain Nemo," as he styled himself, and a copy of *The Voices of Poor People* copied on a typewriter.

CZARNECKA   What a bizarre combination! And how did your manuscripts happen to survive?

MILOSZ   That's a very complicated story.

CZARNECKA   I'm asking because in a short essay in *Ironwood* magazine, your translator Robert Hass said that you had written your manuscripts on your own skin. This may be a striking image, but it must be pure fantasy.

MILOSZ   It's nonsense. On August 1, 1944, the day the Warsaw Uprising broke out, I had no idea that it had begun. I was walking down the street and I had no manuscripts with me, of course. I could not go back to where my wife and I were living. We were living on the outskirts, close to the fields. Because our street was under fire from German tanks, we took shelter with friends who lived on the next street over. When the firing died down a little—it must have been the second day—my wife went back to our house to get her mother, who was still there. And while she was at the house, my wife took a number of my manuscripts. The building was destroyed by artillery fire a short while later. It was at the very edge of the fields, which made it a good target.

CZARNECKA   What happened later on, when you left the city?

MILOSZ   I've said elsewhere that it was because of a nun that I was not sent to a forced-labor camp in Germany.

CZARNECKA   But what happened to those manuscripts?

MILOSZ   I had them with me and I took them wherever I went. What happened when we ended up in the transit camp? I don't think they took anything away from us there.

CZARNECKA   How many manuscripts were there? A suitcase-full? A briefcase-full?

MILOSZ   I didn't have any suitcases with me, just a briefcase with the manuscripts, that's all.

CZARNECKA   You mean you didn't take any of your books with you?

MILOSZ   No, there was no question of that. All my books were lost.

CZARNECKA   Apparently not all, because I remember seeing a copy of *Three Winters* with a bullet hole in the cover in your library in California. . . .

MILOSZ   The floor we lived on collapsed when the shell hit the building. Later on, after the war, we searched through the rubble for our things. That was when we found that book, and there really was a bullet hole through it.

CZARNECKA   So, then, something did survive.

MILOSZ   Big deal . . .

After the War

CZARNECKA   From a purely arithmetical point of view, you have spent most of your life as an émigré, or, rather, an exile—the two words don't mean the same thing and have different philosophical and emotional connotations. Can you tell me something about your life in France between 1951 and 1960?

MILOSZ   First and foremost, I have to say that I emigrated from Wilno in 1937. . . .

CZARNECKA   I know. I included that in my calculation.

MILOSZ   . . . And so I was an émigré of a sort during my years in Warsaw, except that I was in a country where my language was spoken. The years in America, France, and so on came later. Now I have some perspective and don't see any reason to make much ado about a person's living where he likes it best.

CZARNECKA   And California is where you like it best?

MILOSZ   Rather, it's that I'm not living where I would very much dislike to live. Let's put it like that. I feel very much at home in France, even though I'm glad I live in America. There's

90

something that's difficult to define, the antennae a person has, which tend to pick up certain vibrations peculiar to a country. And the vibrations in France have a good effect on me.

CZARNECKA In one of your essays, and in "Rue Descartes" as well, you develop a very interesting theme—the centers from which culture radiates. Paris was the last such center, the capital of the world. But in "Rue Descartes" you say explicitly that the world no longer has a capital, that France has lost that position.

MILOSZ Well, political processes occur at a slow rate. I think Paris was the capital of the world as long as the books published in Paris and the ideas coming out of France could permeate Europe all the way to the Urals. The division of Europe into two parts had a great deal to do with the end of Paris as the capital of the world. I think Paris's fate was somehow tied to Central Europe, that in some way Paris found its completion in Prague, Warsaw, Budapest, or even Belgrade. The situation that exists today is not only unhealthy for our countries but for Paris as well. This coincides in time with the disappearance of French as the international language. I raised this issue in a lecture at Ann Arbor, an issue that Milan Kundera dealt with recently—the fact that Central Europe always gravitated to the West. And, obviously, the West was symbolized by Paris. Throughout the nineteenth century all educated people knew French. And, of course, the paradox of today's situation is that Central Europe has been forced into the Russian orbit. But Central Europe is not drawn there culturally; it does not gravitate toward Moscow. Moscow has none of what Central Europe is looking for.

CZARNECKA That's the essay I was thinking about when I asked you that last question.

MILOSZ Moscow doesn't have what Central Europe's looking for. It wants to look to the West, where it discovers a curious lack of any center, any single capital.

CZARNECKA   What about New York? Isn't that the new capital?

MILOSZ   English has ousted French, that's clear. But it's difficult to say to what degree New York has now become a center of the sort Paris once was. That strikes me as somewhat dubious. New York is not a metropolis in the way Paris was; America is a very decentralized country. And, as we know, New York is a very unique conglomeration. Paris was France, but New York is not a distillation of America.

CZARNECKA   Yet New York has assumed mythic proportions.

MILOSZ   What you're saying about mythologizing is very much to the point. Yes, one of Paris's basic features as the capital of the world was a certain mythology that grew up around it gradually, through literature. Take Balzac—not to mention the French Revolution, which made a myth of Paris. A whole army of poets and writers worked on that myth. Something similar may happen with New York. But if it becomes the new capital of the world, that would make for an even more paradoxical situation. Culturally, Paris was the capital during the nineteenth century within a European political system that was more or less homogeneous. People traveled without passports, except in Russia. And even so, at the turn of the twentieth century, Russia was already a part of cosmopolitan Europe. But today New York is the city of the enemy—if seen from the viewpoint of the Eastern European police. Politics and cultures are at cross-purposes. Our part of Europe has been tossed into that other vat, but the fashions young people follow in music, film, and painting make them gravitate toward New York.

CZARNECKA   In a conversation with Aleksander Fiut that took place, if I'm not mistaken, in 1979, you called America a land of great loneliness. Has anything changed in your attitude toward America since then? You've become known and recognized here, and some of your readers even think of you as a poet of the English language.

MILOSZ   All that came as a great surprise to me. It didn't come all of a sudden with the Nobel Prize, because first, in 1977, I received an honorary doctorate from the University of Michigan in Ann Arbor, and then the Neustadt International Prize in 1978. The Nobel came later. Yes, I did gradually establish contact with the American public, and undoubtedly that changed my attitude toward America, even though I did not begin writing in English. I was never tempted to write in English. I simply realized that I wasn't able to. And I am not tempted to write in English now, either.

CZARNECKA   All the same, has America remained a "land of great loneliness" in your opinion?

MILOSZ   There is no question that for someone raised in the extremely gregarious society typical of the countries in our part of Europe, where there is great warmth and closeness between people, there's a feeling that something is missing here. It's the loneliness of Anglo-Saxon society that makes it alien to us. You have to admit, a party where people stand around with drinks and make small talk is not something that brings people closer to one another. Those parties can serve as a symbol of human relations in America. And also it shouldn't be forgotten that my revolt against capitalism ran very deep. My service to People's Poland was not devoid of those considerations.

   Like millions of other Europeans of my generation, I was not in a position of my own choosing. The system had been changed in our country without our approval. And Poland's subjugation, the occupation that began in 1945, was a hideous thing. It's very difficult to resign yourself to your country's loss of sovereignty. The system introduced into our part of Europe in 1945 is analogous to what Russia experienced under the Tartar yoke, meaning that a prince had to have the khan's blessing in order to rule his own little state. The princes vied with one another in their servility toward the Khan and in denouncing one another, with the more zealous one getting the position. To sum up, it was a serious situation. Of course, at the same time I had been opposed to the situation in pre-war Poland, one that had been very difficult to accept. It had been a society of extremely strong class divisions. The over-whelming majority of people simply had no chance of ad-vancing in society. Poland could not industrialize, because of a lack of capital. My point in all this is not to put socialism and capitalism in opposition, comparing what's good and what's bad about each. That's a comparison that shouldn't be made, because it doesn't lead anywhere. We know there's no parallelism. The communist system is simply parasitic. It couldn't exist if there weren't some margin where people could pursue private economic activities. The main point here is that considering one system unbearable doesn't mean you ac-cept the other systems with open arms. I'm laughing—be-cause this may just be the way life is. But that doesn't mean that a person has no dreams, no vision of some different and better society.

CZARNECKA   What haven't you spoken of yet? What things of importance have you skipped?

MILOSZ   Certain details of my life often go almost unmen-tioned; at least they have in these conversations. We've skipped my entire personal life, haven't we? And it undoubtedly influ-enced my decisions in politics, literature, and so on; there's none of that here, for reasons I think are obvious: there's a certain modesty about those things, a desire to keep one's private life apart. Anyhow, it's very difficult to speak of those matters. As we know, psychoanalysts earn a great deal of money for listening to their patients' confidences. Naturally, I could speak for hours on the subject and fill a few books of interviews, which would all be beside the point. I've de-scribed some of my adventures in my books, and I don't feel any need to go back to that. Besides, certain biographical de-tails would be too difficult for Western readers to understand, since they're bound up with purely Polish situations; those points would require detailed description, a familiarity with Polish affairs, the players' names, and so forth.

One thing here interests people—the fact that for a time after the war I was in the diplomatic service of the Poland created in 1945, and that five years later I decided to break with it. The circumstances in which I decided to serve the new government would also require very detailed information about Poland's situation after the war, when the country had a coalition government, at least in name—that is, it wasn't only Communist Party members who had opportunities open to them but also people of other parties and people who weren't in any party. Another key factor in deciding whether to break with the new government was my reluctance to live abroad as an émigré, since I thought that, as a Polish poet, I'd have nothing to do there. (My career as an author who received the Nobel Prize for works written in Polish, known to the Swedish Academy only in translation, should be considered something of a miracle.) I tried to avoid the censor's reach in Poland while at the same time publishing there, as far as possible. In any case, the point was to maintain contact with Poland.

The reason I was not able to do that for very long . . . Anyone who knows my work well can trace this in my writing, infer the mounting crisis. I think one of the key events was an evening and night in Warsaw in 1949 after I had arrived back from America. At that time I moved in very high circles, with people who were well dressed and had good apartments—simply put, Poland's ruling elite of the time. I attended a reception where people in those "highest circles" drank and danced. We were on our way home at four o'clock in the morning; it was summer, but the night was cold. And I saw jeeps carrying prisoners, people just arrested. The soldiers guarding them were wearing sheepskin coats, but the prisoners were in suit jackets with the collars turned up, shivering from the cold. It was then that I realized what I was part of.

There was also the matter of the Peace Congress in 1948. I

think the whole idea was the brainchild of Jerzy Borejsza, someone who is only of historical interest now. In any case, I had to take part in the congress, because Albert Einstein's support was being sought. I was introduced to Albert Einstein by some very important people. I no longer remember how it happened, but I think it was through some old friends of Oskar Milosz in America. So, if it was then that I met Einstein, and I even wrote a poem about him. I don't think anyone who knew Einstein could fail to be taken with him as a person. Absolutely charming. Enchanting. Einstein wrote a memorandum calling on all governments to unite in controlling atomic energy and in not allowing it to be used for weapons—otherwise all mankind would face extinction. He appended a short letter with well wishes to the congress and sent the material to Wrocław with his friend Professor Nathan. The Russians in Wrocław were against the memorandum's being published. Einstein's short letter was printed as if it were all he had sent. Then Einstein published the full text of his memorandum in *The New York Times*.

I was terribly embarrassed. I explained to him that I had absolutely no responsibility for that, and that I had acted in good faith. Einstein said, "Of course. I don't hold it against you." Later on, in 1949, when I came back from Poland in the midst of my crisis, I went to Einstein and asked him what I should do. And Einstein, who was actually a tenderhearted liberal, said to me, "You know, you can't break from your country. A poet should not break with his country. I know it's very difficult, but things have to change, it can't go on like that." And so he was somewhat opposed to my becoming an émigré, like many émigrés who know how hard it is and prefer to advise people to remain in their own country. In any case, I maintain tremendous admiration for him as a person. He was a warmhearted man. But by then the situation was changing. The year 1949 was a key one for Poland. I was still part of the elite when I was transferred to the embassy in Paris. I went to receptions with Éluard, Aragon, Pablo Neruda. I was *très privilégié*. At that time in France there could be nothing better—in terms of prestige—than to be a diplomat from one of the socialist countries or a country moving toward socialism. . . .

CZARNECKA   So, then, your decision to break with Poland was dictated by moral indignation?

MILOSZ   You could say that. There were some things I couldn't stomach.

CZARNECKA   Finally, how are you bearing up to the Nobel Prize?

MILOSZ   You have to separate out all the fuss that comes right after receiving it. The first year is very difficult, because of the whole commotion that comes with being a celebrity. That subsides later on. I look at the Nobel Prize this way: there's a board with a heavy weight on one end, and then someone throws a weight on the other end to balance it out. I had suffered all sorts of contortions and pain; the Nobel Prize was the weight that restored my balance. That's all. Instead of having the other end of the board go up in the air, instead of having it all go to my head, instead of starting to think of myself as a genius. I recently heard what Saul Bellow said when asked about winning the Nobel Prize. He said that it was the "kiss of death" for a writer and meant the end of his real career. But Thomas Mann, for example, wrote a great many books after receiving the Nobel Prize. So Bellow's wrong there. After winning the prize, I had no thought of writing some great work that would be worthy . . .

CZARNECKA   . . . of the prize. . . .

MILOSZ   Precisely. On the contrary, I turned to some very private writing. I wrote poems in Polish without worrying if they'd ever be translated or if they were translatable. And I'm not concerned in the least with writing some great work in the future. I'd like to add that from the start, ever since I was a little boy, I've had the feeling that I was in the grip of some force, that I was passive, that nothing actually depended on me. And in a sense that's proved true. At the same time, I've had moments of intutition in which my future was revealed to me but as through a glass darkly. Of course, I cannot say that I understand my life, but there's one thing I'm sure of: that it's been composed of a series of strange circumstances. After all, it would have been hard to anticipate that I'd gradually be able to achieve a place in literature outside of Poland. But various other events also indicate that some hand has guided and directed me to do things that were completely absurd from the point of view of common sense, but which later proved to make good sense.

Part Two

Three Winters

CZARNECKA   At the beginning of *The Land of Ulro* you say that you don't understand your life or your work. Toward the end of the book you state that everything has worked out harmoniously and that the old professor from Berkeley, the catastrophist poet, and the little boy are one and the same person. Which of the two statements is true?

MILOSZ   They both are. It's just that on one level you don't understand your life, and on another level, with a different degree of consciousness, you do. Those two statements are not of the same order, not of the same degree of intensity or knowledge. At the end of *The Land of Ulro* I say that somehow or other my life has taken logical form because writing books gives life form. But it's also true that when I face reality squarely, I come to the conclusion that I don't understand my life.

CZARNECKA   Did you have a sense of a calling early in life?

MILOSZ   I don't know if that can be said. In fact, all prophecies of that sort are typically self-fulfilling. As soon as a person begins predicting his fate, his future, it begins crystallizing in that very act. There's the same danger in writing apocalyptic or pessimistic predictions. A certain number of people will start believing in them, and so they will start coming true. It's the same in one's private life—both positively and negatively. Very often a person engineers his own fate in advance, which is why his fate works out as it does. Those are Romantic patterns.

CZARNECKA   But you don't try to avoid the Romantic patterns, do you?

MILOSZ   Naturally I tried to avoid them, but at the same time they are very much alive in Polish poetry, more alive there than anywhere else. A certain number of prerequisites, a certain amount of suffering, is prescribed for a poet.

CZARNECKA   You were around fifteen when you began writing poetry?

MILOSZ   Something like that. In the beginning I treated it solely as an exercise in style. Some people, of course, start writing at once. Take Sartre's *Les Mots.* He describes his childhood there, a childhood spent writing madly. As a ten-year-old boy, he was always sitting and writing novels. I didn't have that tendency. I didn't write literary works. I was actively involved with other things—atlases on the natural sciences, botany, ornithology. I even took an interest in lumbering—I wanted to be a forester. That was my calling, naturalist or forester.

CZARNECKA   Apart from two poems, your later collections don't include anything from *Poem on Frozen Time,* the volume with which you made your debut.

MILOSZ   I don't like that volume. I wrote all kinds of poetry and went through several different phases when I was a young man. The phases had nothing to do with one another. My first volume is the trace of one of those phases, and I don't actually see any reason to confer special privileges on that phase as opposed to the others. Now, of course, they're digging up prewar poetry of mine that was published in periodicals but never included in any of the books. Some of it can make you feel rather stupid. Some of those poems are interesting and no worse, and maybe even better, than the ones published in *Poem on Frozen Time.* I don't know why that volume should be of any importance. I'd be glad to write it off as a loss.

CZARNECKA   *Poem on Frozen Time* appeared in 1933. Three years later you published *Three Winters.* But you don't repudiate that volume, do you?

MILOSZ   As I say, the poetry I wrote before *Three Winters* has a long history of its own. It may not be long in terms of years, but in terms of changes it is. To my mind, 1928–29 is prehistory. I have an image of that period as a specific place and action, of me writing in notebooks and on scraps of paper. At the time I was living in Miss Klecka's boardinghouse, where all the lodgers were university students. I was probably the only high-school student, in my last year. That was a year of great expectations for me. You take a deep breath and off you march, especially in the fall. For me there's something tart and intoxicating about fall in Wilno. The streets are full of leaves. I can clearly remember the wooden sidewalks on the small streets near my house as I wandered through the city drunk on the promise of some ill-defined future. The poetry I wrote then may have been very classical, influenced by Joachim du Bellay, a Pléiade poet. I was very systematic and cool about it. That was the beginning of the prehistory. Over the next few years there were a great many changes in my emotional life, and nearly every year brought completely new styles, new tendencies, a great lyrical drive. By the way, when I think of my last year in high school, I'm amazed by how life doesn't change—the sensuous details, the hands, the faces, the physical aspect of life.

So, then, what is the meaning of all the time that has passed since 1928–29? On the one hand, there's a certain awe at change—so many things have happened, today's world is completely different from what it was in 1928–29, and yet life is exactly the same. Exotic as Wilno was, biologically, life was the same there. Klecka, the woman who owned the boardinghouse, and who fussed around the table smoking cigarettes, serving the food, is part of the present to me. That's it exactly, the consistency of life, dishes that do not change over the centuries. And the faces of the boys and girls who sat at that table are still somehow very close to me.

CZARNECKA   It's interesting that my question about *Three Winters* elicited memories of harmony and ecstasy with the world. Meanwhile, the subject of *Three Winters* is closer to the idea of the artist as cut off from other people, gifted with an ill-fated power.

MILOSZ   I think that in 1928–29 I was more an advocate of enthusiasm than tragedy. The years that followed were very difficult for me, and perhaps I was seeking a way out. The end result of my youthful experiences and conflicts was shifted onto society in the volume *Poem on Frozen Time*, even though we should note that the title itself, *Frozen Time*, signals a certain iciness, a coolness. It was then that Zbigniew Folejewski and I published the *Anthology of Social Poetry*, which I do not include as part of my work. I consider that volume weak and to some degree it may be marked by a flight from the real issues.

Three Winters was another incarnation, though that volume should not be viewed as (a) an idea and (b) its execution. It's a collection of poems written over a period of time. I think that my attempts to deal with my youthful conflicts achieved better expression here because things were approached on a much deeper level. And let's not forget that this volume has some ecstasy in it, too. For example, "The Song" is to a great extent an ecstatic poem. It's also a Manichean poem in a certain sense, because the woman who appears in it is connected with the earth, and that's the source of the praise of the earth and also the bitterness toward the earth. Depending on the edition, the woman is called either

Anna or Ona. "Ona" is "Anna" in Lithuanian. I was devouring Saint Augustine's *Confessions* at the time I wrote "The Song." There is a great deal of the ecstatic in "A Dialogue," whereas I consider "Gates of the Arsenal" or "Birds" as almost surrealistic in their technique.

I was under tremendous pressure when I was writing those poems. I remember walking around Paris, close to the breaking point, repeating one line for days on end, unable to go any further, because what I wanted to express was so impossible to catch hold of. The pressure was so great that it finally blocked me. An extremely strong and strange experience. In fact, I think what makes it worthwhile to be a poet is that it allows you to know what that sort of suffering is. At the same time, in retrospect, it all seems extremely odd: a guy walking around a city trying to find an incantation to match his inner conflicts.

CZARNECKA   There are many contradictions in "Birds." The first part of the poem does not foreshadow the dark vision of destruction, the icy landscape with bloody trees. The "year of renewals" in the first line promises hope, rebirth. That vision is shattered by the "disciple of dreams" who descends below.

MILOSZ   The phrase "the year of renewals" may come from Paul Valéry's "*Le vent se lève . . .*," the ending of "Le Cimitière marin." But I don't think Valéry had any deep or lasting influence on me.

CZARNECKA   Did you come to know his work when you were in Paris?

MILOSZ   Yes, my reading of Valéry coincides with my years in Paris. We should bear in mind that no one knows exactly what "Le Cimitière marin" means. Valéry is very hard to interpret. Some people go so far as to say that Valéry perfected a rhetoric in which the phrases seem to have some meaning but are in reality no more than extremely beautiful combinations of words. Though those phrases may have a great emotional meaning, they cannot be translated into the language of discourse.

CZARNECKA   It seems to me that the fundamental difference between the poems in *Three Winters* and your later work is that earlier you create a reality whereas later on you're reconstructing one. But this is more of a footnote. Let's go back to that sense of being cut off.

MILOSZ   That sense of being cut off from people is of essential importance. Naturally, it's expressed throughout that volume, which illustrates my inner drama as I felt it at the time. I think that I have evolved toward the surmounting of that isolation, even though it took decades. Today I am much warmer, both in my poetry and with people, more at ease. I was very isolated then because of my timidity, and that also had an effect on my political views and my inability to feel at ease in Poland. I was horribly ashamed when I published my first poems, which seemed the height of immodesty to me. I felt that ordinary people could have nothing but contempt for something like that. I felt like a freak.

CZARNECKA   But at the same time you assigned yourself an exceptional role as a poet. The subject of "Birds" is the "disciple of dreams," the "conqueror of dreams," "perhaps the last bearer of retribution," who, like Dante, can descend into hell. In other words, your approach was very ambivalent.

MILOSZ   Yes, it was. Perhaps because I was raised on the Romantic poets, I had an intuition that to be a poet meant to suffer solitude and exile, and I prayed for that.

CZARNECKA   That poem contains the lines:

Everything that can be conceived from your depths,
is dead before it crosses the border of birth.

That sounds like a credo. Is that the nihilistic aspect of art?

MILOSZ   I don't think that's what I had in mind. Those lines can be seen as a variation on "The tongue belies the voice, and the voice belies the thought." That's one thing. And we should also remember that ultimately that book is full of playful elements and self-contained phrases which have their own autonomy. I would call them emotional operations, because lines like the ones you quoted are very dramatic and seem automatically to express the tragic side of life. Various lines can be extracted from that poem and analyzed as gestures of dramatic speech. That's how I see it now. If someone had asked me about it twenty or thirty years ago, I would have interpreted it differently, of course, but that's the way it looks to me now. In classical poetry—Racine, for example—phrases become autonomous, gestures of speech, the human voice. Here we come to an issue Jan Błoński raised in his essay on the polyphonic nature of my poetry. It's as if there were countless dramatic voices speaking within me. The image of the flock of birds stands for the division of personality into a multitude of voices. I may be going too far here, but there might be something to this.

CZARNECKA   Basically, hymns are works written in praise of God or a divinity. But your "Hymn" leads to a certain clash. Is this a struggle for power over people's souls?

MILOSZ   In spite of everything, I see this as a poem of ecstasy. The line "There is no one between you and me" is addressed to God. Quite shameless. A bit like Mickiewicz's "Improvisation." I think of Mickiewicz when I think of pride. I find this a very strange poem myself. I was ashamed after it was published—the immodesty of it. The poem is an extremely strong display of a heightened sense of individual existence. Reality flows by, life is constant change and decay, but I somehow endure.

> I have no wisdom, no skills, and no faith
> but I received strength, it tears the world apart.
> I shall break, a heavy wave, against its shores
> and a young wave will cover my trace. . . .

There is also a sort of delight in transience here.

> How many times I have floated with you,
> transfixed in the middle of the night,
> hearing some voice above your horror-stricken church;
> a cry of grouse, a rustle of the heath were stalking in
>   you
> and two apples shone on the table
> or open scissors glittered—
> and we were alike:
> apples, scissors, darkness and I
> under the same immobile
> Assyrian, Egyptian and Roman
> moon.

I would say that this is the ecstasy of connection with the world and at the same time a manifestation of a special . . .

CZARNECKA   . . . Relationship with God, is that it? That means that the line "There is no one between you and me," which is repeated three times with a different word order, expresses a special relationship between God and the subject of the poem? Is this communication without any intermediaries?

MILOSZ   No. I would say this is the most pantheistic of all my poems. To tell the truth, it's even difficult for me to analyze, because the poem was almost *écriture automatique,* written under the daimonion's influence. I clearly remember how I wrote that poem. In one go. The daimonion dictated it and I wrote it. In any case, this is the ecstasy of union with God, who is also the world, a feeling of a special relationship with God. The poem expresses two desires: for unity in change, in death, without a personal existence, and a longing to be separate and opposed to all that. Which would mean to be against the whole world but at the same time connected with what is divine in the world, of which even transience is a part. *Voilà!*

CZARNECKA   Those same contradictions.

MILOSZ   That's true, the entire poem is built on contradictions, but there's a philosophical explanation for that. We
might even use a Blakean interpretation here, though I hadn't
heard of Blake at that time. Neo-Platonism may have had a
certain influence on Blake—the marvel of enduring form despite the passing of love and hatred. What can you do when
a daimonion orders you to write a poem that even you, the
author, have to wrack your brains to understand? But "Hymn"
does reveal some of my basic tendencies. For me these are
constants: on the one hand, an inclination to ecstasy, to union
with the world of things, a desire to experience everything,
touch everything, to be in the stream of life, and, at the same
time, a negative anxiety that may have mellowed over the
years. I'm thinking out loud here—"Hymn" is actually a prayer
to go to heaven. But that heaven is the whole world in all its
specificity, substance, sensuality, and somehow transferred to
another dimension. "Hymn" is not about disconnection from
the world, but it might be compared with a poem written
several years later, a poem that is entirely in the Gnostic tradition, "Incarnation," where there is an absolute opposition
between "me" and "them," people and the world, as there is
in *Hymn to a Pearl*. In "Incarnation," the whole earth—
meaning the Warsaw of that time, where the poem was written, in 1937, I believe—is revealed as the Egypt that appears
in *Hymn to a Pearl*, as a great longing for salvation that also
includes an intuition of crucifixion, or a desire for it. It's a
very unpleasant poem, and I dislike it for that reason. But I
published it, so, well, let it stand. "Hymn" is much more on
the side of ecstasy with the world, and both poems could be
said to be pedals on the same piano. The stress is either on
separation and salvation (the Platonic and the Manichean
aren't so far apart—there was a very strong dualism in Plato),
or on merging with change and movement. Including the ecstasy of dying. I'd like to draw your attention to that. I experienced very ecstatic feelings when reading or thinking about

death—very sweet feelings. That could be called masochistic or whatever the proper psychological term is. That's the reason I liked Jarosław Iwaszkiewicz's poetry so much when I read it as a young man—because of its constant erotic and thanatological sweetness.

CZARNECKA   There's the following line in "Gates of the Arsenal": "What lives dies from the light." The motif reappears in other poems in *Three Winters*.

MILOSZ   To a large extent that comes from my dreams. At that time I frequently dreamed of a light that pursued me and pierced me clean through. A sort of death ray, a laser, that was killing me. That was a leitmotif in my anxiety dreams: fleeing, pursued by a light, a fire, a ray, that pierced me like a sword. I don't know what it meant, because in my poetry light also appears as a source of delight, ecstasy, wonder. Everything changes into light in the sense that things become luminous, transparent, transformed into a purer form. That's one aspect. The other aspect is the cruel, inhuman light that is against life. There are always those contradictions—I was born under the sign of Cancer, after all.

CZARNECKA   In "Gates of the Arsenal" there's a constant stress on flaws: the crooked pony, the hunchbacked angel, but primarily the "child born of Slavic blood" who is almost a monster.

MILOSZ   That's my obsession with doom—very strong in me.

CZARNECKA   Does that same motif appear in *The Separate Notebooks* cycle as the Wormwood Star? A person burdened with bad genes?

MILOSZ   Yes, of course. And that may also link me to the Manicheans in the sense that they were against procreation because the world is evil. But I both think that the world is evil and that I might be marked in a way similar to Thomas

Mann's Buddenbrooks, who became an artist, a contamination of the line.

CZARNECKA   I think that you reveal your poetic credo of that period in the poem "A Dialogue." In comparison with the other poems in *Three Winters,* it's very lucid. Were the mediumistic poems written in Paris or after you returned from Paris?

MILOSZ   The poems most representative of my work were written before I left for France, in the spring of 1934: "The Song," "A Dialogue," and "To Father Ch." That was an important and intoxicating spring for me. Then came the mediumistic, surrealistic poems—"Gates of the Arsenal," "Birds," and "Hymn"—which were written in Paris. These were followed by the poems written directly after I returned from Paris—"Statue of a Couple" and "Clouds"—which have a very important personal aspect. Chronologically, the last poems in the volume were written after I spent some time in Wilno in 1936: "Slow River" and "Assizes." I think "Assizes" may actually have been first. "Slow River" must have been the last poem I wrote that went into that volume. Summer of 1936—June, to be precise.

CZARKECKA   Let's go back to "A Dialogue." The poem is arranged for two voices—the Master and the Disciples. Are they the ego and the alter ego?

MILOSZ   No. What I see there is the influence of Iwaszkiewicz, who—and he may have also borrowed a little from Stefan George—constantly used the motif of the master and the apprentice, the elder and the younger—very Germanic, it must be said. That motif also recurs in the works of Hermann Hesse. I have the impression that this motif came to me by way of Iwaszkiewicz. Besides, I'm still very much drawn to the search for the brotherhood of the guild, and I long deeply for a master figure. In fact, my relationship to Oskar Milosz had the features of a master-disciple relationship. That desire is expressed in the poem "To Father Ch." It may contain some criticism, but fundamentally the relationship is that of teacher and student.

CZARNECKA   Your dark and icy vision, so typical of *Three Winters,* is perhaps most evident in "Statue of a Couple." It isn't really a statue but their tombstone.

MILOSZ   Yes, that's a very personal poem.

CZARNECKA   The line "And you have led me, as once an angel led Tobias . . ." sounds like something from Sło-wacki. . . .

MILOSZ   That's an allusion to a painting of the angel leading Tobias, with the landscape of Lombardy in the background. It was painted by Pollaiuolo, a fifteenth-century Italian mannerist. I had a specific painting in mind.

CZARNECKA   And what's the source of the Italian thuja and the marshes of Lombardy in the poem? Does it have anything to with landscapes you saw and remembered?

MILOSZ   I hadn't been to Italy yet, but in the poem it would appear that I had been and was describing what I'd seen.

CZARNECKA   Private drama and expectation of disaster interweave in that volume.

MILOSZ   Yes, there's a clear premonition of war.

CZARNECKA   There's anxiety and tension in the poem "The Wind at Evening," for example.

MILOSZ   The poem is interesting insofar as it shows a great leap, a transposition of reality. And there's the time and the place it was written. I wrote that poem in Krasnogruda in

1934. I had relatives in Krasnogruda who lived by the lake near Sejny, in the Suwałki region. But the landscape there doesn't justify the sort of images I used in "The Wind at Evening." Where does that gold cross come from, the silk flag, those odd accessories? It's an attempt to distance myself. Obviously, there are also some details taken from that region. There was a lot of wind there. The highlands, the apple trees, the rowans, and the sleeping dog were part and parcel of that region. But there's also the apocalyptic dimension: the three-prop planes (there were no jets then), the golden cross. It's not clear what it means, but it does forebode something ominous. If I were looking for kindred work, I'd certainly point to *The Coming of the Enemy*, by my colleague of the time Jerzy Zagórski, which has the same atmosphere. Catastrophism was at its height in 1934, 1935. The volume *The Coming of the Enemy* was not reissued in Poland after the war, because it contains too many odd things—the birth of the Antichrist, armies marching through the Caucasus, polar bears—too many prophecies that came true. It's probably the most surrealistic book in all Polish poetry. In *Three Winters* the apocalyptic element is found in poems like "The Book," "Slow River," and "Elegy." There's also a poem that I published later but which belongs to that cycle—"Fragment," written in Paris in 1935. The poem speaks of "Germanic Junoes."

CZARNECKA   You mentioned *écriture automatique*. Was "Slow River" also written in a trance?

MILOSZ   No, that was different. I remember how I wrote it. Very slowly—I would get up in the morning and write a line or two before going to the office. The poem ripened slowly. That's a technique I've been using for years now. The poem grows at its own pace.

CZARNECKA   In "Slow River" you introduce a series of voices, setting each one off with quotation marks.

MILOSZ   Yes, various characters speak. That distances the subject a little. I mean, there's the poet's voice, but other voices also join in.

CZARNECKA   You said once that from the beginning the voices in your poetry were distinctly different, pronounced, just as they are in "Slow River," but later on they began increasingly to fuse into one.

MILOSZ   I said that? Let's leave that for the critics. Maybe it's true—how should I know? Ultimately, I think that Jan Błoński wrote a very fine essay on "Slow River" but, after Mikhail Bakhtin's book on Dostoevsky's poetics, it had become a bit fashionable to interpret works in terms of polyphony. If you read that poem closely, you'll see it's far from polyphonic. But a great many various voices really can emerge at times when a person has a great many conflicts and contradictions. A person is never all of a piece. People are exposed to various influences, ideologies, books. We're under constant assault from many sides today. Anyway, when I lecture on Dostoevsky, I do tell my students that his heroes represent a variety of voices. In the nineteenth century the intelligentsia was exposed to different voices. And the same is true of the twentieth—people who, for various personal, nonsocietal reasons, are full of contradiction fit in well with their times.

CZARNECKA   I'm intrigued by one aspect of "Slow River"— you present two contrasting images of the earth and people. In the first, the world is like a garden, a granary, a "house of joy" and a moment later the happy crowd is depicted as follows:

> —Ah, dark rabble at their vernal feasts
> and crematoria rising like white cliffs
> and smoke seeping from the dead wasps' nests.
> In a stammer of mandolins, a dust-cloud of scythes,
> on heaps of food and mosses stomped ash-gray,
> the new sun rises on another day.

Did the crematoria have the same sinister significance for you
then that they've had for us since World War II?

MILOSZ   No. I think that the crematoria had a different sort
of sinister significance for me—they symbolized a hygienic
society. There were no crematoria in Poland before the war,
but I must have read about them somewhere, most likely in
books like Huxley's *Brave New World*. In the poem the crematoria figure more as an aspect of that new world, where
everything is nice and hygienic. The crematoria here are
something of a pendant to the Młodziak family in Gombrowicz's *Ferdydurke*. That hygienic life and hygienic death
fill me with disgust. In "Slow River" I use the word "rabble"—a very Eastern European form of contempt. High-
minded Eastern Europeans dislike it when the rabble have
cars, eat well, and lead a dull, materialistic life. That same
note is struck constantly by poets like Różewicz. "Non-stop
Show," Różewicz's poem about Munich, is full of horrible
disgust.

CZARNECKA   At the end of the poem you say:

> Three times must the wheel of blindness
> turn, before I look without fear at the power
> sleeping in my own hand, and recognize spring,
> the sky, the seas, and the dark, massed land.
> Three times will the liars have conquered
> before the great truth appears alive. . . .

Is that a prophecy or an incantation?

MILOSZ   The "three times" makes it more of an incantation.
What we have here is catastrophism but not despair. In fact,
much of my work is very eschatological—in that it foresees
cycles. After all, that's the eschatological pattern—first you
have to descend to the bottom so that some rebirth can take
place later on. "Three times will the liars have conquered" is
more of an incantation. In any case, I'd be able to say the

same thing today. That's not so very far from all my thinking, because all the horrors of this century can be interpreted as a preliminary, transitional phase. First, all those illiterate tribes that scratched their food from the ground and had never seen a pair of shoes have to reach some median level of civilization. When I was growing up, people were not all the same. You could tell who they were by the way they dressed or what sort of caps they wore. Now those differences are being obliterated. In the cities it's increasingly difficult to tell a young worker from a bank clerk. Clothing is only symbolic. I don't know how high a price will have to be paid for this, that's a separate subject. But perhaps this is a preparatory stage, and later on a new hierarchy will be formed. It's difficult to foresee how that will take place. Perhaps there'll be something like what Oskar Milosz foresaw in his vision of a theocratic society, a government of philosophers.

CZARNECKA   A world community with each nation preserving its identity.

MILOSZ   Yes, a world government. The United States of Earth. In *Les Arcanes* he spoke of those who did great work in unifying humanity—people like Napoleon, who despite themselves helped unify mankind. A very strange business; Oskar Milosz made some very curious predictions that are just now beginning to come true before our very eyes. But, going back to the incantation in "Slow River," I'd like to add that my work is very strongly marked by the expectation of a new era. That's very Romantic. The Third Epoch of the Spirit, the age of eschatology.

The Poetry of the Years 1937–43

CZARNECKA   An element in *Three Winters* that is not accentuated becomes very prominent in your later work. I'm referring to irony at your own expense.

MILOSZ   There's none there? Could be.

CZARNECKA   Nowadays, ironic distance is assigned a very large role in poetry. But isn't that a defensive gesture, to not overly reveal oneself to the reader?

MILOSZ   Well, it depends on the purpose the ironic distance serves. Actually, it might be true that there is little irony at my own expense in *Three Winters*. I was very solemn when I was young. There were elements of that irony in some poems I wrote at the time, but I may not have published them. The fact is that it was not until the war that I began writing ironic poetry. In the twentieth century it's hard to get along without irony, the grotesque, buffoonery—those are the tools of our century. Tragic writers like Beckett use slapstick, and in a sense this is connected with the times. That's a specific type of irony, because, if we take the poetry Oskar Milosz wrote before World War I, for example, it's full of irony toward himself but it's of a different sort: an extremely romantic irony. In general, you can't manage without it, but it depends on

117

what the irony serves. There's something that isn't good about irony itself, a certain fear of exposing oneself. But it can be used to good purposes. We can say that *The World: A Naïve Poem,* which was written during the war, is a work of pure irony, but an irony very far removed from what is called sarcasm.

CZARNECKA   It seems to me that there is neither sarcasm nor irony in *Three Winters.* It reaches for the heights, and you can hear a furious clash of inner forces at work in it. That's why I think I've treated that volume as a *Sturm und Drang* period in your work. The poems of the years 1937–39 that appeared in your next volume, *Rescue,* are more toned down, not so visionary. The apocalypse is muted, as if it were an echo of *Three Winters.* And the number of lyrical elements seems to have increased.

MILOSZ   That's a possible way to look at it. In any case, there are periods in my—let's call it—professional life that I dislike. Specifically, the period after *Three Winters,* which I would extend more or less to 1943. I don't like that period. It seems to me there are times of search. You search blindly; you try one thing, then you try another; but there's a great underlying sense of being unsettled, lacking the knowledge of what you really want to do. And it's not clear whether things really do take shape and crystallize from time to time. Something gets written, and it seems to be a crystallization. But actually it's all a great inner chaos.

CZARNECKA   After a period of such turmoil, it must be difficult to find the strength in yourself to express the next phase with equal force.

MILOSZ   You see, it all looks different when viewed in retrospect. You can take the story of a life you know well, and I'm more or less familiar with my own, and can check to what degree history is arranged according to fixed patterns and how much it has in common with the actual course of events. A volume of poetry is composed of pieces that were created in a certain time period. That period contains various subperiods, which are very definite and often completely different. And all that is included together between the same covers and represents your latest phase. But that's not entirely true. My next volume of poetry appeared in a mimeographed edition in 1940—under a pseudonym, of course. I included some of those poems in *Rescue* and I rejected others. So, all those divisions are relative. You say that it must have been difficult to maintain that degree of density after *Three Winters*. I've said that I don't understand my own life, and I have even less understanding of how it takes shape in my poetry, and the two are very closely connected. But there's no question that I felt completely lost after *Three Winters* was published. That was a time when I was at sea in the world. When I was fired from Radio Wilno, I had a certain amount of free time before assuming my duties in Warsaw. Oh, did I sigh with relief. Not having to go to the office, what bliss! And I treated myself to a trip abroad.

CZARNECKA   In *Visions from San Francisco Bay*, you wrote: time you spent in Italy important for your work?

MILOSZ   Everything was important. Anyway, I couldn't free myself from my obsession with Signorelli's frescoes in Orvieto—they preyed on me. Years later I wrote an essay about Solovyov and the coming of the Antichrist, and even the book in which that essay was printed, *The Emperor of the Earth*, had three of the principal images from Signorelli's frescoes on its cover. That had made a very deep impression on me. It must have suited my interest in the apocalyptic.

CZARNECKA   What did you find so fascinating about those frescoes?

MILOSZ   What fascinated me most was the idea of depicting the Antichrist in the image of Christ. From a distance, you see a stereotyped iconography of Christ. But when you take a closer look, you see a hideous face. The devil is whispering in his ear. That was not an original idea of Signorelli's. I've read that there was a practice of portraying the Antichrist as Christ in Italian folk woodcuts. Just about that same time, 1500.

CZARNECKA   You say that you dislike the poetry you wrote between 1937 and 1943. Yet there have to be some things of interest, some things that are important to the author. . . .

MILOSZ   All right, I'd say it was an interesting soup but not a great soup.

CZARNECKA   Because they're too personal?

MILOSZ   They probably are too personal. I don't feel any relationship to them. I've already spoken about my poem "Incarnation." I dealt with it recently because I was translating a work of Gnostic literature, but not as part of my interest in the esoteric. It was simply that, while teaching a course on Manicheanism at the university, I had my students use a book on Gnosticism by Hans Jonas, a German professor. He quotes various text in his book, including a classic of Gnostic literature, the story of the pearl. I translated that story as *Hymn to a Pearl*. I didn't translate it from the original, of course, which I think was in Syrian. And it was in connection with that translation that I had a look at my poem "Incarnation." I was embarrassed, because the author and the persona in that poem are somehow shamelessly close; there is too little distance on the persona. And that makes for a certain immodesty. I want to publish "Incarnation" along with a commentary in which I say: It's tough, but you have to own up to such things. "Incarnation" is similar to *Hymn to the Pearl,* that classic of Gnostic literature which tells of a king's son who was dispatched to Egypt; there he's constantly saying that he has "descended to the depth" because his kingdom is somewhere up high, on a mountain. Anyway, in Egypt the king's son has to carry off a pearl that is guarded by an enormous dragon and bring it to his father's kingdom. But he stops at an inn, begins drinking and eating with some Egyptians, and forgets about his mission. Then he gets a letter, which comes flying through the air to him and speaks to him in a language that is not human. The letter reminds him of what he is supposed to do. In the end, the king's son carries off the pearl and returns home. Egypt, of course, is always a symbol of materialism. Crass materialism. That goes back to the Bible. It's the same in Blake's symbolism, where Egypt is the house of bondage, matter. The pearl guarded by the dragon has been set in matter, in Egypt. This is the descent of the soul into matter in search of the treasure of divine knowledge. As soon as the soul seizes the pearl, it returns to the kingdom, the father. When writing "Incarnation" I did not consider myself a Gnostic, nor had I read much on the subject, a very exotic realm. But I had certain unhealthy inclinations toward what could be called Platonism. The dualism of spirit and matter. And that's what "Incarnation" is actually about.

CZARNECKA   When did you begin seriously studying Gnosticism? When were you seriously drawn into meditating on evil in the world? In *The Land of Ulro* you say that the question *"unde malum,"* "where does evil come from," began to prey on you rather early.

MILOSZ   You see, you can't speak of any serious knowledge at the beginning. Young people get together, they read a page of something here, a page there. It's the books you carry around with you that are the most important. And what I carried around was a history of the Church, with accounts of the various heresies. That was my main source. Later on, I had the sort of lust for the occult and the theosophical that is widespread in America today. I don't think those feelings lasted very long, because I realized they were suspect. At that time I was reading Maeterlinck, who was very popular in Poland in the twenties. There was a Danish writer, Gjellerup, a Nobel

Prize winner, influenced by Hinduism, occultism, reincarnation. And of course there was Schopenhauer. Those elements were already part of the scene. Whenever I think about that period, I come to the conclusion that this might be one reason my poetry had so strangely many aspects and contradictions then. I came under extremely strange, simultaneous cultural influences, on various levels and in various areas. But sometimes a person writes something and then feels ashamed of himself afterward. "Incarnation" is a very immodest poem.

CZARNECKA   Do you often censure your own work so severely and not print some pieces for years?

MILOSZ   No, just sometimes. When I'm ashamed of not having been true to myself.

CZARNECKA   But isn't it impossible not to reveal oneself in one's poetry?

MILOSZ   That's an important question. I don't know to what degree. . . . I always had tremendous misgivings about revealing myself. That may be one of my unhealthy aspects. I wouldn't have had these conversations with you five years ago. And fifteen years ago they would have been entirely out of the question. So there's some hope that, if you're patient, we may yet speak of all sorts of things.

CZARNECKA   How is it that you guard your privacy so carefully?

MILOSZ   Difficult to say, for various reasons. I'm speaking here about a certain general tendency toward feeling shame. I spoke of the poem "Incarnation." Someone else might not have been ashamed of it, but I was. There are many things that other people would accept without any scruples. But if a person is inclined toward self-torture and pangs of conscience, his sense of guilt will latch on to any pretext.

CZARNECKA   Do you still have a taste for "Manichean poison"?

MILOSZ   Of course, more than ever.

CZARNECKA   In *Visions from San Francisco Bay*, you wrote:

When our descendants seek to define our times, they will probably make use of the term "neo-Manichaeanism" to describe our characteristic resentment of evil Matter to which we desperately oppose value, but value no longer flowing from a divine source and now exclusively human. . . . For the old fear of hell-fire has not vanished; hell (as with Mani's old disciples) has taken root in our very subjugation to and helplessness against the natural forces residing in us, which today are the domain of the biologist, doctor, psychiatrist.

MILOSZ   Yes, what I had in mind were general trends in the literature and art of our century that are expressed in cruelty toward the body, toward matter, and depict the meaningless of physical human life in its more hideous aspects—something that, oddly enough, goes very nicely with an overall liberalization and an incitement to be as physical as possible. There's a story by Marek Hłasko, "The Eighth Day of the Week," one of his first, written at the start of his very sad career. Let's overlook the fact that Hłasko could be considered a typical representative, not just of one generation but of a few. That story displays a real hatred of the material world; there is a search for a love that elevates matter to a higher level.

CZARNECKA   Don't you always find a moralist when you scratch a nihilist like that? All that so-called *noire* literature is a danger signal, a warning.

MILOSZ   Of course, it can be interpreted that way, too. Różewicz's so-called casket-oriented somatism is moralism of a sort. There's a very fine line between moral longings and self-torture. As a heresy, Manicheanism is known to have arisen out of a search for purity. If the world is so evil, it must have been created by an evil demiurge. To the evil God the Manicheans opposed a bright God who had the face of Christ.

CZARNECKA   But the Gnostics commonly placed the principles of knowledge above faith, which means that esoteric knowledge was more important to them than faith.

MILOSZ   That's more or less correct. And that's probably precisely the reason they failed. Those were elitist movements, which had inherited from late Greek thought a division of people into the initiated, those who know, and ordinary people, ordinary mortals. And that, I think, is what doomed them to defeat in relation to Christianity. Because Christianity was more orthodox, more universal, and it stressed faith, not initiation and knowledge, like the Gnostics.

CZARNECKA   A delight in the beauty of the world, immediately colliding with a disgust for nature, a sense of contamination, is one of the themes most typical of your work. When did that suspicion of nature actually arise in you?

MILOSZ   A very difficult question. I think it's connected somehow with what I experienced in school, in my first year of high school. I had been living a happy and autonomous life until then. I thought that everything was just as it should be. In general, I didn't even think about it. And then all of a sudden there I was, the youngest boy in the class. Some of the students were awfully big, because that was the period after the wars. They sat in the last row. I was weaker than they were, and that was when I began to feel the cruelty of the world. So that must be one aspect—that encounter with a human society that was quite cruel and primitive, more or less like something out of Jack London. London is a writer of cruelty and naturalism, educated on a very primitive sort of Darwinism. He studied here, in Berkeley. He was a dropout from our university. By the way, his novel *Martin Eden* takes place in San Francisco. I liked *Martin Eden* very much, and it had an unusually strong effect on me. It has a wonderful quote from Swinburne:

> From too much love of living,
>   From hope and fear set free,
> We thank with brief thanksgiving
>   Whatever gods may be
>
> That no life lives forever;
> That dead men rise up never;
>   That even the weariest river
> Wind; somewhere safe to sea.

I recall that the hero of Martin Eden commits suicide by jumping into the ocean, just as Hart Crane would do later. Yes, all that naturalistic American literature is another source of my aversion to nature. And so is hunting. Studying nature, studying Darwin's theory in school. Besides, the passage from childhood to youth is a time of *Weltschmerz*.

"The World" and
"The Voices of Poor People"

CZARNECKA   For several years you were searching for a new voice, and the year 1943 makes for a certain turning point. In 1943 you wrote "The World: A Naïve Poem" and the cycle "The Voices of Poor People." Was your finding that new diction at that particular time caused by any changes in you, or was it connected with books you had read, personal experiences?

MILOSZ   A great many factors went into it, and I wouldn't want to be imprecise or oversimplify. Something very complex happened within me. It wouldn't be right to reduce it to a single element. In any case, I had the feeling that something was being revealed to me. It was as if the prewar era were still alive for me. It seemed to have ended, but it still hadn't been overcome in me. For various complex reasons, the prewar period ended for me in 1943. Only then did I have a sense of a new beginning. That's how it was.

CZARNECKA   You were working on English literature at that time, translating Shakespeare. Was that a form of therapy, given what the world around you was like?

MILOSZ   Yes, it may have been some form of therapy. I was studying English; I had had an interest in the language even

126

before the war. Besides, Edmund Wierciński of the Underground Theatre Council wanted me to translate *As You Like
It.*

CZARNECKA   Before the war you translated the poetry of the
seventeenth-century English poet Thomas Traherne. In *The
Garden of Knowledge* you wrote about his metaphysical prose
poems, which glorify the earth as a paradise given individually to every person on condition that he preserve a childlike
innocence. Is the genesis of "The World" connected with your
reading of Traherne?

MILOSZ   I think so. I liked Traherne's poetry very much. This
might also be connected with certain Thomistic reflections,
Saint Thomas Aquinas's endorsement of life as *esse.* I consider "The World" a very strange work. What's truly strange
is that it could have been written in that period, 1943 in Warsaw. The key to "The World" is that it's a poem about the
way the world should be. It was written in terrible circumstances. Warsaw in 1943—that was hitting bottom. But all
it took was an act of magic to depict the exact opposite. Because, given the way the world was, if you actually wanted
to say something about it, you'd have had to scream, not
speak. It was the exact opposite of the world that I decided
to depict—a rather ironic operation.

CZARNECKA   Because of your point of departure?

MILOSZ   Yes, because of the point of departure. And that's
why I get very irritated when the poems "Faith," "Hope,"
and "Love" are selected from "The World" and published
separately in anthologies. That takes them out of context. It
is precisely in an ironic context that they have their meaning.
In and of themselves, they could have been written for school
readers—they're that positive. And someone could be de-
luded into thinking that the entire cycle is sunny and child-
ishly positive. That's why the date when it was written is
important. I don't know if I was aware at the time of the

procedure William Blake used when juxtaposing *Songs of Innocence* and *Songs of Experience*. I knew a little Blake then, of course, but I did not see the full extent of his irony in juxtaposing those two cycles.

CZARNECKA Blake defined those cycles as an image of the two opposed states of the human soul.

MILOSZ Yes, but I'm not sure I realized that at the time. And so for me "The World" can be termed a sort of intuitive launching of a process that the perspective of time has made more or less obvious to me. In fact, "The World" does contain an identification with a naïve view of the world.

CZARNECKA But wasn't writing that poem also a form of escape into the domain of hierarchy, order, safety, where the father is the highest authority, the protector?

MILOSZ Naturally, this is the creation of an artificial world as a defense against the horror. I say this is a very strange work, because it lays the fullest possible emphasis on the basic disagreement that had come between me and the young Warsaw poets from the "Art and the Nation" group, and Krzysztof Baczyński's group as well. Their poetry was condensed, a magma of images, because of the enormous pressure of nightmarish reality. There was something similar in Tadeusz Borowski's poetry. But I was striving for a pure, calligraphic line. I was very fond of *The Chinese Flute* in Leopold Staff's translation, which I may have read then or perhaps earlier, in 1942. I rebelled strongly against being swept away by events. *They* were all submerged, but *I* didn't want to be!

CZARNECKA At one point you wrote about the sources of your poetry: the May devotions to the Blessed Virgin, the Bible, ritual, tradition, the books you read as a child. And so "The World: A Naïve Poem" could have been the purest example of all that. By the way, do you remember this poem by

Maria Konopnicka from your childhood: "Down the road the children go, a sister and a brother, and they cannot help but wonder at the beauty of the world"?

MILOSZ   Yes, I remember it.

CZARNECKA   Do you know why I asked?

MILOSZ   Yes. It's very possible there are echoes of it in "The World."

CZARNECKA   Besides, in *The Land of Ulro* you say that reading Blake's poetry, which you found in an anthology in occupied Warsaw, returned you to your childlike sense of enchantment, of experience, the child's sensual feeling for things.

MILOSZ   Yes, but to write a work of that sort under those circumstances was a way of going against the grain. It turns out that all my work had gone against the grain. In a certain sense, I was sticking out my tongue at the world, sometimes consciously, sometimes less so. But I wasn't thumbing my nose, not jeering. "The World: A Naïve Poem" is similar to *The Issa Valley:* unfashionable writing. Ultimately, those Warsaw poets had inherited the avant garde and the reality of the times, all in one legacy. I freely admit I found that an ungainly combination. And that's the reason I attempted what I called a calligraphic purification of the image free of any trace of the Nazi experience. What is *The Issa Valley?* That book, which was written in Paris, is also an assault against all modern literature. I am not a primitive, after all. I was capable of writing avant-garde books.

CZARNECKA   This would also be in keeping with poetry's salutary function, the opposition to negation and nihilism: to save the world by writing "The World," to preserve basic values. Still, that cycle is something of an exception, because in your other works of this period the pressure of the actual reality of the occupation is very strongly felt. Primarily in the cycle "The Voices of Poor People," which can be viewed as a counterpart to Blake's *Songs of Experience* if we take "The World: A Naïve Poem" as a counterpart to *Songs of Innocence*. Especially since those two cycles are always printed together when published in book form.

MILOSZ   That's true, but my entire image as a poet is constantly changing. As I see it, that's something over which an author has very little control. Since I wrote a certain number of poems that are civic-minded in some way—for example, "The Voices of Poor People" or "Campo dei Fiori"—there's a whole school that wants to make an ideological bard out of me. The poems chosen for some anthologies make me appear noble, the bard of the nation. That's not in the least to my taste.

CZARNECKA   You once said that "Campo dei Fiori" is a very immoral poem.

MILOSZ   Why?

CZARNECKA   Because it was written from the point of view of an observer about people who were dying.

MILOSZ   Where did I say that?

CZARNECKA   In New York, at a meeting with young poets, in the fall of 1978.

MILOSZ   Of course. There's an essay in *The Garden of Knowledge* entitled "The Immorality of Art" where I speak of the immorality of writing when confronted with some horror of the world or of life, the so-called conflict of life and art. I quote Thomas Mann there, because he was constantly oppressed by the split between life and art. That essay is a reworking of a talk I gave at the University of Michigan and was published in English in the *Michigan Review*.

CZARNECKA Do you call a poem like "Campo dei Fiori" civic-minded because it's about people's indifference to the death of others?

MILOSZ Yes, it was written out of a moral reaction.

CZARNECKA In that case, what's the civic aspect of the poem?

MILOSZ Well, let's not forget what a very large amount of civic-minded writing stems from a moral reaction. Civic-minded writing is a form of protest, and it derives from moral indignation. No conclusions are necessarily to be drawn from this. For what conclusions could be drawn? That poem is a bit of a touchy subject for me. Several Hebrew translations were published recently. Why do I say that in a certain sense "Campo dei Fiori" is a civic-minded poem? Because conclusions can be drawn from it. First, there are the horrors of Nazism, and second, the indifference of people in the streets of Warsaw. You might ask if people in the streets of Warsaw were really like that then. They were and they weren't. They were because there were merry-go-rounds near the ghetto, and they weren't because the people of Warsaw behaved differently at other times, in other parts of the city—so there's no question of leveling any accusations here. That poem was an ordinary human reaction in the spring of 1943.

CZARNECKA When was the cycle "The Voices of Poor People" written?

MILOSZ At the end of '43, the beginning of '44. Roughly speaking, to the best of my memory. But I rebel against any attempt to reduce me to those poems, even though there's something very noble about having poems like those as part of one's work. I was a poet before the war, and so I went into the war mature in years, which doesn't mean that I was mentally or emotionally mature. If my poetry is to be treated as a whole, then those poems have their place as part of the background, of my entire evolution. I always avoided noble rhetoric, even if at one point I did happen to write poems out of moral indignation. Of course, I prefer some of the poems from *Three Winters* or *The World*, because they contain affirmations and have a certain metaphysical background. Later on— for example, in the volume *The Light of Day*—there was a great deal of civic-minded poetry, protest, and so forth. But writing that kind of poetry always had a bad effect on me. You have to understand why I don't like *Poem on Frozen Time*. Precisely because it's a book of civic-minded poems. Even the noblest works, conceived out of moral indignation, are based in rhetoric. And so I can be said to move constantly between a poetry of social and historical reality, and the purer reaches. *Va et viens!*

CZARNECKA   Not everything is clear to me in the eight poems of the cycle "The Voices of Poor People." Could you tell me who the guardian mole is in the poem "A Poor Christian Looks at the Ghetto"? It appears in the third stanza:

Slowly, boring a tunnel, a guardian mole makes his
     way,
With a small red lamp fastened to his forehead.
He touches buried bodies, counts them, pushes on.
He distinguishes human ashes by their luminous vapor,
The ashes of each man by a different part of the spec-
     trum.

MILOSZ   I don't know who the guardian mole is. The poem is simply an image of an earth full of ashes.

CZARNECKA   Not just ashes, because skin, hair, and various artifacts appear in the first two stanzas. You give a whole list of things that were subjected to apocalyptic destruction.

MILOSZ   No, that's on the surface, whereas, inside, the earth is filled with ashes, which are not entirely dead matter.

CZARNECKA   Is that the reason they emanate a part of the spectrum?

MILOSZ   Yes. People's images of eschatological space—
heaven, hell, Hades, the Old Testament Sheol—are strange,
very loose, fluid, but they always have a spatial aspect. So,
one can imagine a subterranean space where something alive
is moving. If that's how it moves, it must be a mole. What
other creatures move through the ground? That's how I reconstruct it now. When I was writing the poem, I wasn't
thinking as systematically as I am now, interpreting it after
the fact. Of course, the point is that Sheol or Hades is being
visited by some creature from the world of the living. What
else moves like that? It must be a mole . . .

CZARNECKA   . . . which turns into a judge with the heavy-
lidded eyes of a patriarch. I understand that you didn't choose
your symbols systematically. Does that mean you consider
the cycle "The Voices of Poor People" *écriture automatique?*
You mentioned that you wrote the poems in *Three Winters*
as a sort of recording device. In some of your later essays you
say that art is actually craft, constant labor.

MILOSZ   Either both statements are true or both statements
are false. Of course art is craft in the sense that you have to
sit down and work. You asked me if I had pondered that
image, if I attempted to be systematic in creating it. No, it
just appeared, that's all. All the "depth" theories of art have
something to them. This isn't a cerebral, intellectual matter,
after all. Far from it! An image arises; it has a logic of its
own, and it has power over us. And then you have to work
and be stubborn. . . . The daimonion and hard work go hand
in hand.

CZARNECKA   A recurrent theme in the poems you wrote during the war—and in later poems, too—is a sense of guilt
toward those who were killed. This seems to be the burden
of a survivor's guilt, and is explicit in "Café," one of the poems
in "The Voices of Poor People."

MILOSZ   For me that poem lacks universality—it's too closely
connected to actual historical circumstances. The problem of

being a survivor is an enormous issue, one that recurs both for me and for a great many others who wrote in Poland after the war. For Różewicz, it's a total obsession. I don't know how much attention this has been given in Poland, but the poems in "The Voices of Poor People" anticipate Różewicz in a certain sense. Still, I think that to discover anything of importance here, you would have to dig much deeper than that. The magnitude of the trauma of those times is a subject in itself. There was the ghetto, for God's sake, and the liquidation of three million Polish Jews, a sin that cries out—on the earth, in all of Poland—to be absolved. I think this is a difficult subject to discuss.

CZARNECKA   For me, "Outskirts" is the most amazing poem in "The Voices of Poor People." You had not been interested in the urban, lumpen-proletarian subculture before then. Is this a fascination with mediocrity? That doesn't fit in with the rest of your work. How did that sudden turnabout take place? There's a scene by a clay pit, the ruins of the city in the background, near a railroad line used for prisoner transports—where a group of Warsaw wiseguys is playing cards, drinking vodka, trying to pick up a girl.

MILOSZ   That aspect of reality seems to me to have been very strong, very prevalent in Warsaw toward the end of the war.

CZARNECKA   Meaning crudeness?

MILOSZ   Yes. There was plenty of moonshine, cork-soled slippers, girls wiggling their butts. That was very typical of the atmosphere toward the end of the occupation, and I don't think it was confined to Warsaw. Something of the sort existed throughout German-occupied Europe. There was a certain amount of contact in that period, for example, between Warsaw and Paris, via the Reich; people did business, they traveled. "Outskirts" may be a bit the result of reading English poets—there may be a little T. S. Eliot in there. That poem has been called extremely deep for its image of all Europe at that time, and because it links the historical with the personal. And it truly is a landscape of the night of the occupation, not as seen from the city but from the outskirts of the city.

CZARNECKA   Though "The Poor Poet" is part of "the Voices of Poor People," it is not one of the group of poems that you called civic-minded. . . .

MILOSZ   This is a polemic with art, a constant turning against art.

> I poise the pen and it puts forth twigs and leaves, it is
>   covered with blossoms
> And the scent of that tree is impudent, for there, on the
>   real earth
> Such trees do not grow, and like an insult
> To suffering humanity is the scent of that tree.

This is the immorality of art.

CZARNECKA   Is that why the poem also says:

> I sit, a sly and angry poet
> With malevolently squinted eyes.

MILOSZ   Yes, "I plot revenge."

CZARNECKA   Against art?

MILOSZ   "To me is given the hope of revenge on others and on myself." That's interesting when looked at from this perspective. I wonder how someone else might have written that poem. I've mentioned Różewicz. All his work is marked by an immense falling out with art and culture. It comes down to something like: You can talk about culture and art, but please do have a look at what happened here. My poem is somewhat along those lines. The revenge the poor poet plots is more or less the one Różewicz carried out. Except that I was never a consistent nihilist. This is part of the complex that turns against European culture, against art, which, if the truth be told, had a lot that needed throwing out, a great deal that was disgraceful. This is what Gombrowicz praised me for, my self-contradiction: "Being Milosz, I do not wish to be Milosz."

CZARNECKA   You once wrote that Polish literature always has to be viewed in terms of dates. Do you include your own work in that?

MIOLSZ   It would certainly be very nice to view a poem apart from its date and circumstances, but that can't be done. Besides, what do we want—marble, unshakable canons, beauty? I'm no Mallarmé. Dates are important. We've spoken of "The World" being an odd work, but if it had been written in other circumstances, it would only have been an oddity. I don't know; maybe in two hundred years there won't be a scrap of information left on the origin of various poems. Some poems will filter through and become part of the anthologies. . . .

CZARNECKA   In "The Songs of Adrian Zieliński" you express a desire to break free of the nightmare around you, to escape to "happy cities" on some distant islands. In a poem written right after the end of the war, "In Warsaw," you say:

> Was I created for this,
> To mourn and lament?
> I want to sing of the banquets,
> The joyous groves to which
> I was led by Shakespeare.
> Leave the poets a moment of joy
> Or your world will die.

Didn't this become the subject of a heated polemic in the reviews of your volume *Rescue?*

MILOSZ   In 1946, Kazimierz Wyka published an article, "Somnambulist Gardens and Pastoral Gardens," in which he

wrote about my Arcadian complex. I objected in a reply, because I think that what Wyka called my Arcardian tendency
is in fact a desire to contrast the world of twentieth-century
evil with some almost utopian image of peace, beauty, equilibrium. The Islands of Happiness, or Arcadia, represent a
search for a realm to contradict reality and thereby create a
certain dynamism. It's difficult to be a poet only of despair,
only of sadness. An element of joy, located somewhere in an
imaginary future, is the other side of catastrophism. But, going
back to the poem "In Warsaw," which you asked about: that
poem was jotted down on a scrap of paper in half a minute.
And—as is often the case with my poems—I don't consider
it a poem, just a note. That poem also arose as a moral reaction, like "The Poor Christian" or "Campo dei Fiori."

CZARNECKA   In the volume *Rescue* you appear as a "mourner
and lamenter"—even though in "Dedication" you observe
the ritual of Forefathers' Eve and entreat the spirits of the
dead not to visit you any more—and at the same time you
are an artist bidding farewell to an era. It's interesting that
for this role you make use of disguise, stylization, references
to other literary or historical times. I'm thinking here of two
poems: "Complaint of the Ladies of a Bygone Era" and
"Farewell." Is the former allusion to Villon?

MILOSZ   Probably not. Ultimately, that's a sort of a general
cultural cliché. Naturally you can say that there's some *"Où
sont les neiges d'antan"* here, but that's already a part of the
language. This poem takes place at a certain boundary. That
means that the so-called eternal element is repeated—the ladies of bygone years (Villon asks where this lady is, where
that lady is . . . not that his were so ladylike). This is a dance
of death, a universal *danse macabre,* but at the same time one
that takes place in a specific historical setting. After all, the
time here is the end of the war, when those women truly were
becoming a thing of the past. One way or the other, the poem
contains an awareness of enormous change. The Russians will

be arriving any minute, there will be a new, different world. There's even a certain sense of resignation here: tough luck, bid the ladies farewell, there's nothing you can do about it.

CZARNECKA

> Our elegant coiffures in which the master's skill
> Wove silver stars, flowers, plumes from birds of para-
> dise
> Have come asunder and fall like ashes into darkness.

Why are those ladies in eighteenth-century costume, splendid wigs? By analogy to the fate of ladies during the French Revolution?

MILOSZ   No. I think this is a way of distancing, through the use of extravagant accessories, costumes. Ultimately, when you think of ladies, you imagine them in eighteenth-century dress.

CZARNECKA   In the poem "Farewell" you use Verona as a mask, though one may assume that it's Wilno you're bidding farewell to. And even though the poem says, "To reject, to reject everything," that cannot be reconciled with a world stripped of the sensual. This is, after all, only an ironic acceptance of a world without Verona, without Romeo and Juliet.

MILOSZ   I don't know if this poem's about Wilno. You have to understand the circumstances in which that poem was written: Cracow, in the spring of 1945. As long as I walked on Saint Thomas Street, where I lived, to the Old Market, to Mary Square, and later to the writers' union at No. 22 Krupnicza Street, it was bearable. But the security police's building was right there, and it was filled with the young people Wajda tried to portray in the movie *Ashes and Diamonds*. The scenes at the train station were straight out of Dante. It was a migration of nations. Millions of homeless people coming from the east and the west. The terrible world of the spring of 1945. That reality is reflected in this poem.

I'm always amazed at how little reality filters into literature. Very little, in fact. Sometimes it happens by chance, by some odd turn of events. The greater part of the reality of people's lives somehow disappears without a trace. And it cannot be re-created afterward. Let's take the Napoleonic Wars, for example. How much of the Napoleonic Wars actually filtered into literature? Not descriptions of campaigns and battles, but the immediate, day-to-day reality. Of course, the writers felt that there was something wrong about all those heroic scenes. Stendhal tried. Tolstoy tried by placing Pierre Bezukhov at Borodino when describing the chaos of battle. And there's a prisoner-of-war camp in *War and Peace.* Still, most of it is lost. And then, all of a sudden, reality slips into a poem as atmosphere, background. Sometimes a single line is enough, a detail. We spoke about "Outskirts." Something of that reality remains in the poem, some atmosphere. But I don't know if there's any reflection of reality in "Farewell." I only described Cracow anecdotally in that poem. But I think it contains both despair and an acceptance of the new world.

CZARNECKA   Does the poem "Fate" also contain an acceptance of the new world? And—despite everything—a faith in poetry? One no longer hears the voice of the "poor poet" who plots revenge because he has no faith in art, but the voice of an artist conscious that his work will endure: "To me is given coal, oak, and a ring, and the foaming wave."

MILOSZ   That's a sort of poetic exercise with a certain ideological content, and it is based on cutting oneself off from the past, on forgetting, making a new beginning, which was nothing unusual in those circumstances. Loyalty to everything that prewar Poland represented was not such a simple matter during the occupation. In any case, it wasn't for me. I felt much freer as soon as I came to the conclusion that certain of the holy of holies had started to become boring. But no one actually wrote anything about all that. Dygat may have tried in his novel *Farewell,* whose action takes place outside Komorów, that area, after the fall of Warsaw. A couple of the heroes finally break with their loyalty to long-suffering Poland; they want to live. "We won't run away to the West," they say. "We'll see what life'll be like here—no matter what, it'll be life." This comes close, close, but it doesn't catch—all the complexities. The poem you're asking about is a joyful one—a turning away from the past, an affirmation of life masked as a stylistic exercise, as was done during the Baroque.

CZARNECKA   *Rescue* was the only volume of your poetry published in postwar Poland until 1980.

MILOSZ   Yes, the only one. *Treatise on Morals* was published in the journal *Twórczość* in 1948. I was surprised it was allowed. It was just before the Socialist and Communist parties were united, and the onset of all that indoctrination.

Treatise on Morals and
The Captive Mind

CZARNECKA   Was your first stay in America between 1946 and 1950 good for you as a poet, creatively?

MILOSZ   It was quite creative. Yes, I wrote a certain number of poems of which I am not ashamed. At the time I was trying to do work that helped me make sense of things. I translated a good deal from English and Spanish. Spanish is very easy for someone who knows French. And I had also happened upon some wonderful bilingual editions: Spanish poetry with the English across from it. So, in a way, I was discovering that poetry for myself and read a great deal of it at the time. That period was marked by a sense of obligation. I had to do something to counteract the grayness in Poland. As a poet, I could inject a little color. Poets writing in Spanish—the Mexicans, for example—are very colorful and baroque. I also translated some Chinese poets from English. Jerzy Borejsza was glad to publish those translations in People's Poland, for reasons of prestige and propaganda, because even if he did have an image of a communist literature, it wasn't like the Russians'. Those poems may have suited his needs, but what I wanted was to counteract the grayness. But such desires often prove in the end to be delusions, illusions. A person likes to work, wants to do something, and then he turns out to be helping the propaganda machine by lending it his name.

It's quite a tricky game. But there's no question that I wanted to introduce Spanish and English poetry to Polish literature, which before the war had nearly no knowledge of the entire huge body of world poetry. They only translated from the French. By that time I was trying to translate Różewicz into English—his poems are easy to translate. When I showed them to Americans, no one understood them. But people liked those same poems when I printed them recently. A certain evolution has occurred in America—some things can now be understood. But back then an even greater distance existed between Poland and America than does today. Those were two very different worlds.

CZARNECKA   Between 1946 and 1950 you wrote many poems that didn't appear in print until the volume *The Light of Day,* published in the West in 1953. But were some of the American poems published in Polish literary journals before you emigrated?

MILOSZ   Yes. We mentioned *Treatise on Morals,* a poem that mocks socialist realism published right before socialist realism was introduced in Poland. Afterward, there was no longer any question of publishing a poem like that.

CZARNECKA   To whom were you addressing *Treatise on Morals*—your fellow poets, yourself?

MILOSZ   It could be said that, before writing *The Captive Mind,* I sketched it out in the form of *Treatise on Morals* and then developed the idea in prose. Whom was I addressing? I don't know. I appear to be speaking as one who has a better understanding of things. I wrote *Treatise on Morals* in Washington, and perhaps distance gave me the feeling that I had a clearer view of things.

CZARNECKA   Should the title be taken at face value, or as irony?

MILOSZ   I don't know. That's how it came out. I don't think
it should be read as a moral treatise as opposed to an immoral one. It's a treatise on the subject of morality. Besides,
everything is put clearly, I think. Here, for example, I'm writing about the security police, of course:

> When the devils plant their pitchforks in the damned
> Lying on their beds in hell,
> The sight is familiar, though hideous.
> Anyway, they are masters of disguise.
> So, don't take this description as literal.

And this fragment is about Gomułka:

> Avoid those who in their own circle,
> Having made their political bets, sit
> While the fire crackles in the hearth, and
> Call out: the people, but whisper—putty.
> Who call out: the nation, but whisper—shit.
> I think they're acting very badly
> Because they're drunk on appearances.
> They are only meteors themselves
> And long years await them in the earth,
> And much water will flow in the Vistula
> Before anyone gives a peep about them again.

I was surprised when Gomułka returned to power in '56. I
thought that my poem had been proved incorrect, but that
was only temporary.

CZARNECKA   In *Treatise on Morals* you give certain pointers
on how to live according to ethical standards when on the
brink of disaster. This is, after all, a world on the "razor's
edge." *Treatise on Morals* concludes with a prediction of
coming annihilation.

MILOSZ   I thought that we truly were heading for the "heart
of darkness." I don't suppose I would think differently now.
I did not see any hope then. And, to a considerable extent,

I'm still a catastrophist today. Back then, in 1947, to say that the "heart of darkness" was up ahead of us was completely justified.

CZARNECKA   Let's switch to developing the idea of *Treatise on Morals* in prose, in *The Captive Mind*. How long did you work on that book?

MILOSZ   I began it in the spring of 1951 and finished it in the late fall.

CZARNECKA   And when exactly did you request asylum in France?

MILOSZ   February 1, 1951.

CZARNECKA   In your introduction to *The Captive Mind* you say that you hoped never to deal with that subject again.

MILOSZ   That was quite sincere on my part. I always felt that way. Obviously, that subject was to a degree imposed by circumstance. I had my back to the wall, and I wrote the book, but that isn't my line. *The Captive Mind* got excellent reviews in American sociology journals. I could actually have based a career on it. Today, that book is still considered a key work in the field. So, it created some opportunities for me at universities, but in sociology or political science. In France, of course, I could have specialized in writing political articles, like those Eastern Europeans who style themselves as experts on communism. The prevailing atmosphere among the French intellectuals was leftist, but some of them had somehow worked it so that they were making a leftist critique of communism. And that was what I was trying to steer clear of.

CZARNECKA   Was *The Captive Mind* written primarily with the Western reader in mind?

MILOSZ   Yes, perhaps with the hope that it might explain something about the greater world to that reader.

CZARNECKA   There's a certain irony of fate here: you wrote *The Captive Mind* out of need, and the book brought you fame.

MILOSZ   What sort of fame? I prefer a different sort of fame. Yes, the book continues to be quoted and republished. However, I find it far away from my real interests.

CZARNECKA   How many languages was *The Captive Mind* translated into?

MILOSZ   I don't remember exactly. I actually translated it into French myself. André Prudhommeaux corrected the style, and the translation appeared under his name. There were translations into English, German, Italian, Spanish, and some of the more exotic languages. I'll tell you an odd incident that happened to me at a poetry festival in Rotterdam in 1975. There was a poet there from Indonesia who was apparently very famous and who recited his own poems in his native language. His style of recitation was something like Mayakovsky's or Voznesensky's. High emotion, gestures—a very revolutionary poet. When he found out my name, he said, "You don't know this, but you are one of our national heroes." "What do you mean?" I said. "It's because we translated your book *The Captive Mind* and distributed it. It's our main weapon in the struggle with the current regime." "But your government is rightist," I said. And his answer was: "That's right, but what difference does that make? It's totalitarian all the same. Your book is against absolutism. Your book is the gospel for our intellectuals who are opposed to the government." A host of Indonesians were at the reading, and there is a photograph of me among them. What adventures I've had in my life—a national hero of Indonesia!
I had all sorts of difficulties with those translations. Of

course, I don't include the languages I don't know—at least I don't have to worry about *them*. I suspect some of them are terrible. In fact, an author loses complete control over translations into other languages. At least *The Captive Mind* was translated into English by a very good translator. Some of the translations were done by friends of mine, with a lot of hard work and dedication, and with unbearable nitpicking on my part. I'm a taskmaster when it comes to precision.

CZARNECKA   *The Captive Mind* does not have the distance, the remove, the cool eye, that is characteristic of your other work. And in replying to criticism, you yourself stated that the book was written in blood, which obviously calls neither its value nor its truthfulness into question.

MILOSZ   I did write the book at a time of very great inner conflict. I was wrestling with myself, because I, too, had been affected by all that historical necessity, Hegelianism. Which is why I wanted to free myself from all that, immediately after writing the book. But I realized that the book had marked me in a certain way. Someone else might have accepted that and made good use of it. In an article I once said that Pasternak was in a horrible situation when they gave him the Nobel Prize for *Doctor Zhivago*. He got the prize for a novel, not for the poetry that was his life. Here, in the West, it took me many years to be recognized as a poet, and not as the author of *The Captive Mind*. Writing that book did me no harm in the Polish world. Quite the reverse, because if people can read Polish, they can also read my poems and my other books, and get a sense of my work as a whole. *The Captive Mind* is nothing to be ashamed of. But foreigners who know only a part of what I've written have a distorted image of me. For Polish readers I can write *The Captive Mind* and still be viewed as a poet. Essays are part of my equipment, one of the instruments I play.

CZARNECKA   In *The Captive Mind* you included portraits of four writers, which could of course be treated as synthetic portraits except that it requires no effort to decipher them. So, then, why did you replace their names with letters of the alphabet while providing so much information about them?

MILOSZ   Because I didn't want to be a gossipmonger. Ultimately, it sets a rather unpleasant example if a person flees his country and then slings mud at his friends and colleagues, tells tales. Even if I did write for the foreign reader, Poland was still the source of my material. But my intention was to depict a worldwide phenomenon, not a local, Polish one. Poland exemplifies it. Why should I have mentioned those people by name? I think what I have against the book is that dash of gossip, which is what interests people. Here we encounter a certain basic issue—namely, that everything that interests most people is in some way second-rate. And that, unfortunately, means that the actual demands I place on literature would probably have eliminated everything of interest to people. The single artistic reservation I have about *The Captive Mind* is those portraits. But at least I was discreet enough not to use their names. Who knows them outside Poland!

CZARNECKA   What if you were to write *The Captive Mind* now?

MILOSZ   I certainly would not write *The Captive Mind* now. Even when I was writing it, I felt that it was fragmentary, just part of the truth, because things went deeper than that. Later on, in various essays and books, I tried to reach the source of the entire issue of communism in the twentieth century, the older sources, touching on a philosophical current that can be studied by going back to the eighteenth and nineteenth centuries: Hegel, the fascination with historicity. I tried to elucidate those issues. My colleague Herling-Grudziński thinks that I invented this problem in *The Captive Mind*. What I wrote was true with regard to a certain number of people in Poland. It's just that there were very few such people in Poland. In the end, this book describes the conversion to Marxism, if such a thing exists. In the conclusion of his book *The*

Main Currents of Marxism, Leszek Kołakowski says Marxism doesn't exist. But people believe that it does. Someone said that in Honduras anyone able to read ten lines of print in an hour considers himself a Marxist.

CZARNECKA   Do you think that the mechanism for making the transition to the New Faith, a mechanism that you described in the chapter "Murti-Bing," is still binding? According to you, one accepts a doctrine in which one doesn't believe out of fear of isolation, an indefinite sense of historical necessity, and, finally, in order to achieve fame or success.

MILOSZ   I have to admit I've lost interest in that issue. It's ceased to be relevant in Poland. And I have to be sensitive to that one country, because what's written, said, and thought in Polish matters to me. Everything in Poland is much less complicated in that no one there believes in the magic power of Marxist philosophy. On the other hand, in the world as a whole, nothing could be more relevant for a great many people who are just learning to read and write than their genuine concern with Marxism.

CZARNECKA   It seems to me that in part *The Captive Mind* is a polemic with Stanisław Witkacy's pessimistic vision of the future. In other words, you are attracted by his catastrophism but at the same time you're protecting yourself against a no-exit situation where religion, philosophy, and art have been eliminated and society is composed of automatons who are kept happy by artificial means. In the chapter "Man, This Enemy," you express a certain hope for a renewal, a liberation from the New Faith. You mention the workers and the Church as the most likely sources of opposition. And that has proved true in the Polish situation.

MILOSZ   Yes indeed. Witkacy's novel *Insatiability* definitely had a powerful effect on me and my colleagues. Witkacy did not interest us as a playwright, and we did not see any of his plays. Secondly, we were not in the least attracted by his theory of the theatre. On the other hand, his pessimistic vision of history was very compelling. I don't think he was original in that pessimism; there were others, an entire current. Pessimistic science fiction had existed since Wells's *Time Machine,* which appeared in 1895. In any case, at the time when people were leaning toward Marxism, leftism, Witkacy was on people's minds. It seems to me now that I was fully justified both in accepting Witkacy's pessimistic, catastrophist vision and in protecting myself against it. That's probably a correct reaction, because Witkacy's historiosophical vision has proved true to a large extent but the world has not come to an end. All that conformity, that grayness, has come to pass. On the other hand, it's still a long way to the end of religion, philosophy, and art.

CZARNECKA   I wonder if the Polish émigrés' violent reaction to *The Captive Mind* was connected with your prewar leftist sympathies and then later on, your "Hegelian bug." Those who wanted a negative image of Polish society felt threatened by your dialectics. Some people considered this book a veiled apology for Marxism. In an article written a few years later, you acknowledge that Marxism has at least one value. Allow me to quote a passage from your article "Speaking of Mammals":

The centuries that separate us from the Middle Ages are not a tablet that can be wiped clean with a sponge; when launching satellites into space, we cannot accept Dante's world view as our own. That static image of the world is inaccesible to us. It was not known then that man is a creature of history and subordinate to society so that he constantly breathes the air of conditioning. The significance of Marxism, always present in European disputes, is that it does not allow us to forget that fact—and, despite all the hopelessness of the controversy between the hostile camps, it may at some point contribute to a fuller grasp of elusive truth. But man cannot be reduced to his role in history, which is unable to pass moral judgment.

MILOSZ   Granted, Marxism has vulgarized the idea of history, because it is a philosophy for simple souls. In the current historical situation, it's for yokels, young people. I'm not being contemptuous here. I consider Marxism a false and harmful philosophy, as I've said many times before. On the other hand, I don't deny that it has given people an awareness of history. In America, thinking in historical categories is something very new and difficult to master. I think this is the fault of the secondary schools to a large extent. And there's also what drove the poet Norwid from America—the lack of old stones. I'd like to add that I was commissioned to write the article "Speaking of Mammals" by Henry Kissinger, who was a young Harvard professor at the time and the editor of the magazine *Confluence*.

CZARNECKA   The final section of *The Captive Mind* is devoted to the fate of the Baltic countries. Was that chapter part of your original intention?

MILOSZ   I remember that I hesitated about it but finally included it for what I might call sentimental reasons. That chapter may stand out because all the rest of the book is about Poland while the focus of the last chapter is outside Poland. I thought that I should include it because of my great sorrow and compassion for the fate of the Lithuanians, and the Baltic states in general. No matter what, I was born there, it's my native land.

The Light of Day

CZARNECKA   *The Light of Day* is the first volume of poetry you published after you emigrated. It contains work from various periods. . . .

MILOSZ   Yes, largely because there were many poems I couldn't publish in Poland. The situation there had changed. *The Light of Day* is not a very well-ordered collection; it's rather haphazard. It lacks a unifying principle. I'm not very fond of it as a whole; I write it off as a loss. The book's structure is chaotic, because of my difficult personal situation and the pressure of the political atmosphere, which had been alienating me from poetry for a number of years.

CZARNECKA   Which poems in that volume do you still think highly of?

MILOSZ   One moment—I have to remember what I included there.

CZARNECKA   The volume opens with the poem "To Jonathan Swift."

MILOSZ   Personally, I'm very fond of that poem.

CZARNECKA   Let's talk about it a little, then. Why did you choose Swift as your patron at that point, comparing your own fate to the adventures of the hero of *Gulliver's Travels?*

151

MILOSZ   Because I still felt trapped, and I couldn't vent my great rage and despair. Actually, that was the despair of moral indignation and conscience. I was in a very awkward situation. It might have been a good one had I been concerned with making my way in life—in 1947 I was in America. I don't want to depict myself as a paragon of virtue. Still, it's a fact that, as a Polish poet, I didn't have very much to do in America, especially after my experience of the war and with all those Polish dramas and imbroglios that make no sense to Americans. I never felt at ease. I was extremely caustic about the situation in Poland, the foreign domination in particular. Everything was clear to me. Since I could read Russian, I had an excellent idea of that period, which was described much later by Solzhenitsyn. It was a very difficult situation. Let's say that poems like "To Jonathan Swift" were a refuge in satire, for which I swear I had no penchant before the war. That came as a complete surprise to me. Besides, at the time, I found myself drawn to the classical, in the eighteenth-century sense. Not as I had before the war, when I might have been under the influence of Paul Valéry, meaning a French neoclassicism coupled with strange surrealist images. But in Washington it was the eighteenth century that interested me. That may have been the result of my contact with Juliusz Tadeusz Kroński, who was a great champion of classicism in literature, the classical stance as opposed to the Romantic. If I look back at the various styles in my poetry, I myself find them strange. I did not think of myself as talented in fashioning stanzas of that sort, but those poems toy with the classical conventions and constitute a type of parody. "To Jonathan Swift" is obviously a stylization of the eighteenth century. The form is cut and dry—an experiment in dry form. If you recall, Heraclitus said that dry souls are the best and that moist ones are very bad.

CZARNECKA   In the poem "Central Park," which is dedicated to Juliusz Kroński, the Cassandra voice is used again. The poem is a warning addressed to America, where "nature becomes theatre." That's the ahistorical America, indifferent to

Europe's experience. But the poem also contains the hope that good will triumph over evil:

> Gazing calmly upon force, we know
> That those who wish to rule the world will pass,
> And we realize that it is not always necessary
> To live with knife or gun in hand.
> The cunning of weapons turns to misfortune
> And strong winds tear standards to tatters,
> But glory, our heritage from Greece,
> Will last as long as mankind lasts.

MILOSZ   That poem reveals a great fascination with the philosophy of history, with events. At the same time, there's something prophetic about it: for rebirth to occur, one first has to enter the heart of darkness. I express faith in Europe. During the war, Kroński wrote an essay, "Fascism and the European Tradition," which appeared, though perhaps not in full, in his book *Reflections on Hegel*. The essay is actually not about fascism but about totalitarianism of any sort. Kroński stressed faith in Europe, European culture, which, he held, shone through despite all its diseases. A very nineteenth-century residue of faith in a world of values, even though bottom had already been hit several times. "Central Park" is a bit reminiscent of *Treatise on Morals*, since it was written at more or less the same time. In *Treatise on Morals* I said that a little light was shining "in France, the China of Europe," a world was re-emerging from the flood, and it would continue to shine.

CZARNECKA   Were you counting on a rebirth in France in particular?

MILOSZ   No, that was more of a chance usage, no prophecy intended. It was simply a prediction of renewal. Poems like "Central Park," "To Jonathan Swift," and *Treatise on Morals* are a sort of invocation, a faith in another shore, a modified eschatology, because it's a very fine line indeed between a reborn world that comes in history and a reborn world, the

Kingdom of God, that comes after the end of history. Those things interweave; one is connected with the other. All Christian eschatology concerns that borderline. In the Apocalypse of Saint John there are a thousand years of peace and of a world reborn before the complete end of history—in other words, there is no clear division. The Kingdom of God, and the kingdom of humanity reborn on earth before the end of history, are very intimately connected.

CZARNECKA   You included many poems on American subjects in *The Light of Day*. It's not an overly sympathetic image of America that emerges from those poems. The sterility of life in a poem like "Without Vision." A world subordinated to the laws of nature, unaware of history, as in your poem "Native Land" . . .

MILOSZ   Well, you know, I have plenty of company in that. And that's why probably all postwar Polish writers are, to one degree or another, worried about the West—America is not the point here. I was not enchanted by America in the sense that I had a strong desire to live here. If it hadn't been for all those chance events—too complicated to go into here— if it weren't for the nightmare of Poland under foreign domination, I wouldn't have wanted to live in the West. But those are complex issues, and it would be easy to be untrue and overly simple here. Conversations like this are very dangerous because there are a thousand things you're aware of and don't mention. All the biographical aspects, the motives, are definitely falsified in conversation.

You asked me about my attitude toward America. Of course there are poems that have something to say on the subject. The stance in those texts is one of great distance. The poems "Child of Europe" and "Mid-Twentieth-Century Portrait" are, however, the most important for that period. I treat them together because they complement each other, develop the same ideas. "Child of Europe" has to be read *à rebours*, of course, because it becomes cynical if taken literally. I wrote it in a state of fury, anger. This poem, too, came out of moral pain. At the time I was probably the only person who reacted to the situation in Poland, our experience, in such fashion. I mean the only person who reacted that way in writing. A great many people were probably thinking that way at the time. Many poems have that ironic tone in Polish literature today.

CZARNECKA The same theme is probably also in the poem "A Nation," in which you enumerate the Poles' heroic acts and high-mindedness and contrast that with their prosaic faults and low-mindedness.

MILOSZ Yes, that's a bitter poem. That was a poem written entirely outside my control, in the sense that something comes, grabs my hand, and orders me to write. There's nothing I can do about it. You're faced with a *fait accompli*, and you're surprised by it afterward. The more I think about my so-called life as a writer, the more I'm convinced that I function as a medium. Something arises in me, but just how is a mystery.

CZARNECKA There's an ecstatic tone in "Song of a Bird over the Shore of the Potomac," a tone that is rare in *The Light of Day*. There's also an effort to forget, which can be assisted by America's lack of a sense of history, otherwise so alien to you. . . .

MILOSZ Yes, that was a part of my ongoing effort to cut myself free from the past. Still, the amputation of Lithuania is a painful thing. When I lived in Wilno, I pretended to revolt against its provincialism, but nevertheless a great deal bound me to that place. After all, when writing that poem, I was aware of that enormous country to the east that would come and destroy local cultures for the indefinite future. I was not like those Polish émigrés who at that time were waiting for a new war to break out at any moment. And so it was necessary to adapt. Those poems express a variety of renunciations in an agonizing code. In fact, this was an attempt to convince myself that I had to turn away from the past. I thought that you shouldn't allow yourself to be caught up in it. However, later on, in *The Issa Valley* and various poems, a certain reclaiming takes place. First there was the cutting off and then there was an appropriation of something that is not part of current reality but belongs to the past and can be a subject for art.

CZARNECKA   I think that what you reclaimed paralleled what was amputated. For example, in "The Legend," which you wrote in 1949, you say: "Because a country is nothing without its past," and the poem ends with the line "And from then on history was our home." I think that poem is connected to Lithuania, Wilno.

MILOSZ   No, to Mazovia and Warsaw. Polish history is transposed into a metahistorical dimension, in the sense that the Apocalypse is metahistory. Sergei Bulgakov, the Russian theologian, analyzed the Apocalypse of Saint John from that point of view. Saint John drew on the situation in the Roman Empire of his time, but he simultaneously changed the dimensions of a situation that recurs in human history, turning it into metahistory. What that means is that you take situations that recur in history in general and raise them to the level of paradigm. That's how I would interpret "The Legend." It's an attempt to create History out of the history of Poland.

CZARNECKA   Unless I'm mistaken, the poem "Mittelbergheim" is one of the few poems in *The Light of Day* written in France. Doesn't the volume consist mainly of poems written in America?

MILOSZ   Yes. As I said, I was at an impasse in France. I couldn't write poetry. For me just contemplating the world was sufficiently absorbing, interesting in the ontological sense. On the other hand, the situation was such that it was difficult to protect myself against history and society. All that kept pulling me away. I was in a tailspin. I had gotten involved in

Hegelianism of a sort—under Kroński's influence, to a great extent.

CZARNECKA   Did you carry on a correspondence with Kroński? I remember you mentioning in *Native Realm* that you sent him your poems.

MILOSZ   Yes, but not right away, because I lost touch with him for a while. I didn't know where the Krońskis were. First they had been deported to Germany, where they were liberated, and afterward they worked as interpreters with the British army. It was only later that they made their way to Paris and found out that I was in America. That's when our correspondence began. But that must not have been until 1948.

So, as I say, I had gotten involved in Hegelianism, which was very unhealthy for me. There's no doubt that Kroński's Hegelian influence was liberating to some degree. It liberated me from the past, from a certain Polish "God-and-country" complex. Therefore in a certain sense it proved necessary. But, on the other hand, it was very alien to my nature and made me sterile as a poet. Which is why *The Issa Valley* was therapeutic. Even though some poems of that period, especially ones like "The Concert," are eminently "mine." I mean there's no incursion of civic-minded poetry. "Mittelbergheim" is also very much "my" poem.

CZARNECKA   The poem is inwardly directed, an expectation of maturation like that of wine in barrels. The very title of the poem is symbolic—"Mittelberg" means "midmountain."

MILOSZ   Yes, it's a poem of convalescence. It gave me my perspective back for a time. It was written in Alsace in 1951. I was living in Maisons-Laffitte, outside of Paris, then, and I made a trip to Mittelbergheim.

The Seizure of Power

CZARNECKA It seems to me that you're reluctant to acknowledge having written *The Seizure of Power*, that it's your unloved child. For a book that doesn't number much over a hundred and sixty pages, the novel is conceived on a broad scale, with a great many characters and plot lines. Is *The Seizure of Power* in some sense an offshoot of *The Captive Mind?*

MILOSZ Yes, of course.

CZARNECKA It's a political novel that reveals the mechanisms used to manipulate people, but it also has its philosophical side. A good many things you'd written about before reappear in that book, and it also contains the seeds of themes you deal with in your later work. I remember that you wrote the book in great haste. *The Seizure of Power* didn't appear in Polish until 1955, but hadn't the French edition come out first?

MILOSZ Yes. The book received a prize in 1953. I learned of the award in the winter of 1952–53. I wrote the book during two summer months of 1952, but I don't like that book. You ask me why. Because there is such a thing as a calling. People who depart too far from it are unable to accomplish anything of value. A person must stick pretty much to his calling. And to write books on historical tragedies is not my calling. Political action, or any sort of action, was never my calling. Those are subjects that should be written about by people who have engaged in action directly and experienced the conflicts produced by genuine political involvement. In my opinion, *The Seizure of Power* is clearly outside my area of competence. Besides, considering my knowledge about the reality of that time, the relationship of my book to that reality is like the relationship of a mathematical formula to a world full of colors, tints, and individual shadings. It's conceptual; it makes extracts of people's standpoints. And yet it does not contain all of the elements that proved decisive. The reality of Poland was very specific. No people like Piotr Kwinto actually existed, and there my opponents have a very good argument. The standpoints I described in *The Captive Mind* were present in some numbers, but there were very few people with Piotr Kwinto's mentality who arrived with the army from the east.

CZARNECKA   What sort of mentality do you mean?

MILOSZ   The mentality of the Jewish intellectual. The truth is that in prewar Poland the leftists were mainly Jews. There's no racial mystery in any of that. They simply had an international outlook, whereas since the nineteenth century the Poles had had a very strong tradition of fighting for independence. The Poland that had reappeared on the map of Europe seemed so precious to them that the very idea of any end to the unique arrangement that allowed Poland to exist was unthinkable. A whole series of imponderables prohibited any sympathy for the Communist Party. Somewhere I used the example that the Communist Party in prewar Poland would be like a a party in Mexico that called for incorporation into the United States. It's doubtful that party would have much chance of success.

CZARNECKA   *The Seizure of Power* probably has a place of some importance among other works of fiction written in Poland or by émigrés, because it describes a very interesting period of history without presenting just one side. It is a comprehensive attempt at depicting reality.

MILOSZ   No question of that, which is why the book should be cursed by all sides.

CZARNECKA   That's what it has come to. Especially since you are very critical of the Home Army resistance movement and the London government-in-exile.

MILOSZ   There you have it—I exceeded the limits of my competence. The conclusion is that poets shouldn't write novels. I entered the novel in a competition. You had to submit a manuscript in one of the European languages. Polish was obviously disqualified, because there wouldn't have been any juror able to judge it. For that reason, I submitted a French translation to the jury for books in French. I don't know who the competition was, but in any case my book made it through and was nominated for the international prize by the French jury. In other words, a certain threshold had been crossed. The manuscript had been labeled as a translation from Polish; the French made no secret of it. Then there was a further selection of the books proposed by the French jury, the German, the Italian, the Swiss. . . . The prize was funded by Les Guildes du Livre, which is located in Switzerland. The prize was divided between me and a German writer, Werner Warsinsky. I had written *The Seizure of Power* for that competition as a sort of exercise, casually, without taking it much to heart. With Witkacy's theory in mind, I proceeded from the assumption that the novel is a sack into which you can stick whatever you want, that it is not an art form. That relaxed me. I told myself that any trick could be used. Material could be taken from life, from literature, more or less the way all novelists do. But that procedure makes me too uneasy. I have too many inhibitions to be able to write novels.

CZARNECKA   All right, but you don't renounce your other novel, *The Issa Valley*. . . .

MILOSZ   No, though some things about it do embarrass me—everything that departs from how things really were. In other words, the fiction. I would like to write only about how things really were.

CZARNECKA   Can that be achieved in poetry?

MILOSZ   Well, it can be approached in poetry. But one has the justification that poems are tightly bound by form. We start out as if we are trying to come as close to reality as possible, but, at the same time, we're always bound by convention even if we aren't writing sonnets. The sonnet is an example of the contrast between the passion for Laura and prescribed form. I wrote about that fundamental contradiction in an essay on classicism. Poetry is the distillation of form, but it's also the dream of biting off as much meat, reality, as possible. To my mind, a novel's only proper task is to describe how things really were. But that can't be done. It'd make me blush for shame.

CZARNECKA   It seems to me that you endowed Piotr Kwinto with a few traits of your own. Kwinto is an admirer of Paul Valéry's poetry, which you valued as a young man. The mishap that occurs when he attempts an illegal border crossing while fleeing Wilno could have happened to you. And then you, not just the hero of your novel, would have ended up being deported.

MILOSZ   Yes, definitely. I'll tell you a secret. The name Kwinto is from my district. When I was little, I was always hearing about Mrs. Kwinto who lived on the other side of the river.

CZARNECKA   Is *The Seizure of Power* a *roman à clef?*

MILOSZ   No, but no doubt some characters are easy to identify.

CZARNECKA   In *The Seizure of Power* you employed a technique like that of a screenwriter. Very short chapters, almost always in the present tense, changing points of view . . .

MILOSZ   As soon as that competition was announced, I said to myself: "All right, I'll give it a try. If it works, fine, if not, that's fine, too." I decided to write one chapter a day.

CZARNECKA   So that's why they're so short! Did you really write that novel in as many days as it has chapters?

MILOSZ   More or less.

CZARNECKA   The first part of the novel in particular is written like a film script. By the way, you had already co-authored a film script with Jerzy Andrzejewski—*The Robinson Crusoe of Warsaw.*

MILOSZ   Yes, but that was much earlier, the spring of 1945. Still, let's not forget that in the twentieth century everyone has been influenced by film, and so you don't have to be a screenwriter to use those tricks in literature. After all, film technique has become a part of literature.

The Issa Valley

CZARNECKA Many readers treat *The Issa Valley* as an auto-biographical work and identify you with Thomas.

MILOSZ Yes, many people think those are my reminiscences of childhood. Naturally, a great many elements were taken from life, as they say. But the plot is something else entirely. It has its own symbolic structure. The characters and the plot are two different things. For example, the person who served as my model for the character Balthazar was named Ausku-raitis. And he really was a forester. I recently learned from my brother what happened to Auskuraitis during the German occupation. He was drinking heavily. Then the Russians came in and he gave a lot of aid to the Lithuanian partisans. He was threatened with deportation, and so he married a Mongolian woman, to protect himself. Later on, his wife died and he started drinking more and more. His hut was at the border of the large forests where the anti-Soviet partisans hid. That's the last anyone knows of him. Auskuraitis was a Lithuanian nationalist, one hundred per cent.

CZARNECKA And just what is *The Issa Valley*'s symbolic structure?

MILOSZ Let's leave that to the literary critics.

CZARNECKA   In one of your essays you mention that Stanisław Vincenz induced you to write *The Issa Valley*.

MILOSZ   I didn't say that he induced me, but I may have been unconsciously influenced by my conversations with Vincenz, his deep attachment to the Carpathanian region, his constant harking back to the one specific spot where his family was from. In what he said and wrote, Vincenz showed that this little enclave far from the beaten track of Europe—the virgin forest on the slopes of Czarnohora was there until the end of the nineteenth century—had everything. Besides, he had a theory of a Europe of homelands. For him Europe did not consist of states, because states were artificial creations, but of little regions that often did not even have a name. Naturally, it was a great pleasure to converse with Vincenz, because he was the complete opposite of a Polish nationalist. After all, my own conflict was chiefly a conflict with Polish nationalism, which was very popular—victorious—but there were older traditions: those of the Polish Republic, the various provinces. Had there been more people like Vincenz, everything might have turned out differently. Moreover, when a person is living in a very difficult period and is thrown completely out of orbit and has to begin life all over again, he reaches for his treasures, his childhood. That's a theme of *The Brothers Karamazov*—it's not my discovery. The critics have pointed out that some of Dostoevsky's characters make a sacrament of their childhood, which is a sort of radiant memory for them; they return to it and it saves them at trying times. For example, Alyosha Karamazov is constantly remembering his mother, who held him up in front of an icon, and Dmitri, who gets into terrible trouble because of his passions and rages, remembers that when he was little and completely forlorn a German doctor gave him a pound of nuts and taught him the prayers that now save him at critical moments. Happy moments in childhood have great therapeutic importance, and that is why they return to a person. But there's also the question of Proustian distancing. I was not thinking about whether the book would sell or not when I wrote *The Issa Valley*. I simply wrote it for myself. I had to.

CZARNECKA   But the world it depicts is not Arcadian in the least. Thomas's realization of death and transience makes for a painful initiation.

MILOSZ   Of course. There are various problems, various conflicts of mine there. Some of the pages are a return to the sacramental, bright, serene experiences of childhood, and others are an expression of inner pain, anguish, perplexity, a general settling of accounts with life.

CZARNECKA   Earlier you mentioned that *The Issa Valley* is something of a nineteenth-century tale, that you purposely used an unfashionable form of stylization. . . .

MILOSZ   Yes, it was probably rather unfashionable. I asked Albert Camus, who at the the time was one of the directors of Gallimard publishers, what the narration reminded him of. He said, "Russian prose of the nineteenth century, Tolstoy's tale about childhood." Camus liked *The Issa Valley* very much and after reading it immediately accepted it for Gallimard, which published it in 1956, I think. The German translation was very widely reviewed, to the point where it made me a little uncomfortable. I thought: What the hell is this, is it the *Natur* that interests them so much? The Germans detected similarities between *The Issa Valley* and Faulkner's novels.

CZARNECKA   The narrator does not have a cold eye, even though you've so often stressed the need for distancing, and your narrator betrays his affection for Thomas.

MILOSZ   That's just it; when I read those chapters, I was struck by their large dose of irony. I'm not even sure it can be called irony. It probably can, because irony has various shades and meanings. This has nothing to do with sarcasm but, rather, with irony in the sense that Blake is an ironic poet. And so I read those chapters—the most prosaic ones, hunting scenes, details about dogs—and I was surprised, because this is, after all, tongue-in-cheek. That made me somewhat uneasy. I want to point out that none of the characters are the target of ridicule. But at moments the amount of comedy is disturbing, and I wonder if there isn't too much. I don't know, I could be wrong: a reader might take the book literally. I'd say that it's somewhat akin to the humor in *Pan Tadeusz*, which was not my intention in the slightest. Let's say the scenes in *Pan Tadeusz* that describe the preparation of coffee or hunter's stew, or the treatise on fowl.

CZARNECKA   One other similarity: in *The Garden of Knowledge* you refer to George Rapall Noyes's opinion of *Pan Tadeusz*. Noyes, the founder of the Slavic department at Berkeley, was enchanted by that poem and discovered features in common with Traherne's poetry, because both poets present the world from a child's perspective while remaining fully aware that this is a child's point of view. That remark could also apply to *The Issa Valley*. But then Thomas would have been an innocent. For Traherne, childhood is free of sin.

MILOSZ   Really? I don't know anything about that. Thomas is burdened with original sin. Nature is corrupt. But what about all the sadistic aspects of Thomas, don't they count?

CZARNECKA   In any case, at one point Thomas reflects on the nature of evil and wonders, "Maybe there's a hidden helplessness in every evil." Is Dominic Thomas's alter ego, or is he the initiator of the evil?

MILOSZ   That strikes me as an overly psychological approach. I don't view *The Issa Valley* as a novel where the characters have to be grounded psychologically. It's simply a fairy tale. Of course, the problem of evil is there—the discovery of the world of murder, nature, the hunt.

CZARNECKA   I think that Thomas is innocent until the idea of a separate ego comes into his head.

MILOSZ   That probably means guilt is connected with an awareness that other people's eyes are on us. Judging us. The eyes of another person. So innocence would always be joined with a perfect naturalness, a complete lack of concern of how you appear in other people's eyes. From that point of view, the child's innocence is, however, highly problematical. Let's be frank: such innocence doesn't exist, because children have such a strong desire to perform and show off, and that indicates that their awareness is already very developed. I had a very limited number of human contacts when I was a child. I ran and played in beautiful gardens, usually by myself. I had my own fantasy world, a world of my own. But when you take a closer look, you can say that by the time I was seven I was rich in my experience of the Fall of Man. By the time I was about five, I began to live in the society of other people and other children, and I was keenly aware of my drive to show off. It was only later that I ended up in the country, in the great gardens. I returned to Lithuania in the spring of 1918. And it was then that I was entirely alone. Not that there weren't any people around, but I was perfectly happy in the world of nature. I have an extremely strong sensual feel for the beauty of nature. Those were conditions that favored a sense of innocence, one based on the lack of temptation. Had I gone to kindergarten, things certainly would have been different. It was simply that my spontaneity did not disturb or offend other people. To a large extent my innocence was based on my not being tested by anyone. I wasn't forced to think that someone was better than I or that I was worse than someone else. The end of innocence must come quite early. I'm entering autobiographical territory here. And I definitely would not have said anything on that subject if I truly knew anything about it. Those are mysteries, because the mind of a child cannot be re-created.

CZARNECKA   Let's go back to the problem of evil in your novel.

MILOSZ   I think it was Louis Iribarne, who translated *The Issa Valley* into English, who called it a theological treatise in disguise. Because it deals with the discovery of evil in nature . . .

CZARNECKA   . . . and in human nature.

MILOSZ   Yes, the passage from childhood and the discovery of the world of grownups, which is the world of nature. The erotic plays a very strong role in that world. In fact, the erotic is an incursion of a very pitiless element. That was always the most drastic aspect for the Manicheans: procreation means the continuation of an evil world. And Thomas's attitude toward adults is very interesting in that regard. He discovers both the cruelty of the hunt and the cruelty of adult life at the same time. *The Issa Valley* accentuates the drama of life, the drama of cruelty. It's the world of innocence and the world of experience, as in Blake. This book stands apart from the rest of my prose, because it has neither precedent nor sequel. *The Issa Valley* can be interpreted as standing at the boundary of my poetry and intimately connected with it. And no doubt it also has a connection with other works, like "The World." The same theme is shared a bit—the world as it could be, should be. But the critics are intelligent and they can figure what to say about that novel. I don't know anything about it apart from its secret, hidden code, which I understand. Whether or not other people can crack that code no longer concerns me.

CZARNECKA   You said that you'd be perfectly willing to write about how things really were but that an author exposes too much of himself in a novel. How do you rate *The Issa Valley* on that scale of truth and fiction?

MILOSZ   I've already said that that the characters in the novel
are modeled on real people, people I observed. It's also relia-
bly accurate in its topography, even though several different
districts are described. It's not just a question of place. Józef
Mackiewicz, whose criterion for all literature is accuracy, wrote
that there are no inaccuracies in *The Issa Valley* as far as
birds, descriptions of nature, and hunting are concerned, with
one exception: Balthazar shoots at a prisoner of war with a
sawed-off rifle and so he can't take a bead on him because
the barrel's not long enough. To go through Mackiewicz's
wringer and come out in one piece, that's really something!
In the book I also described a near-mystical experience, very
strange. In the part about the princess.

CZARNECKA   Do you mean the dream about Magdalena?

MILOSZ   Yes. That's an actual experience I had as a child. I
think I was about ten years old at the time. I was at my aunt's,
outside Kaunas, on the Niewiaża. There was a little chapel at
the crossroads. The entrance was bricked up, but somehow I
managed to get in. Inside, I saw a shattered coffin containing
the silk dress and shoes of the young woman who had been
buried there. I dreamed of her all that night. I had such a
strange feeling of the passage of time. . . . I thought of her
as a princess.

CZARNECKA   Why did you call your native river, the Niewiaża, by another name?

MILOSZ   To create a sense of distance. I couldn't write about
the Niewiaża, because it's not a fictional name but the real
name of the river. That would have made it too personal. I
was undergoing a major crisis, I was at a great impasse when
writing *The Issa Valley*. I couldn't write poetry. This was an
attempt at therapy. I started writing *The Issa Valley* in the
fall of 1953, and I think I finished in June of 1954, in small
French towns, first in Bon, on Lake Leman, and later in Brie-
Comte-Robert outside of Paris. After finishing it, I began
gradually returning to poetry.

CZARNECKA   You mentioned earlier that you didn't write *The Issa Valley* with any market in mind. . . .

MILOSZ   Yes, I'd been living in France long enough, and by the time I had received the prize for *The Seizure of Power* and Gallimard had published *The Captive Mind*, I had made something of a name for myself. I had a certain fame, a very suspect sort of fame, but, in any case, I had a name. All I had to do was step on the gas and go. It was then I began writing *The Issa Valley* and later *Treatise on Poetry*, which was not practical in the least. After all, *The Issa Valley* is the absolute antithesis of what I should have been doing at the time, a crazy project for someone who had made a name as a political writer. That's my contrariness again. When I was young, people thought me terribly arrogant. And I probably was. But I must have already sensed the whole problem then: mediocrity pursues us constantly, in the sense that concessions have to be made. Mallarmé said, "No concessions," and turned his back on the public. Absolutely no concessions! And his poetry was written for an extremely small circle of admiring friends. That really was a heroic credo. I don't say that because I like Mallarmé, since I'm very anti-aesthetic. But the problem of which concessions to make is a very real one. Being a professor at the University of California at Berkeley is an ideal solution: you don't have to write for the market; you can write what you want.

CZARNECKA   But even in France, where your situation was worse and you did not have the security of a university position, you must also have told yourself: No concessions to the market.

MILOSZ   Yes, I was absolutely unable to . . . Another conflict: the refusal to integrate with the environment.

CZARNECKA   As a footnote, in *The Land of Ulro* you say that whenever you tried to write prose at your home on Grizzly Peak Boulevard in Berkeley, it always came out as some sort of dismal Kafkaesque story. That sounds as if you wrote your poetry with a different hand, so to speak. Is that true?

MILOSZ   Yes, naturally. Gombrowicz used to say to me, "Why don't you write novels?" I'd say, "Because I don't know how." "What does that mean? You've proved that you can." I'll try to answer your question as if it had been asked by one of my students. But perhaps my answer will be too superficial. The very idea of poetry presupposes immense transformation. In poetry, form is profoundly of the essence, completely apart from meter, rhyme, or whatever other stylistic approach is taken. The very essence of the act is to distill the material of life. In prose, on the other hand—and here we return to the autobiographical elements again—the distinction is not so explicit at all, meaning that it's much more difficult to find a form. I admire writers like Gombrowicz who are so able to distill their work that it is separate from the author as a person. Gombrowicz's work has distance. He was really a poet. His novels are not reflections of self.

I've said that I'm repelled by novels. Pick up any novel, open it to any page, and you say to yourself: I'm not going to read this undistilled self-involvement. You can see right through it to the paltry personality of an author who hasn't found his voice as an artist. This applies to 99 percent of all novels. I can't read them; they bore me. I don't understand that mentality, that total exhibitionism. Is the guy saying that absolutely nothing is sacred to him? Dostoevsky was something of a marvel in that regard. In *The Idiot* there's a crazy general who tell stories about his heroic exploits. He says that he lost a leg during the war with Napoleon, and so he buried the leg and put a gravestone over it. And then he tells what the inscription on the stone says. In reality, that was the inscription on Dostoevsky's mother's gravestone. I find that horrifying, absolutely awful. How could he do it! I'll tell you something about myself here. Once, when I was a little boy, I was playing with some other children and, as part of a game, they started making little rhymes while hopping around. When I said, "Mummy, mummy," they started shouting, "Mummyscummy." I attacked one little boy and started kicking him. Because I felt that something sacred had been violated. I had that same sense of horror in relation to Dostoevsky.

CZARNECKA   But, after all, those autobiographical borrowings don't have anything to do with treating Dostoevsky's works as great novels.

MILOSZ   Maybe there's some secret here. Maybe as a person Dostoevsky was so abstracted from himself that he could make use of everything, even the most sacred aspects of his own life. Excellent justifications can be found for this, of course. But I'd like to add here that in the nineteenth century the historical spirit, the *Zeitgeist*, was on the side of the novel. People like Flaubert, Dostoevsky, and Stendhal, who were called on to perform exacting and difficult tasks, found fulfillment in the novel. But I think that that spirit deserted the novel in the twentieth century. I may be wrong; I may be praising my own horse too much, meaning my bias against the novel.

Treatise on Poetry

CZARNECKA   *Treatise on Poetry* appeared in book form in 1957, but you had already published the first three parts in the June 1956 issue of the journal of *Kultura* and the fourth there in December 1956. How long did it take to write it?

MILOSZ   I don't remember exactly how long I worked on *Treatise* because I was involved with other things at the time, but it was more or less six months. I started writing it at the end of 1955 and finished it 1956, in the spring.

CZARNECKA   Did the poem go through several rewrites, or did you hit on the form right away?

MILOSZ   I had tried to write something of the sort a few times before, but those weren't earlier versions, just sketches, starts. A few lines, a few ideas. For a long time I couldn't hit on it— I'd start one way, then another, but nothing would come of it. Later on it came.

CZARNECKA   Why does the poem have such a dry, formal title?

MILOSZ   *Treatise on Poetry?* Well, it was meant to be dry. This is definitely connected with the search for a dry form in poems like "Central Park," "To Jonathan Swift," *Treatise on*

Morals, or "A Toast." You could call them purely logical reasoning, a response to the excess of moist, emotional poetry which surrounds us. The poetry of subjective perceptions, personal metaphors, is a moist poetry. There's one other aspect here—certain aesthetic tastes at work in me, and not just my conversations with Juliusz Kroński on the classic stance. For example, I have an absolute horror of Tchaikovsky's music, which is in fact a variation on what the Russians call Gypsy songs. It makes my hair stand on end, horrible. That's the source of my search for a dry and seemly form.

CZARNECKA　You must have been well aware of the difficulties in store for readers of *Treatise on Poetry* because, when publishing the fourth part in *Kultura,* you supplied it with a short commentary of your own. It's interesting that the first three parts, published earlier in *Kultura,* were not provided with a key of this sort. "Beautiful Days" and "The Capital" should not be especially hermetic to readers familiar with twentieth-century Polish literature, but the third and fourth part of *Treatise,* "The Spirit of History" and "Nature," are very rich and complex. The narrative is jagged, the images change constantly, and, even though they make reference to specific events, the main problem in those two sections is philosophic. Perhaps we could begin with the apocalyptic vision of an "inferior God," the Spirit of History, adorned with a chain of severed heads. . . .

MILOSZ　That section of *Treatise* is based on my question as to whether Hegel's Spirit of History is the same spirit that rules the cruel world of nature. I ask in what respect history is a continuation of nature.

CZARNECKA　As necessity, extreme determinism?

MILOSZ　Yes. Ultimately, this may in some way be connected with the two schools of Marxism, which Stanisław Brzozowski wrote about in the early part of this century. One orientation is more materialistic, while the other is more dialectic. The concept of dialectical materialism is a *contradicto in adiecto*. There are two pedals, dialectics and materialism. The materialistic tendency is very strongly represented in Engels's *Anti-Dühring* and others of his works. Brzozowski accused the materialistic Marxists of viewing history as a continuation of nature; everything is determined. Our will counts for nothing since the laws of history, which we have to divine, lead automatically to a communist society because of the same necessities that are at work in the world of nature. The dialectical approach, which is the reverse position, attempts to view nature and history as opposites. That's in Marx. Sartre took that line in his polemic with the Marxists—that there are no *a priori* dialectical laws for the development of society, only man can introduce that dialectic into society. There may be an echo of that opposition in *Treatise on Poetry*, because I pose the question of whether that Spirit of History is the spirit of nature in disguise, whether we face the same necessity in both. In any case, the poem presents a problem that some people were facing in the winter of 1944–45—I don't know how many people thought in such categories, but that doesn't matter. The point is that the problem could arise given Poland's situation, the fact that it was to be thrown into that Russian melting pot. I may not have expressed myself clearly. It's not 1944–45 that matters, because from 1943 on it was already more or less obvious what would happen.

CZARNECKA In an article published in *Kultura* in December 1957, you discuss an anthology of Polish clandestine poetry and you say that for young poets during the occupation the principal artistic motivation was like that of Słowacki's hero Anheli—that is, a "renunciation of the earth, a willingness to sacrifice their lives, and, even more than that, to seek sainthood in battle." Is the fragment of *Treatise on Poetry* that begins "You, Warsaw's twentieth-century poets . . ." in fact addressed to them?

MILOSZ   Yes. To the god-and-country nationalists grouped in Art and Nation, with their belief that "an empire will arise from out blood"—all those demented right-wing ideas of Polish domination. But they're treated kindly there, with great sympathy. And then:

> Then the living ran from themselves
> through the fields, knowing a century would pass
> before they returned. Ahead of them were the shifting
>   sands
> on which a tree is turned into
> nothing, an antitree, where no boundary
> divides form from form, and the golden house, the
>   word
> IS, collapses with a roar
> and from now on BECOMES shall be in power.

This is not about the young poets. These are the people who are running away. The process of shifting to the so-called new reality has already begun—the reality of People's Poland, in a word. "Becomes" is the opposite of "to be," "*esse*," a fundamental concept in Thomistic ontology and for the whole philosophy of being in general.

CZARNECKA   "Becoming" in the Heraclitean sense of the word as constant flow? Is the part that begins "O King of the centuries, boundless Movement" those people's prayer?

MILOSZ   It's pure Hegelianism. Those people had become followers of a new god under the influence of the entire trauma and of the feeling that they had been thrown into the melting pot.

> O Antithesis which ripens in thesis.
> Now we are like gods
> understanding through you that we do not exist.

We don't exist, only historical processes exist. It's like something that was said to me during the war by an eminent communist, a well-known figure during the German occupation. I had told him that I couldn't accept the labor camps and collectivization. His answer was: "What difference do a million people make, either way?" Even though

> The pain of the twentieth century has revealed to us
> that we could ascend the heights
> where the Spirit of History's hand wields its instru-
> ment.

In his memoirs, *My Century*, Aleksander Wat tells the story of an NKVD man, an Asiatic, trying to convince him that he should confess and sign a statement, with this argument: "Be humble, Allah creates the situation." I'll quote some more from the *Treatise:*

> And everyone kept
> a dead hope that time's domains
> had an expiration date.

That's correct, dialectically: suffering and terror have their limits. There is even a personal hope—that these people will live something of a personal life.

> That one day, once only,
> They will be allowed to look upon a flowering branch
> In a moment unlike any other.

This is a strictly personal moment, unique.

> To lull the ocean to sleep and stop the hourglass,
> And listen as the clocks fall silent.

The ocean, the hourglass, clocks, they all represent the flood of time.

CZARNECKA   This oath, or prayer, is immediately followed by a ghetto Jew lamenting his own death, hurling a curse at the earth of contempt and hatred. What connection does this have to the next fragment, "The ungainly speech of Slavic farmers"?

MILOSZ   That structure has the logic of historical events. "Twentieth-century poets of Warsaw"—that's the time of the occupation. Next a Hegelian problem is sketched, and then a sort of balance is struck, the end of the German occupation, because the hymn sung by those who pray to Hegel is about a time when everything is a foregone conclusion. The dead man's poem refers to the final liquidation of the ghetto, the slaughter of the Jews. And then all that's left is an earth that is burdened, blood-stained, desecrated. It's not clear what sort of political structure will be formed on it. And the question arises, What will be left in the end? Grass, pickles, that's the essence of Polishness. The crime burdening the land was the crime against the Jews. The past is Mickiewicz, culture is Mickiewicz, but the reality is:

> Pickled cucumbers with a stalk of dill
> Ferment in sweat-beaded jars.

That's the real Poland. Everything has been wiped out, but the pickles remain. "Misty and flat all the way to the Urals." This is Poland reduced to its essence. Mickiewicz's "A castle on the shoulders of a hill in Nowogródek"—that's a luxury now. Even the "wooded hills" are a luxury, because there's nothing but a plain.

> That Mickiewicz is too hard for us
> What does the learning of lords and Jews have to do
>   with us.

A total mess.

CZARNECKA   The fourth part of *A Treatise on Poetry*, "Nature," opens with an image that is in contrast to that gray, hopeless expanse. This is the sensual land of the fairy tale. . . .

MILOSZ   The first three lines:

> The garden of nature opens.
> The grass at the threshold shines green.
> An almond tree blossoms.

were written much earlier than the rest of the poem and included in it later. The Latin text that follows these three lines is the incantation used by Faust in Marlowe's *Doctor Faustus*. Translated, it says: "May the gods of Acheron be friendly, praised be the triple name of Jehovah, welcome, spirits of fire, air, water, and earth." Nature here is magical, straight from a fairy tale. Ariel, who lives in a palace of apple trees, Mephistopheles, the pentagram, are connected with Faust and the magic that seeks control of the forces of nature.

CZARNECKA   Could you explain how this fragment is to be understood?

> Here there is sun. And he who as a child believed
> It is enough to understand acts and action
> To break the repetition of things,
> Is degraded, rots in the skin of others
> And looks upon the butterfly's colors with a wonder,
> Mute, formless, and hostile to art.

MILOSZ   Yes, that's very difficult. As a child, I thought that if something was described it could not be repeated a second time. All you have to do is describe something and people will know it, do it differently the next time, not repeat what was described. A very strange state of mind. It's a reflection on the world: people act the way they do because something has never been seen or described from the outside. To describe something would appear to prove that it has a form. Then people will know what it is and be able to avoid it, because it has been dealt with, checked off the list. A strange theory, isn't it?

CZARNECKA   A very high degree of abstraction for a child's theory.

MILOSZ   It's as if the world existed to be described and then to move on to new forms. There really is a great deal of abstraction in this stanza. All things that are subject to nature are recurrent, but consciousness is somehow alien. It enters into that recurrence and introduces something new, but is there anything to that theory that it's enough to describe something to check it off the list? Recurrence is broken when something new arises. But since this involves someone "who believed as a child," the idea doesn't turn out to be true, and recurrence continues. To put it in plainer terms, you can say that, for example, since the bad ends tyrants come to have been described so many times, they will have no successors, because the end that awaits them is already known. But no, there are always new people willing to give it a try. "Is degraded, rots in the skins of others"—that means he cannot be so much the individual, he sees himself as a part of the statistical pattern of the human species. "And looks upon the butterfly's colors with a wonder that is mute, formless, and hostile to art." That means he admires the butterfly, but art, which was supposed to be an incantation and break that cycle of recurrence, protect against it, turns out not to have been very effective; the power of recurrence, the power of the natural order, is very strong. So that's how he looks at the butterfly: Sure, it's pretty, but so what?

CZARNECKA   Now we come to the image of America. Is this the America of your childhood reading or of personal experience?

MILOSZ   This is an accurate description of a lake in northern Pennsylvania. I tried to spy on the beavers—there were beaver lodges there. This is a real America. When the beavers hid, I was left alone in the night.

CZARNECKA   Are you setting up an opposition between man and animal here through your meditations on the animal world?

MILOSZ   Man is memory, historical memory. That's why I use images from history here—the wedding in Basel. The wine cups in Savoy really do have drinking spouts for six people. They could all drink at the same time. I'm identifying very closely with those people getting married in Basel and no longer know if it's my wedding or theirs. Or perhaps it's just a feeling of community with the people of history. The next stanza shifts to personal matters. History and the personal flow into each other.

CZARNECKA   The following stanza strikes me as the key to this section of *Treatise on Poetry*:

> Yesterday a snake was darting across the road at dusk.
> Run over by a car, it writhed on the asphalt.
> But we are both the snake and the wheel. There are
>   two
> Dimensions. Here is the truth
> Of unattainable essence, here, at the edge
> Of what lasts and what does not, two lines intersect.
> Time lifted above time by time.

MILOSZ   Well, yes, that's the basic motif. To put it without going to great length: the search for eternal values, eternal truths, by denying the flow of time. Of course this tendency has emerged often in European civilization. There have always been those movements for a return to immutable beauty and the immutable values. A very Platonic outlook, the search for eternal truths, eternal values. But when it came to discussing an eternity utterly devoid of the flow of time, the theologians concluded that there still must be some sort of time in an eternity conceived as paradise, heaven; so they introduced the concept *aevum* instead of *aeternum*, a time different from earth's but still a variation on it, because man cannot imagine anything outside of time, nothing can exist without developing. But I feel closer to the view that man lives in time and in some way has to build those eternal or lasting values out of time. Time is given to man for his use. But he should not allow himself to be completely carried away by time, because then he will be lost in relativism and utter fluidity and be smashed to bits. That motif also appears in my poem "Bon on Lake Leman," where I say, "To pluck an eternal moment from movement."

czarnecka   What does "Time lifted above time by time" mean?

milosz   First, time is only biological continuity; then comes historical time, connected with memory, and then—I don't know—contact with God, the acquiring of lasting, immutable values, but through a rootedness in time. Here's an example. If you make something, it's done in some amount of time. It doesn't happen outside of time. This is more or less what T. S. Eliot called "redeeming time." I have always been fascinated with time, as Simone Weil was. Because time is the sole pledge of immortality and of man's individuality in comparison with nature. In fact, without time and death, who knows what would have become of us. The most horrible things would have happened to us. I tell my students that I'm not afraid of Gombrowicz's relativism because one can defend oneself against it fiercely in the name of an unchanging human nature and the unique personality of the individual.

> From smashed armor, from eyes stricken
> By time's command, and returned
> To the jurisdiction of mold and fermentation,
> Comes our hope.

czarnecka   Is this a line of defense against relativism?

milosz   Exactly. Our hope is in the historical. This is what Brzozowski called "*storicismo polacco*"; he thought that philosophy was given a new beginning in the work of Giovanni Battista Vico because history as time, but time remembered, is something different from nature's time. Our hope lies in a heightened sense of history, not in an escape to Saint Thomas Aquinas. There's a static quality to Thomism, and it allots a very weak role to historical change. Medieval people had no feeling at all for that dimension. Some claim otherwise and defend Thomas Aquinas. But, basically, that was a world of immutable essence and human nature. The historical dimension was very weak. Naturally, a line of defense against the invasion of the historical was taken by various figures in the twentieth century. Marxism, of course, sides with movement, constant historical thinking. Our hope lies in assimilating that germ of the historical and then leaving it for the mataphysical, to seek the ontological dimension after passing through the purgatory of historical thought, historicism. That has some connection with Juliusz Tadeusz Kroński. Kroński admired this section of *Treatise on Poetry*, because it touched some other shore, after passing through the heart of darkness. In fact, that is the poem's eschatological, religious vision. This eschatological motif is quite strong in my work. The poem continues:

> Yes, to unite the beaver's furriness and the smell of
>   the bulrushes
> And the wrinkles on the hand holding a pitcher
> from which wine trickles.

Those are images of nature and man. The point is to accept our animal nature while at the same time not allowing ourselves to be diminished. Sufficiently intense thought about history leads to a dimension that is truly divine, because the entire idea of the history of secular progress, dialectical movement, and change is in fact taken from the Bible, modified and translated into secular language. The Old Testament and the New Testament are one great reflection on history. All European culture comes from a transposition of the Bible. All thinking since the beginning of the nineteenth century secularizes historical religion, because, after all, Judaism and Christianity are a single historical religion, as opposed to religion in Greece or Rome, which was concentrated around nature.

> Why cry out
> That the historical ravages our substance,
> If it is given to us
> As a weapon and instrument,
> The Muse of gray father Herodotus?
> Though it is not easy to use and increase its power
> So that once again like lead with a pure center of gold
> It will serve to save people.

In other words, it doesn't serve people now, and will only at some future point. Ultimately, who are the dissidents? People who first had to pass through Marxism, that historical dimension. Of course, Poland also has an entire dissident movement that is directly connected to the nineteenth-century tradition of the struggle for independence, but in fact all this began with people who had been through Marxism— that is, the historical. That's the only source of ferment, isn't it? This section of *Treatise on Poetry* is also very closely bound with my experience in America when I was here, in 1949, 1950. Very painful and difficult issues prompted these thoughts. Even if I had wanted to forget about my poetry, my language, America would have still been completely static for me. To choose to live in America would have meant choosing to live outside of time. If you settle on an American farm—I could have chosen that fate, for example—there's nothing but fall, spring, winter, nature.

CZARNECKA   Only nature's time . . .

MILOSZ   That's all! Nothing else! America appears as nature in this poem. What concern of mine were those presidential elections, the Democrats, the Republicans—I could not feel the rhythm of time in any of that. That was not a place where I could feel the granularity of historical time. Thus what remained was nature. That section of the *Treatise* was quite deliberately entitled "Nature." I still perceive America exclusively as nature. For me America is recurrence.

CZARNECKA   The poem in *Treatise on Poetry*—"O City, O Society, O Capital"—reminds me a little of your later poem "Three Talks on Civilization."

MILOSZ   That's interesting, because "O City" was a separate poem I included in the *Treatise*. Some of the poems were written separately and then included later on.

> O City, O Society, O Capital,
> You have revealed your steaming entrails.

> You will never be what you were before.
> Your songs no longer gratify our hearts.

What's said here is more or less that if one acquires a fuller historical vision, and if historicism enters a higher dimension, then all society, all service, the entire state that calls for our service, whether it be a socialist state or another sort, starts to fade for us. It no longer exists for us. A deeper historical vision gives us distance, and we search for something else. All our loyalties are now directed toward those higher demands. Since poems are not philosophical or political treatises, I don't say that this is any prediction of a theocratic system, any prophecy on my part. It might not come about at all. But this is a search for a higher dimension through the medium of intense reflection on history, the past. Thinking of bones in clothing from the late Second Empire provides a sense of connection. In *The Land of Ulro* I wrote about the historical and the supernatural in Mickiewicz's *Forefathers' Eve* because the "communion of saints" —communion with the souls of our ancestors, and the historical—and communing with the country's past intersect there. Ancestor cults are of course very old in all civilizations, older than the Old Testament's image of a life after death. In a certain sense this was the historical thinking primitive people were capable of—families, tribes. What makes *Forefathers' Eve* such an unusual work is that intersection of the supernatural and the historical, ancestral rites and political action. And in the poem "O City, O Society" I depict the relatively short-lived period in which society and the state are able to place unlimited demands on us.

CZARNECKA   In that poem you say, "And where was the covenant broken?" Is this the covenant between the citizen and the state? The covenant between science and religion?

MILOSZ   I'm asking the question—it's not clear. In the end it may turn out that the last war was the beginning of the breakdown of the purely sociological approach to man and the end, as a serious subject, of what is known as alienation.

> At twilight, as the towers go flying by,
> Did you ever look from your train across a desert of
>   tracks
> To a window out past the locomotives
> Where a girl examines her sullen, narrow face
> In a mirror, and ties a ribbon
> To her hair pierced by the sparks of curling papers.

What that scene in the window shows is a woman worker in a deeply alienated society. The locomotives are there for a reason—they set the scene in time. This is a meditation on what Oskar Milosz called the suffering of the modern masses— a life that is not entirely human, that seems to be one of consumption only. New York is an example of that sort of life, where there is no higher order, no real reaching for anything apart from the day at hand, which is spent on work, entertainment, pleasure, drinking. I can be attacked here because I'm saying something suspect. I could be told, "Here you're a latent totalitarian because you want to transform ordinary people into angels." I do appear that way here, of course. What's essential in this poem is the horoscope cast, the prediction of some breakthrough that has occurred. It's not clear when, but it's spoken of as having already occurred.

> Those walls of yours are walls of shadow
> And your light has disappeared forever.
> No monolith of the world, just our works,
> Stand beneath the sun in an altered space.

It's as if Gombrowicz were speaking. Society has been seen in its entirety, and some distance has been gained on it. There are certain points of contact between me and Gombrowicz, but, after all, there are also certain points of contact between Gombrowicz and Marxism.

> From walls and mirrors, glass and paintings,
> tearing aside curtains of silver and cotton,
> Comes man, naked and mortal.

This stance is very close to Gombrowicz, and it came precisely through duly thinking about history, historicism. "Weep, O Republic. In vain do you call out: on your knees!" This is an attempt at indoctrination. I don't think there's a direct influence here of Gombrowicz's *The Wedding*, which I didn't understand for a long time and had set aside. This is, rather, some basic aspiration, tendency, intersection with Gombrowicz. To a large extent this part of *Treatise on Poetry* is rooted in Kroński's influence, but in the good sense. This is not bondage to the historical. There's a way out, a way of going beyond.

CZARNECKA   Later stanzas are about the nature of America, its lack of a sense of history. Is that why "Herodotus will lie unopened"?

MILOSZ   Yes, and this is connected with a very specific temptation. Thornton Wilder tried to convince me—we'd become very good friends—that I was totally wrong in wanting to return to Poland, that he had a clear vision of my future in America. He'd set me up on a farm where I'd sit and write poems. . . .

CZARNECKA   You must have found that tempting.

MILOSZ   Yes, especially for a person who understood what was going on in Poland. But, for some reason, I didn't go for it. That temptation of nature is echoed in *Treatise on Poetry*. And that is the reason for the song about the rose. The rose is a symbol of sexual love, the beauty of nature, "and we find songs of it in dreams." This is a song of temptation, because life, apart from history and historical thinking, offers a sufficient number of themes to be explored. All you have to do is take the rose and immerse yourself in it, take a journey of imagination—into the depths of everything, into all nature's forms, going deep into the trunk of a tree. There's a strong element of the fairy tale in my work—becoming little, for example. The world is full of mysteries and a variety of dimensions, so why involve yourself in the history and immediate issues of the twentieth century. This, then, is a temptation:

> May the names of the months mean only
> What they mean. And not live on in the thundering
>   guns of
> any Aurora. . . .
> Why not sit at rough-hewn country tables
> And write odes the old-fashioned way.

And then later I move on to an ode, "O October." In October 1956 people said that I had predicted those events. . . .

CZARNECKA   Really? That's odd, because the ode has a soothing quality.

MILOSZ   It's an ordinary October. Later, I say:

> Great reproach will be made us, great,
> Because, having been given a chance, we rejected the
>   peaceful life.

That's about the American farm.

> Silences, and dreams about the structure of the world,
>   which deserve
> respect. The eternal questions
> did not attract us as they should, nor did purity.
> Quite the reverse, everyday we wanted
> to raise the dust of names and events with our
>   voices. . . .
> And, albeit reluctantly, we paid the price.

This is about my decision to leave America. I'm dealing with important things here. It surprises even me how much can be put into a poem.

CZARNECKA   But the code here is very complex. In the prologue to *Treatise* you promised directness and clarity of expression, but gradually you move on to higher and higher levels. When I hear your explanation and commentary, I'm able to understand the puzzles in *Treatise*. But without them it would be difficult to find the right path at once.

MILOSZ   Yes, I agree. *Treatise on Poetry* was written just as I began to struggle with that entire tangle of politics and historiosophy, Hegelianism, Kroński. I had to liberate myself from all that. But the poem also contains an approval of the choice I had made. An approval of my not wanting to stay in America. Eventually I wrote *The Captive Mind*—that is, I became committed. I suppose that I cut off another road by not staying. I probably would have started studying Hebrew and Greek earlier.

> And yet the accusers lamenting the evil
> Of this age are mistaken
> If they see us only as angels
> Hurled into the abyss and from the abyss,
> Brandishing a fist at the works of God.

That refers to all those who said, "I've been gypped." I wouldn't want to generalize on that—this is not necessarily about Marxism or communism, but in general about emotional involvement with twentieth-century issues.

> Certainly a great many were destroyed ingloriously
> Because they suddenly discovered time and relativity
> Like an illiterate discovering chemistry.

I also felt the desiccating, destructive influence of that fascination. And I'm afraid that if I had returned to Poland for good, it would definitely have been very hard to liberate myself from it in one sense or the other. So how do you save yourself from that fascination?

> For others the very concavity of a stone
> When picked up on the bank of a river
> Was a teaching.

This is the role played by the ontological weight of specific, natural things. *To on* in Greek means "being." The entire fascination with time, history, what the French call *devenir*, is the opposite of being.

What is the main value of Thomas Aquinas's philosophy and the Thomist inspiration? That's a world in which being, *esse*, has enormous weight. That's the reason that the essence of Thomism, the essence of Scholastic philosophy, is ultimately meditation on the meaning of "to be." What does it mean that this table *is?* The attribute the French call *esséité* is attached to the table. "The very concavity of a stone was a teaching." This moment suffices. Or "a perch's bloody gills"— also a specific thing that exists, completely tangible. Suddenly it turns out that our quest for equilibrium is aided by the tangibility of things that have their own existence. In short, to save yourself from leaning too much toward movement, toward Hegelianism, you have to write *The Issa Valley*. "Because contemplation fades when it meets no resistance. / It must be forbidden out of love for it." That's a very dangerous aphorism but an interesting one. Contemplation as a means of preventing oneself from being immersed in fluidity also restores one's balance. Here nature appears as the abode of a host of things that are real. And that's good medicine. But why did I say "Because"? A very strange transition. I should, rather, have said: "Although contemplation fades when it meets no resistance." I interpret it like this: "Because" refers to the entire operation—I mean, I left America, I didn't want to settle on a farm, I was always fascinated by the movement of time. Meanwhile, ontological contemplation is my very essence, the thing to which I feel closest. In other words, nothing could be more congenial for me than to live on a farm and engage in contemplation, but "it must be forbidden out of love for it." Very perverse. It's like Thomas in *The Issa Valley*, who loved bows and for that reason did not allow himself to draw pictures of them. Something of that sort.

CZARNECKA   But you've said many times that poetry has to be more than contemplation.

MILOSZ   Yes, it has to. Those really are very important passages, because they reveal the mechanism Gombrowicz was
using when he wrote: "I am Milosz. I do not wish to be Milosz, being Milosz I must be Milosz. I kill Milosz in myself so
that, being Milosz, I am Milosz all the more." Because, as I
say here, out of love for contemplation in poetry, I turned
against contemplation in poetry, and toward the immediate,
time, fluidity. But then I say:

> And we were certainly happier than those
> Who imbibed sadness from Schopenhauer's books
> In their garrets hearing somewhere down below
> The roar of a dance hall.

This refers to the beginning of the twentieth century, the Young
Poland period, and the difference between my generation and
that of the Symbolists. There were not many of them in Poland, but of course they read Schopenhauer and wanted poetry about eternity and the soul, not history. And I say that,
for us,

> . . . philosophy, poetry, and action
> Were not divided, as they were for them.
> Were they united into a single freedom? Unfreedom?
> That was the reward, vexing at times.

This means that Young Poland, Symbolism, suffered from a
certain paralysis. At that time, poetry, philosophy, and action
did go their own ways, and could not be united. Their poetry
did not have a great capacity for intellectual content. In *Treatise on Poetry* I assert that at least we achieved some content
through our interest in time. To whom does "we" refer? Perhaps I'm writing about Kroński and me here. At times we did
achieve that unity; in any event we strove for a sense of unity.
Philosophy is not a teaching that stands apart from everything and has no connection with anything. In some measure,
Treatise on Poetry is proof that philosophy, poetry, and action can be united.

CZARNECKA   Is there a liberation from nature in favor of historical thinking in the last stanza of *Treatise?*

MILOSZ   I describe my journey back to Europe from America. in a certain sense, this is also a farewell to that farm. That's the reason I conclude by quoting Horace:

> *Iam Cytherea choros ducit Venus imminente luna.*
> (Now Venus leads Cytherian choirs under the rising
>   moon.)

A farewell to the farm, and to the rose as well. A very complicated poem.

Native Realm

CZARNECKA   *Native Realm* is, as you wrote in the introduction, an attempt to tell other Europeans what it means to be an Eastern European. Your own life story was to serve only as an example, not as an occasion for confessions or laying oneself bare. When writing about your fate since early childhood, you always stress historical and social conditioning, almost in keeping with the slogan "Existence precedes essence." I wonder to what extent it's dangerous to seize upon typical processes, because they efface what is individual about a person in favor of the general. Fortunately, you didn't take those anthropological and sociological principles too literally, and for that reason the book is also a portrait of an individual. I admit to preferring its title in French, *Une Autre Europe*, because it gives a better picture of the Eastern European's status as a "poor relation," which is clearly accentuated in some chapters. On the other hand, *Native Realm* in English and *Rodzinna Europa* [*Native Europe*] in Polish give no sense of the ambiguities or complications.

MILOSZ   I don't recall how I came to that title. I must have been moved by a sense that in the twentieth century I had to define Europe as my native land, as opposed to Asia, Africa, or America. The title is no manifesto about Poland's being a part of Europe, though naturally there's an awareness here of

193

the Polish Republic and the entire past of the region where I was born and grew up. Besides, I write not only about Lithuania and Poland in the book, but also about France and Italy, and even America.

CZARNECKA Do you think you achieved the goal you set yourself—maximum objectivity, looking at yourself as if you were someone else?

MILOSZ Well, some people faulted *Native Realm* for being so Olympian as to be inhuman, in the way it views everything from an enormous distance. As for the view it presents of me, I have no idea. It's difficult for me to answer that question. In any case, I openly admitted in the book that I was not attempting sincerity, because sincerity is impossible, and so I present a picture of myself not as a person but as an individual purposely cut to a sociological measure, let's say. That is what makes the picture untrue. Many things there are untrue, because the whole truth was not told about the hero, the narrator. A great deal was left out. A tightrope act. But, on the other hand, had I started confessing, the book would have run to ten volumes.

CZARNECKA Was that book, which was actually intended for the Western reader, quickly translated into French and English?

MILOSZ Not so quickly. I wrote *Native Realm* after *Treatise on Poetry*, and right after that, or overlapping, I did an anthology of Simone Weil's writings and I put together *Continents*. *Native Realm* came out in Polish in 1958. It's my impression that the German translation was the first to appear. I was in need of money in 1960, shortly before I left for America. I offered the book to Gallimard in the spring of 1960, I think. Gallimard had a communist in charge of foreign books, and he solicited an opinion on the book from a Warsaw writer, a party member, who was in Paris at the time, as that party man told me later with a laugh. My colleague from Warsaw gave it a very good review and Gallimard accepted the book, but I don't recall when it was translated. In any case, it took a lot of time. The French translation is very fine. A student of mine, Catherine Leach, translated it into English. Since that was the first book she had translated, she didn't have too much expertise yet. Certain sections would have to be redone if there were to be a new edition. *Native Realm* didn't appear in English until 1968, as far as I recall.

CZARNECKA   Didn't you ever feel the desire to write a sequel?

MILOSZ   I guess not; the impulse I felt at the time somehow passed.

CZARNECKA   And what was that impulse?

MILOSZ   A desperate desire to communicate certain information to the Western reader, to explain what it meant to come from that other part of Europe, the worst part, the sort of historical complications a person from there has to experience.

CZARNECKA   In that sense, is *Native Realm* a sequel to *The Captive Mind?*

MILOSZ   Yes, but all that's entirely behind me now. For example, *The Land of Ulro* is addressed to a completely different audience—the Polish reader. My orientation had undergone a total change. I had given up, because I had learned that there's no explaining anything. You could strip off your skin and it still wouldn't do any good.

CZARNECKA   As opposed to your other works in prose, *Native Realm,* despite its approach, allows a few glimpses into your private world, providing some information that is more personal in nature. In addition, it seems to foreshadow a theme you pick up later in *The Land of Ulro*. I'm thinking of the chapter "Catholic Education," where you describe your attempt to create an intellectual bridge between religion and the scientific world view. In other words, that theme had been ripening in you for many years. Another example: in *Native Realm* you wrote a short chapter, "The Young Man and the Mysteries," on Oskar Milosz. By the time you wrote *The Land of Ulro*, Oskar Milosz had grown into a central figure. I must say that I view him as a prophet, especially in regard to your fate and the directions your work has taken. A few years ago you translated his metaphysical poems *Ars Magna* and *Les Arcanes* into English, after ruminating on them for years. You have stressed the fact that Oskar Milosz remained close to the Bible and imagined the poetry of the future as having a Biblical line. Now you are translating the Bible, and your own poetry strives for a Biblical line fairly often. You would appear to be Oskar Milosz's spiritual heir, and, like him, you seek in theology the answers to the most important questions. Many years ago he told you things that are now coming true. Just as in 1935 he foretold that a war was imminent, that it would last five years, and that you would survive that war.

MILOSZ   Could be.

CZARNECKA   Was it he who interested you in the Bible as the most important of books?

MILOSZ   No, I was always fascinated by the Bible, but my only access to it was the Gdańsk Bible, which was actually a Protestant Bible; it was the most popular version and on sale everywhere. I was interested in the Bible and always respected it, but nothing much came of that. Oskar Milosz is very important to me because of my incredible fastidiousness and my need for a strict hierarchy. I am very elitist, very fastidious. And, in a certain sense, I think that's good, because, as you know from reading Gombrowicz, literature is very hierarchical. And that was the path I followed. Living in America is ideal for maintaining that hierarchy, by which I mean not writing for the market, but supporting oneself instead by teaching at a university.

CZARNECKA   Several times you've mentioned the attraction you felt to the ultimate issues; your contact with Oskar Milosz could only have heightened that natural penchant.

MILOSZ   Of course. But I did not reveal much of that in *Native Realm*—a tactical move, and one with a large dose of irony in it.

CZARNECKA   In *Native Realm* you touch on a host of issues that are developed later in such prose works as *The Land of Ulro*, and in your poetry as well. For example, your memories of winter in Wilno in 1936 return in metrical form in the final part of your poem "From the Rising of the Sun." Or, to take another example, in *Native Realm* you give a brief account of a performance of a Pirandello play. The lead role was played by Ludmilla Pitoëff, who uses makeup to change on stage from a young girl into an old woman in a matter of minutes. I think that experience later found expression in the poem "A Singsong," which is dramatic in its compression of time. A girl just out of school returns a moment later hunched over, with a cane. . . .

MILOSZ   Could be. But even before I'd seen the Pirandello play, I'd written the poem "The Song," which is similar to "A Singsong." In fact, my poetry contains many references to the drama of a woman's aging. This is the drama of women's relationship with time and earth, women who last as long as their beauty. I feel that very keenly. And I suppose that's why I was so affected by Ludmilla Pitoëff's performance, in which makeup gives us the illusion of witnessing an entire life in five minutes' time.

CZARNECKA   You dedicated the last part of *Native Realm* to Juliusz Tadeusz Kroński, who appears in the book under the pseudonym of Tiger. Did you part company with him as part of your rejection of Hegelianism?

MILOSZ   No, that's not how it happened. Kroński had read *Treatise on Poetry*. He sent me a congratulatory letter and died soon after. I received word of his death while I was writing *Native Realm*. His wife, Irena, was deeply offended by that chapter in *Native Realm*. It was also attacked by many people who had had Kroński as a professor. His former students thought that Kroński had not been depicted correctly at all, that I had turned a common coward, an ordinary cat, into a Tiger. I turned a person who was horribly afraid to speak up into the great philosopher of Ketman. Of course, those who knew Kroński better and knew his diabolical sense of humor—people like Leszek Kołakowski, who to a great extent was formed by Kroński—did not hold that portrait against me. On the other hand, Irena Krońska thought I had somehow diminished the man, not shown his full stature.

CZARNECKA   Do you recall any of the more interesting responses to *Native Realm*—reviews?

MILOSZ   Vaguely. The émigrés were a little put out by my Lithuanianness, the stress I laid on the eastern borderlands, my unorthodox views on Polishness, my lack of nationalism. But all those years when I was living outside the country and writing in Polish were years marked by a lack of critical response. That's probably the weakest aspect of émigré writing.

CZARNECKA   Were some of your works printed for a short time in Poland after 1956?

MILOSZ   That lasted a very short while. A volume of my poetry was supposed to be published. I had already signed a contract, but I was late in delivering the manuscript. That was entirely my fault. Then the chill set in and that was the end of that. I think that was in 1957. The publishing house was not responsible.

CZARNECKA   What works of yours appeared in Poland during the seventies?

MILOSZ   A negligible amount. An anthology of contemporary Polish poetry that appeared in 1973 has an exceptionally large number of my poems. I think that this even caused the anthologists some trouble. That anthology makes me into a patriotic poet. Some of my translations from English also appeared in the three-volume anthology *Poets of the English Language*. The weekly *Tygodnik Powszechny* printed my translation of Ecclesiastes, and the monthly *Znak* published my translation of the Gospel according to Mark. A few of my translations of the Psalms appeared in the journal *Twórczość*. That's nearly everything. There's not a lot.

CZARNECKA   We can add to that list the samizdat publications of your works, the ones published by NOWA.

MILOSZ   That's true. Those were either reproductions of the books published in Paris or typescripts printed in offset. Chojecki gets the credit for that.

King Popiel and Other Poems

CZARNECKA *King Popiel and Other Poems* was published in 1962 and, strictly speaking, was your first self-contained book of poems since *Three Winters*. Both *Rescue* and *The Light of Day* were collections of poems from various years. . . .

MILOSZ Yes, that's true, in the sense that those are poems from more or less the same period and make for a certain whole. Something opened up for me after writing *A Treatise on Poetry*. I went back to poetry.

CZARNECKA In *King Popiel* there's a clear liberation from the tone of "civic-minded poetry," as you call it, and historiosophy yields the forefront to metaphysics. "Teachings" is a meditation on original sin, and "Conversations on Easter 1620" contemplates resurrection and life after death. The book contains as well a few lighter poems—"From Peasant to King," "On the Beheading of a Lady in Waiting," "A Frivolous Conversation"—which are almost bantering court trifles. The volume also contains poems composed of several parts, like "From the Chronicles of the Town of Pornic," the long poem "Throughout Our Lands," and "Album of Dreams." By the way, is that dream album authentic?

MILOSZ Yes, to a great extent "Album of Dreams" is actually based on my dreams.

CZARNECKA   One of the best-known poems in that volume is "Magpiety." The audience always bursts out laughing whenever you recite that poem at a reading.

MILOSZ   Yes, they do. I'm especially fond of that poem.

CZARNECKA   "The same and not the same, I walked through oak forests." Is that a sacred oak forest, as in Lithuania?

MILOSZ   No, that's specifically La Forêt de Sénart, near where I lived in Montgeron, outside of Paris. "The same" means me as I was in the past, in my childhood, but I am also "not the same" because I have been changed by time.

CZARNECKA   Well, if you say that you also encountered a magpie in that forest . . .

MILOSZ   I encountered many magpies there, of course. La Forêt de Sénart is a very beautiful forest of tall oak. At one time it was a royal hunting ground. As for magpies, I believe in "magpiety"—the quality of being a magpie—as I do in human nature. I'm actually very interested in magpiety. This is what Aristotle called "entelechy." It's strange, but the individual species seem to have pre-existing qualities. You know what the argument about universals was—whether the ideas of things exist before the things do, for example, if the idea of magpie exists before the magpie as a creature. The magpie that, so to speak, exists in the world of the ideas, in God, before the actual, created magpie. It's very mysterious. If you look at the jays that live on various continents—in California, for example—there are two species of jays that are very different from European jays. Still, all jays have a basic jayness to them. An astounding trait. Their feathering is of another color entirely, but they have a jayness in common. And all sparrows share a basic sparrowness. I can't help suspecting that there's something wrong with the whole theory of evolution if such a thing as entelechy exists, if the traits of a species are realized in its members. Of course, the theory of evolution explains the passage from one species to another.

But for me the differences among species are so clearly drawn that I can't believe in evolution. How do you get from the fox to the elephant?

CZARNECKA   Your poem "No More" reminds me of your reflections on beauty in *Continents*: "Could the sense of beauty be nothing but a very high degree of interest? In that case the painter, poet, or musician would be a person whose interest in the world achieves exceptional intensity. If that is so, then beauty is indecent. Why should I see beauty, be interested, if millions of people are suffering?"

MILOSZ   And no doubt you'll ask me about these lines from "No More":

> . . . Out of reluctant matter
> What can be gathered? Nothing, beauty at best.

CZARNECKA   Even with the reservations I just quoted, that's still a lot, isn't it?

MILOSZ   Yes, but what we have here is the desire to go beyond beauty, beyond aesthetic values—to reality.

CZARNECKA   We've spoken of how little reality there is in literature.

MILOSZ   Exactly. By conviction, I'm actually a realist. That means that I struggle to seize hold of fragments of reality. After all, that entire poem is an act of compassion for those Venetian courtesans. There may be some influence of art here— a painting by Carpaccio, *The Two Courtesans*. But there's also the specific image of a moment, the skipper of galeons and the courtesan. What we have here is solidarity with and feeling for people who lived long ago. There's a sense of how little of what actually happens can be contained in a poem. There were certain people, there were real, specific moments, and so little of that can be caught in words. Mallarmé's poetry is based on the arrangement of the words. The words, the integrity of the line, are what matter. A line that is so compact that it becomes like a specific tissue. Mallarmé says, *"Purifier les mots de la tribu"*—"to purify the language of the tribe." But in fact the rendering of the specific, the capturing of a moment, recedes into the background in that sort of poetry.

CZARNECKA   Is that why you compare yourself to the Japanese who composed poems about cherry blossoms—that is, timeless things? Cherries were the same three hundred years ago, and they'll be the same three hundred years from now. Nothing about them, no aspect, is connected with the capturing of the transient.

MILOSZ   Yes, poets like that are timeless. I'm expressing a bitter irony in that poem, resignation, and actually protest. "No more"—that's despair but it's also a revolt against the insufficiency of poetry. Roughly what the poem is saying is, What are we talking about, capturing reality! We're all like those Japanese poets who composed verses about cherry blossoms. Anything really concrete is beyond our reach. One of my old poems comes to mind as an example here: "Encounter," written in Wilno in 1937:

> We were riding through frozen fields in a wagon at
>   dawn.
> A red wing rose in the darkness.
>
> And suddenly a hare ran across the road.
> One of us pointed to it with his hand.

That's a moment. A hare really did run across the road. The point there was to catch something that had actually happened. At one moment, one second. Odd that I should feel the need.

CZARNECKA   You've expressed it in many of your poems:

> I wanted to describe this, not that, basket of vegetables
>   with a redheaded doll of a leek laid across it.

And in one of your essays you stressed that what you want to describe is an actual door handle, not the idea of one.

MILOSZ That's the point.

CZARNECKA In the poem "What Was Great" you say, "As long, long ago, I launch my boats of bark." I suspect that this, too, is on some specific moment.

MILOSZ Yes, of course.

CZARNECKA The cold eye that poem casts is typical of the whole volume. The worst troubles are behind you, and now it's time to examine the world from a distance. And you recommend a sober gaze in the poem "Should, Should Not": "A man should not love the moon." But why do you say, "An ax should not lose weight in his hand"?

MILOSZ In a certain idiomatic and symbolic sense, loving the moon means being dreamy. But I'd say that there's a defense of the middle road here. To keep things from becoming too sterile, too hygienic. The ax loses weight when tools that are faster and more efficient are used in its place. Axes are not used very widely today, because they've been replaced by power saws.

> His garden should smell of rotting apples
> And grow a fair amount of nettles.

A well-kept garden doesn't have any rotting apples.
    When conversing, man should not use words that are dear to him. Once again we enter the sphere . . .

CZARNECKA . . . of your carefully guarded privacy. . . .

MILOSZ No, a strange sphere where what is valued most is left untouched, as Thomas does in *The Issa Valley*. A man should not "split open a seed to find out what is inside it." That's a very childish thing to do—to cut open a teddy bear to see what's inside. "He should not drop a crumb of bread, or spit in the fire." That's such a strong taboo that I never throw bread out. And to spit in the fire was a great transgression. I learned that in childhood. It's a profanation, because fire is sacred. You weren't supposed to place a loaf of bread upside down. You weren't supposed to walk backward, because that meant you were measuring your mother's grave. There were all kinds of them. . . .

> When he steps on marble stairs,
> He may, that boor, try to chip them with his boot
> As a reminder that the stairs will not last forever.

Those are the marble steps of the Berkeley library that I was writing about. The poem is really a protest against sterility.

CZARNECKA   Is the seeking to be average in this poem like the anonymity, the merging with the crowd, recommended in "Greek Portrait"?

MILOSZ   Yes. I don't know where those poems come from, given my arrogance, fastidiousness, and aristocratic ways. Even I'm surprised. But recently a friend of mine, Jeanne Hersch, said to me, "You're so much the instrument, I can't understand how you translated the Psalms. You're not a human being, after all, just an instrument."

CZARNECKA   I think that the praise of the average is very ironic in both poems. This is more of a mask, because the character in the poem is also keeping some secret.

MILOSZ   Yes, it's a mask. What can you do with a strange guy who doesn't understand himself? "An instrument, not a human being but a device."

CZARNECKA   The poem "Heraclitus" has something in common with the theme of "No More." It's another attempt to re-create people from bygone eras in sensuous detail. And your fascination with Heraclitus is back. . . .

MILOSZ   I've already said that I wrote my senior essay on Heraclitus's river of time; that fascination dates way back. But I'm not alone in that. On the whole, there's a lot of interest in the pre-Socratics. Heraclitus is intriguing because he left practically nothing except some fragments. Before I wrote that poem, I published my translation of some of those fragments in *Continents*. Stanisław Vincenz assisted me in the translation, because I didn't know Greek then; I only had Latin from school. "Heraclitus" is connected with my conversations with Vincenz and the work we did on the translations.

CZARNECKA   What does the end of the poem mean? The story of Heraclitus breaks off and suddenly there are submarines.

MILOSZ   Aha, that's interesting. Heraclitus was in the mountains, but could see the sea from there. He was living like a hermit, lamenting for history and people, poor people, caught in the flow. At the end of the poem we pick up history at a later date, many centuries after Heraclitus. The monstrance bells, Orlando Furioso's golden clothes—that's the sixteenth century, Ariosto. And then it goes right to the twentieth or the twenty-first century, because there's a radio girl—Soviet, of course.

CZARNECKA   "Album of Dreams" leads me to ask you a personal question: do you keep a diary?

MILOSZ   I don't keep the kind of diary where you record what's happened every day.

CZARNECKA   A notebook, then?

MILOSZ   Well, sometimes I make notes, but they already have some literary form. I've never jotted things down in raw form, but maybe I will someday. In any case, during one period I had very intense, constant dreams, and I wrote them down. I don't remember whether I did it directly in a ready form or a paraphrase. That's how the little album came together. For me this signified that I was emerging from a period that had been quite sterile for poetry. A return to the subjective world, to dreams. I only allow myself this sort of thing very rarely. For one reason or another, I forbid myself indulgence.

CZARNECKA   In the readings you give, you often recite the poem about the hamster from the cycle "Throughout Our Lands." In this poem are you returning to the impossibility of grasping the world, which eludes description?

MILOSZ   The poem is ironic toward itself, of course. Some wisdom is sought but the effort falls short. The world is so ungraspable that our relationship to the world is like that of a hamster to ballet music.

CZARNECKA   This is from that same cycle: "And the word revealed out of darkness was: pear." Does this mean that you don't think in images, only in words, as you once said?

MILOSZ   Yes, the emphasis is on language here. The word "pear" is not evocative enough, but when I name the varieties of pears, I can see different parts of a garden where different varieties of pears grow. It all becomes more specific.

CZARNECKA   Is that why the image keeps expanding?

MILOSZ   Yes, now I can see some people, and more and more of the garden, but I am cut off from all that by space and by time. I am constantly spellbound.

CZARNECKA   For me, the hero of "Throughout Our Lands" is a sort of traveler on a magical journey. I imagine him as someone like Nils Holgersson in Selma Lagerlöf's *The Wonderful Adventures of Nils*.

MILOSZ   Yes. I adore that book. It's an enchanting book.

CZARNECKA   What about Paulina in her room behind the servants' quarters? She's drawn very clearly.

MILOSZ   She should be in *The Issa Valley*. The wife of Szaty-bełko, the steward. She's a very specific person whose image I've touched up here and there. It's interesting—the passage of time has a certain definite effect. The Paulina described in the poem is becoming realer and realer to me, and starting to obscure the actual person. The real model is becoming unreal.

CZARNECKA   Part thirteen of "Throughout Our Lands" begins like this:

> Whiskers of rabbits and downy necks
> of yellow-black ducklings, the flowing fire
> of a fox in the green, touch the heart
> of master and slave. . . .

And then that sensual image collides with a sadistic vision of naked nuns with whips. Why?

MILOSZ   Well, it's all part of the world of the senses. The ducks, the color of the fox in the green, and the ducklings' downy necks "touch the heart / of master and slave"—I bring in historical categories here. Besides, it has a connection, normal or perverse, with the world of nature. Yes, that scene is straight out of de Sade: "To order naked nuns . . . to lash us with a whip as we bite the bedsheets." But I don't know why that part was placed just there. . . .

CZARNECKA   Things are not strictly structured here, of course. The whole cycle is very freely constructed.

MILOSZ   Yes, the imagination moves in many directions. There's great variety. Perhaps the last part, the one about Cabeza, has some connection with the preceding part, the rabbits. That's a true story. Cabeza was in a shipwreck. Everyone lost his life except Cabeza—he was washed up on shore, somewhere in Florida. The Indians saw a wretched white creature crawling out of the sea. Later on, Cabeza wandered the American continent. Those wanderings gave him a special view of the world. After everything he'd seen, all the products of civilization seemed artificial. He laughed at Doña Clara, the lace cuffs, all the fuss and bother. He saw that world nakedly, as if he had been to Conrad's "heart of darkness." Those carved tables and chairs, that life of form and surface. The connection with the Marquis de Sade and all that sensuality is the other side, the underside of civilization. On the surface everything is harmony and order, but underneath it all are those naked girls, those brothel scenes. It's the other side of the coin, the view from underneath. That double awareness appears quite often in my poems. I suppose this part of the poem is a reflection on French civilization. The years I spent in France and my trips to Paris before the war contibuted a lot here. France was and still is very much a country of the double life. The sense of form is keenly felt everywhere. Nineteenth-century French life was incredibly well-ordered on the surface. Everyone was aware of the conventions. Middle-class men went to their little brothels. The double standard was no secret. That's the connection between Cabeza and the rabbit.

Bobo's Metamorphosis

CZARNECKA   The volume *Bobo's Metamorphosis* is a collection of poems written mostly in Berkeley between 1962 and 1965. In the title poem you describe a character you had read about as a child. Why did Bobo stick in your memory? Are the books you read in your childhood still important to you? Did they leave a lasting trace?

MILOSZ   Yes. Zofia Urbanowska, the author of the original *Bobo's Metamorphosis*, wrote children's books. I remember another one of her novels, *Rose Without Thorns*, which takes place in the town of Zakopane, which, you know, was a magical place at the turn of the century. Another book I read as a child, *Doctor Catchfly's Fantastic Adventures in the World of Insects*, by Erazm Majewski, is also set in the Tatra Mountains—Catchfly takes an elixir there. But Urbanowska's book impressed me deeply. It helped form me and stimulate my interest in littleness and bigness. The hero of *Bobo's Metamorphosis*, a nasty boy, was changed into a fly. . . .

CZARNECKA   But we find that out at the end of the poem. For a time we're witnessing a magical journey.

MILOSZ   Do you see it like that? Perhaps it can also be interpreted that way. How should I know? There's a very important passage there:

My eyes closed, I was grown up and small.
I was wearing plumes, silks, ruffles and armor,
Women's dresses, I was licking the rouge.
I was hovering at each flower from the day of creation,
I knocked on the closed doors of the beaver's halls and
    the mole's.

In other words—omnipresence. That's connected with being changed into a fly. You can always see things people can't see, you can fly anywhere. I think that's one of the themes here—flying into the center of things, examining various things that aren't accessible to human beings. A fly can be ubiquitous. In Urbanowska's novel, the metamorphosis was only temporary: Bobo went back to being a boy and could live a normal life, with the chance to mend his ways. That was the uplift aspect. Later on, Bobo wore pressed trousers and had a clipped mustache. Actually, the entire cycle is an exploration of reality from various angles, in various guises. There's a landscape from Shakespeare's *The Tempest*, and the legend of Philemon and Baucis from Ovid. A variety of metamorphoses, constant incarnations in a variety of characters.

CZARNECKA   And part five of "Bobo's Metamorphosis," which describes the death of Pieter Brueghel—is that one of the incarnations? That part begins with the words "I liked him as he did not look for an ideal object."

MILOSZ   No, that's something of a polemic with Zbigniew Herbert. Herbert wrote a poem about abstract art inspired by, I think, a painting by Berlevi. Herbert's poem is called "Study of an Object" and it says:

> The most beautiful object
> is the one which doesn't exist.

So this could be a polemic with the theory of abstract art. I counter it with realistic art, the things that do exist and which I want somehow to name, paint, draw.

CZARNECKA   You frequently refer to Mnemosyne, the god-
dess of memory, as your muse. But in the poem "The Language Changed," you doubt the reliability of memory and
generally distrust the words that are supposed to communicate a memory. It seems that only the dead can communicate.
The eighteenth-century soldier and poet Jakub Jasiński is
talking with Lilian Gish. . . .

MILOSZ   Yes, the comparison is made. After a time, Lilian
Gish leaves for that realm where she is on an equal footing
with Jakub Jasiński, and they speak in a "rattling tongue,
very staccato," because their bones are rattling. But, "elegant
and fading, memory" distorts everything.

> Neither was it as it first seemed
> Nor as you now make it into a story.

It eludes language; it actually eludes our perception of the
world. When we experience something, it seems one way to
us, but later it seems different. It's difficult for us to catch
hold of what it was that shaped that perception, that experience. By the time you turn it into a story, it's far away. But
when is it ever really real? Neither when we experienced it
nor now, when we put it into words. That poem keeps harking back to one thing—the unattainability of the real, what
we want to get our hands on. The language changes and we
change with it. We acquire distance; we are influenced by
language. To be honest and not beat around the bush too
much—I went through a great evolution by constantly
adapting to the changes and the possibilities of language. Ultimately, the thirties, when I began writing, and the sixties
are not the same thing. The whole world is different, and so
is language. Language influences the way experience is formed,
and alters it. Language is always an obstacle to perception.
The questions remains whether there is any such thing as naked experience, or if a person isn't always thinking about
something. What's happening in his head influences the way
he perceives things.

CZARNECKA   The poem "Rivers Grow Small" seems to depict a view of the world seen through the wrong end of binoculars.

MILOSZ   Well, that's a well-known experience. After a while, everything seems smaller.

CZARNECKA   The lake turns into a shaving bowl. . . .

MILOSZ   Yes, the world seems different from that perspective.

CZARNECKA   "The face's features melt like a wax doll plunged into fire." Is this the problem of the particular and the general again?

MILOSZ   Yes, our individual features seem incredibly important to us when we're young. Our personality in all its uniqueness seems so important to us. At the same time we suffer because we're not like others and we feel cut off. Later on, it turns out that all these individual features begin to melt away, more in our minds than in our emotions, because it's difficult to rid oneself of self-love. But through our minds we discover that we share those traits, supposedly so uncommon and individual, with others, and that many people have similar problems. And for that reason, when we look in the mirror we don't see a very individual face, just a human face: eyes, ears, nose, mouth. . . .

CZARNECKA   Are the two next poems in *Bobo's Metamorphosis*—"They will place there telescreens" and "On the other side"—two versions of hell?

MILOSZ   These are descriptions of life after death. Our images of life after death are very fluid, constantly changing. Every age constructs its own heaven and hell out of the means at hand. Hell's technology used to be that of cauldrons and tongs. But why couldn't telescreens be used as a punishment?

CZARNECKA   A hell where films of our memories are projected on large screens reminds me of Lem's *Solaris*, where emanations from the imagination re-create people who have died because the space research station in the novel is on an ocean that is in reality a psyche, a memory.

MILOSZ   Yes, of course.

CZARNECKA   And what is the "Armageddon of women and men" that you write about in that poem?

MILOSZ   Armageddon is a Biblical concept: the place where the final and decisive battle is to be fought between the forces of good and evil just before the end of the world.

CZARNECKA   In the poem "On the other side" you describe hell according to Emanuel Swedenborg's image of it.

MILOSZ   Yes, in a certain sense Swedenborg's hell resembles that of Lem's *Solaris*. Because consciousness emanates not only from people but from everything—the landscape, the entire environment. In my poem, hell is quite modest.

CZARNECKA   Like a poor section on the outskirts of town . . .

MILOSZ   I once wrote an essay on Swedenborg and Dostoevsky. In *Crime and Punishment*, Svidrigailov tells how he imagines life after death, punishment. He's surprised that people imagine hell as great and ominous. It's probably a soot-blackened bathhouse, a little room with spiders in it. That's all, for eternity. I suspect Dostoevsky took the idea from Swedenborg. Whatever the sinner's state of mind is, it stays that way for all eternity.

CZARNECKA   Then there's "Three Talks on Civilization":

> The dark blush of anger
> the impolite reply

the loathing of foreigners
uphold the State.

Is this about one state in particular? Is the acrimony against the West?

MILOSZ   No, it's the state in general. I think there's something sinister about the essence of the state. The state and organized society are upheld by rudeness, brutality, everything that is unpleasant. If the state and society were as soft as a rabbit slipper, they certainly couldn't exist, they'd collapse. The entire poem is full of mockery and ridicule. It's a sort of philosophical discourse. The state would be finished if it were not for "everyday necessity" and "hairy pleasures," if people read Saint Thomas Aquinas's *Summa*. I'd say it's a poem hostile to society. But it can also be interpreted like Herbert's "Elegy of Fortinbras." In the end, Fortinbras says to Hamlet: Everything's fine and dandy for you now, but I have to work on a decree on prostitution. Denmark, he says, is a prison. My poem is somewhat along those lines. Perhaps it's not so much hostile to society as sarcastic. There's a funny misunderstanding connected with the second part of "Three Talks on Civilization," which begins, "Yes, it is true that the landscape changed a little." An American poet told me that he liked this poem very much but did not take it ironically. He viewed it as a protest against the pollution of the environment and what man was doing to nature. But it is not a poem in defense of nature. It's ambivalent, just like the first part.

What do we regret? — I ask. A tiger? A shark?
We created a second Nature in the image of the first
So as not to believe that we live in Paradise.

That's the same as the image of nibbling chocolates in the first part of the poem. Aha, so you'd like to live in paradise, nibble chocolates, be moved by the loves of the shepherd Aminthas, but that's crazy! Nature is nothing to long for, and that second nature created by man, civilization, is also suspect.

CZARNECKA   Why does the narrator turn into Metternich in the third part of "Three Talks on Civilization"?

MILOSZ   Because this is a continuation of the reflections on nature.

I detested those foolish pups of Jean-Jacques,
and envied them their belief in their own noble nature.

This is a negative attitude toward the belief in man's inborn goodness and purity. There's an ambivalence toward the state in the first part and toward society in the second. But in the third part the narrator or hero keeps having horrible dreams because of his guilt complex, his knowledge of his own evil.

Therefore, I think, I wrote to Alexander,
Advising him to curb the youth societies.

Because he was aware of his own evil and did not believe in any romantic fantasies, Metternich advised the tsar to grab all those pupils of Jean-Jacques Rousseau by the scruff of the neck. The year 1820 was a very important one. It was then that Tsar Alexander, who had formerly had very romantic and mystical leanings, turned against the Masons and the young people of his country. It's also very interesting that Alexander suffered constantly from a guilt complex on account of his tacit complicity in the murder of his father, Paul, who had been strangled, with Alexander's knowledge. Here I strongly identify with Metternich in envying Jean-Jacques's pups for believing in their own noble nature. So "Three Talks on Civilization" is very ambivalent, much more so than that American poet thought.

CZARNECKA   You placed your translations of Walt Whitman and Robinson Jeffers at the end of *Bobo's Metamorphosis*. Is Jeffers still an important poet for you?

MILOSZ   I consider him an outstanding poet who is unfairly neglected today. I wrote a poem, "To Robinson Jeffers," which is a sort of debate with his work. We represent two completely different views. That poem is probably so clear that it doesn't need discussing.

CZARNECKA   Were you interested in Whitman earlier?

MILOSZ   Yes, I've written about that in *The Garden of Knowledge*. Actually, it's probably one man who's responsible for my interest in Whitman—Alfred Tom, who translated a number of his poems, and, I think, very well. I read them in a volume of Lam's encyclopedia, the volume on foreign literature. That encyclopedia is very rare today and can only be found in certain libraries. I was very taken by Tom's translations. I was a young man then; later I had a desire to read Whitman in the original. There's some disturbing link between Whitman and Jeffers. They have the same desire to speak directly, apart from all the conventions of literature, to liberate themselves. Except that Whitman had been affected by the entire American philosophy of life and the world, and there had also been some European influences on him, a little Hegel. Jeffers, on the other hand, represents a terribly pessimistic bent, a completely other direction, total misanthropy. He said of America, "Shine, perishing republic!" His entire philosophy stemmed from his reading of Nietzsche. Then there was his naturalism, his passion for the natural sciences, his turning away from the American myth, progress, and history in general, which Jeffers saw as meaningless repetition. He was a poet who tried to oppose the cosmic to the historical. Of course, he's very American in all that.

There's a turning away from Christianity and history in Melville, too. It's interesting that the rejection of Christianity and history go together. Even in his early work, Melville wrote about likable cannibals in the Marquesas Islands, where he ended up by chance as a young sailor. His early books *Typee* and *Omoo* are already disposed against Christianity and the missionaries. There's a search for the cycles of nature and the cycles of man, who is a part of the cosmic rhythm. That's explicit later on in *Moby Dick*. After all, Captain Ahab represents the madness of the white man, while it's Queequeg the Polynesian who has true wisdom. When the whaling boat goes under, Ishmael saves himself by floating on the coffin that Queequeg had had made for himself in advance. The ideal here is a stoicism connected with a cult of the cosmic and an impersonal, pantheistic God. Jeffers is similar, except that he strikes a more sarcastic and bitter note. That's why I'm opposed to Jeffers. I am rooted in those Christian, Slavic dreams. The Kingdom of God, or at least an independent Poland.

City Without a Name

CZARNECKA *City Without a Name*, your next book of poetry, published in 1969, contains poems written mainly in California, but there are fewer and fewer images of America in them.

MILOSZ I don't know. Maybe that's true and maybe it isn't.

CZARNECKA Many of the poems use a Biblical line. Was the idea of translating parts of the Bible already ripening in you back then?

MILOSZ It must have been, it's just that I wasn't aware of it.

CZARNECKA When did you begin studying Greek?

MILOSZ I was sixty years old at the time, because that was in 1971. Do you remember when Joseph went with his father, Jacob, to Egypt, Pharoah asked Jacob how old he was. He answered that he had not lived as long as his ancestors, he was only a hundred and thirty—a short, hard life.

CZARNECKA The heart of this volume is the poem "City Without a Name," which is composed of twelve parts. America appears only sporadically, in the reference to Death Valley or the landscapes of California, Arizona, drawn in a single stroke. The rest of the book keeps looking back toward the past, toward Wilno and Lithuania.

MILOSZ   I would not place any special emphasis on my thoughts' returning to Wilno. Where else could they return? That was the stuff of my life. That's where I was living when I was twenty years old. And there's a mixing of contexts in the book. When I write about the Zealous Lithuanian Lodge in part six, it doesn't mean that I belonged to it. And it's the same for the beginning, where I write about Kontrym, a nineteenth-century figure:

> Who will honor the city without a name,
> So many being dead, and others in distant countries
> Where they pan gold or deal in armaments?

It's true, I went to school with some people like that. I wrote about them in the second stanza:

> What birch-bark-swaddled shepherd's-horn will sound
> On Ponary hills memory of the lost—
> Vagabonds and Pathfinders, brethren of a dissolved
>   lodge?

The Vagabonds—that was our Vagabonds Club at the university. Pathfinders is an allusion to Rymkiewicz's poem "The Pathfinder," and also to pathfinders in general, in Cooper's sense—literature for young people. "The current carried an echo and the timber of rafts." That's a precise detail. "A man in a visored cap"—they used a Russianism for "visor" in those parts. A train of connected rafts was steered from the rear. You had to lean on the enormous steering oar, and the whole train would change direction. There was a little shed where they cooked and slept.

> In the library, below a tower painted with signs of the
>   zodiac,
> Kontrym would smile and take a whiff from his snuff-
>   box.

Kontrym was a librarian at Wilno University and maintained contact with the young people, the secret student society of the Philomaths. Since he was a great Freemason, he was the Freemasons' contact with the young.

CZARNECKA   The second part of the poem begins:

In Death Valley I mused about different styles of
   hairdo,
About a hand that shifted a spotlight at the Students'
   Ball,
In the city from which no voice reaches anymore.

Do your thoughts always return to Wilno, no matter where you are?

MILOSZ   Yes, certainly, but that's a constant refrain in my work. A hairdo is something that basically goes against nature. Here are Death Valley, naked geography, nature; different hairdo styles—that's human time, history, connected with specific places. And I cannot think about historical time if I abstract myself from my past and the places I lived.

CZARNECKA   The Zealous Lithuanian Lodge in part six of the poem, is that a real name?

MILOSZ   Yes, Wilno was full of Masonic lodges, and one was named the Zealous Lithuanian Lodge.

CZARNECKA   In "City Without a Name" there is great stylistic variety in the short forms. There's Baroque stylization, compact three-line units, and short verses that in other parts become elongated phrases joining to form a Biblical line.

MILOSZ   Yes, you asked me about the Biblical line. Naturally, it's no accident that I began translating the Bible. I had been fascinated by the Biblical line from the time I was a young man. It gave me some hope, a way out of metrics, a way of embracing and including more of the world. And so I had been thinking about translating the Bible for quite a long time, but I felt that it couldn't be translated from Latin, because that allowed very little freedom of movement. Everything had already been given form.

CZARNECKA Part eight of "City Without a Name":

> Absent, burning, acrid, salty, sharp.
> Thus the feast of Insubstantiality.

"Insubstantiality"—meaning without content or form? "Even the Summa thins into straw and smoke." Is that the *Summa Theologica*?

MILOSZ Yes, there's even a story that Thomas Aquinas once said that everything he wrote seemed like straw to him. Meaning lacking in presence. Everything should be full of presence, but it isn't. There's always something burning, biting, sharp, and bitter in taste. You can never catch enough; there's a lack of substantiality. And then all of a sudden—"angelic choirs sail over in a pomegranate seed." Dimensions again. From our own large dimension we shrink into one where we can see a choir of angels flying in a pomegranate seed. There's enormous space there. Big and small, as we know, are relative. There's no border between the macro- and the microcosm.

> And the angelic choirs sail over in a pomegranate seed.
> Not for us their leisure and the blowing of trumpets.

Not for us, but for reasons unknown. The poem is shouting: Help! Well, what else can you do?

CZARNECKA "It stands before me, ready, not even the smoke from one chimney is lacking, not one echo, when I step across the rivers that separate us." Is that line about a city restored through faith in apokatastasis?

MILOSZ No, it's simply how I saw Wilno in my imagination.

CZARNECKA   And was the oarsman you mentioned also a real person?

MILOSZ   Yes. The University Sports Association had its own dock on the Wilia. It was normal to see a ship on the Wilia, and skiffs going upriver.

CZARNECKA   There's another tremendous compression of time in the poem "Window"; everything seems to be happening in a dream.

MILOSZ   We've discussed those two themes. Once again it's the elusiveness of reality, the lack of substantiality. Everything dissolves; nothing can be caught. Joseph Brodsky thinks one basic mark of my poetry is the constant regret that human experience eludes description.

CZARNECKA   That's clear in your recent book of poems, *The Separate Notebooks.* . . .

MILOSZ   Yes, it is.

CZARNECKA   Another long cycle—or long poem composed of fragments—in *City Without a Name* is "With Trumpets and Zithers." Is the trumpet your favorite instrument?

MILOSZ   I'm not sure that the instrument is what matters here. What matters, I suppose, is some exploration of language. It's trumpets and flutes that appear most often in the poetry of the past. The trumpet is always played to express joy, ecstasy, praise, ceremony.

CZARNECKA   It's also a very Biblical instrument.

MILOSZ   So is the zither. Both instruments are very Biblical.

CZARNECKA   The first poem in this cycle begins: "The gift was never named. We lived and a hot light created stood in its sphere." Is that the landscape of paradise?

MILOSZ   No, those are mainly quite specific landscapes that I'd seen at one time. And how they assume that particular configuration and not some other is my own alchemical secret.

CZARNECKA   Except for part four, where there is a clear reference to death, in which the hero cannot believe, "With Trumpets and Zithers" does in fact lack one characteristic motif of your poetry: the dread of transience.

MILOSZ   That's true. It's a very Dionysian poem. Every section is a sort of ecstatic experience. Rapture at the beauty of the world: "On many shores at once I am lying cheek on the sand and the same ocean runs in, beating its ecstatic drums." A Dionysian experience, a Dionysian ecstasy with the world, is very difficult to translate into systematic form. In any case, when I say, "I address you, my consciousness," there's some liberation here, albeit brief. Because consciousness weighs our faults and merits. But, under the influence of that ecstatic experience of the world, I don't remember who I am and who I was. Naturally, as you said, death comes right in here. The scenery is Baroque: "Nothing but laughter and weeping. Terror and no defense and arm in arm they drag me to a pit of tangled bones." These are Baroque visions of skeletons. I will be down there with them in a moment. The *danse macabre* belongs to the late Middle Ages but had something of a revival in the Baroque. "With a train of my cloak carried by the Great Jester, not I, just the Sinner to whom a honey-sweet age was brought by a winged Fortune." The Great Jester appears in the seventeenth-century passion play *The Tragedy of the Polish Scilurus*. In that play, devils wait on the Sinner. The Great Jester presides over these ceremonies on the vanity of the world. "Beyond seven rocky mountains I searched for my Teacher and yet I am here, not myself, at a pit of tangled bones." "Not myself"—because I wanted to achieve something, in the sense of knowing the world. I searched for understanding, for a teacher, perhaps Jesus, to have the knowledge of this world. Then suddenly there's no more time. "I am standing on a theatrum, astonished by the last things, the puppet Death has black ribs and still I cannot believe." "Last things" means some ultimate knowledge. And I can't believe that everything will end. On the other hand, the next part is entirely Dionysian: "Borne by an inscrutable power, one century gone, I heard beating in the darkness, the heart of the dead and the living."

CZARNECKA It's like part ten of the poem, where you describe the forest inhabited by animals and people.

MILOSZ Yes, that's the paradise of the senses. But it ends the instant consciousness comes.

CZARNECKA Let's pause at part six of the poem. I would like you to comment on the first two lines:

What separates, falls. Yet my scream "no!" is still heard
    though it burned out in the wind
Only what separates does not fall. All the rest is beyond
    persistence.

MILOSZ There's the old Greek philosophical idea that unity is good and multiplicity is bad. For example, that's why the circle is the most perfect geometric form—because it's closed. The sphere is good because it is self-enclosed, it has unity. Man is splintered off from that unity and exists as an individual; he must pay for that, for existing apart from unity. "What separates, falls"—death and oblivion would seem to be the punishment for individuality. My scream is a protest against transience and disappearance. And I also say, "Only what separates does not fall," which is just the opposite. Because all the rest is beyond persistence. Persistence in time is a function of individual existence. Not being part of the unity, existing separately, this alone makes for persistence. All the rest, perfect unity, would be beyond time, persistence. That's something of a refrain in this section; why all the rest is beyond persistence is exemplified later on. It's what we said at one point about the poem "Bon on Lake Leman"—to pluck a moment of eternity from time. It's the same thing here. I want to record something that exists and persists because it is individual, unique.

> I wanted to describe this, not that, basket of vegetables
> with a redheaded doll of a leek laid across it.
> And a stocking on the arm of a chair, a dress crumpled
> as it was, this way, no other.
> I wanted to describe her, no one else, asleep on her
> belly, made secure by the warmth of his leg.
> Also a cat in the unique tower as purring he composes
> his memorable book.

I know a tower like that.

> Not ships but one ship with a blue patch in the corner
> of its sail.
> Not streets, for once there was a street with a shop
> sign: "Schuhmacher Pupke."

There was such a street. And the sign is authentic.

> In vain I tried because what remains is the ever-recur-
> ring basket.
> And not she, whose skin perhaps I, of all men, loved,
> but a grammatical form.

This entire poem is about my revolt against the Greek philosophical assumption that what separates, falls. I may also have been influenced here by my reading of Lev Shestov, the Russian philosopher, who couldn't bear Greek philosophy. He wrote a book, *Athens and Jerusalem*, a very pointed attack against the Greek obsession that what exists individually is bad and that the general is good. Like the sphere or the circle. Shestov said: Why? I am an individual and I'll scream "no" at annihilation!

CZARNECKA But the hero's arguments are only triumphant for a time in this poem. The last line says, "And the street will always be only one of many streets without name."

MILOSZ I scream "no." Then I propose an idea: only what separates does not fall, all the rest is beyond persistence. That's what I believe. And that's why I strive to give each thing its individual name. Yes, there is an admission of defeat later on. But this admission of defeat does not signify an acceptance of the Greek philosophy.

CZARNECKA Is the poem "How It Was" in *City Without a Name* thematically akin to "Oeconomia Divina" in *From the Rising of the Sun*?

MILOSZ Yes. That poem slightly embarrasses me because it might fit in too well with America's own anti-American feelings. America as a promise unkept, a blind alley, has been a constant refrain of the American mentality in the last couple of decades. They're obsessed with it. Even if things were going perfectly well in America, it wouldn't matter. This poem may not have any special American undertones for me. You could be right that it is like "Oeconomia Divina," and is not about America but, rather, the world.

CZARNECKA Your "Ars Poetica?" is frequently quoted and considered by many as your statement on poetry. Still, why did you use a question mark in the title?

MILOSZ Because I'm not sure myself if what I said is so. Actually, this is my own prescription for my own problems.

CZARNECKA In any case, you can say that you have created a

    . . . more spacious form
    that would be free from the claims of poetry or prose.

You found a way out of metrics and the closed stanza; you join poetry and prose in your long poems.

MILOSZ I've never had the satisfying feeling of having discovered something, that now I had it—no, never!

CZARNECKA   You reiterate that poetry has to be salutary, that the daimonion dictating the poem has to be good. Deep down, you are even skeptical about irony.

MILOSZ   Yes, there's a good deal of irony in my poetry, but I'm very suspicious of it. As I say, I would prefer to write without irony. Except that it's very difficult to speak directly of things, and so you try to catch them in a more roundabout way. Ideally, you would meet your subject head on.

CZARNECKA

  . . . Our house is open, there are no keys in the doors,
  and invisible guests come in and out at will.

You're speaking of poetry's trancelike quality here again.

MILOSZ   Naturally. I'm particularly able to do that because I am often seized by trances. I myself don't know what sort of forces have been seizing me and ordering me to write all these years, perhaps all my life. I am very hardworking and precise, I try to do everything as best I can—but how to explain it? "Ars Poetica?" was written very quickly and without any thought of publishing it someday.

CZARNECKA   The question mark in the title lends the verse an ironic form; basically, the poem itself is not ironic.

MILOSZ   Yes, the question mark makes for irony.

CZARNECKA   Is that because without it the poem would be too much of a statement?

MILOSZ   Yes. I have no desire to write statements. This poem, too, was dictated to me. In fact, I don't write a good portion of my poems as poetry—I just jot them down and then they lie around for a long time. I keep going back to them, not sure that there's anything there, anything worth publishing.

Other poems come slowly and with great effort. You can spend a very long time on them, or else they come—just like that. And you don't know who dictated it, a good spirit or an evil one.

From the Rising of the Sun

CZARNECKA   You only published one volume of poetry in the seventies, and then a long silence set in. Not everyone is aware that the title of the volume *From the Rising of the Sun* is a quotation from one of the Psalms. . . .

MILOSZ   That's true, but it's not in my translation, because I hadn't translated the Psalms at the time. This is a psalm sung at vespers: "From the rising of the sun to the going down of the same."

CZARNECKA   In this volume you've stopped supplying each poem with the date and place it was written.

MILOSZ   Apparently time's been standing still since I started living in Berkeley. Why did I stop using dates? I really don't know.

CZARNECKA   "A Task," the first poem in the book, is a public confession. Don't you think you've already made that public confession many times?

MILOSZ   Aha, so you can't keep confessing the same sin over and over. . . . Do you think it's obsessive? It could be. No doubt I have been confessing the same thing over and over.

230

CZARNECKA   In "A Task" you say:

> We were permitted to shriek in the tongue of dwarfs
>   and demons
> But pure and generous words were forbidden.

But since you also say that you're searching for new dignity for the Polish language, a new hieratic language, in what way are you breaking with the grotesque and the ironic?

MILOSZ   But I'm always the ironist, the shriek of dwarfs and demons is always inside me, and so I'm always falling into the same sins. I'm speaking about my contemporaries and myself. My tongue is constantly itching to say something nasty. And then that sin has to be confessed. Pure words were forbidden.

> Under so stiff a penalty that whoever dared to pro-
>   nounce one
> Considered himself as a lost man.

We were all afraid. Ultimately, if irony were only something superficial, easy to expose—like, let's say, the irony of Ernest Bryll's poems or of those who use it to speak without saying anything and to condemn without condemning—then everything would be simple. But irony is also very connected with our times. Buffoonery, slapstick, and clowning are very deeply ingrained in us. The point is to find a language. If in translating the Psalms I was searching for an elevated, hierarchic language, I had my reasons, because language itself imposes various ambiguous and ambivalent attitudes on us. Spoken Polish, especially on the telephone, relies on hints, exclamations, ironies. And there's a certain fear of bombast and loftiness here, too: we became disgusted with all that in the twentieth century. We saw through all that, and through heroic bombast as well. That doesn't mean I rule out civilization's entering a new phase when people can speak straightforwardly, without irony, when it's again possible to write an ode in honor of a hero.

CZARNECKA   Were you already able to read the Gospels in Greek when you wrote "Readings"?

MILOSZ   Yes.

CZARNECKA   In that poem, time and human history are seen from a vast perspective. We are still part of the same aeon as the first Christians.

MILOSZ   "Aeon" is a very old Greek word, popular in the first centuries after Christ. Some of the Church Fathers speculated on the meaning of the word. The very concept of an aeon assumes enormous cycles, everything renewing itself in some way. The concept can have various meanings, depending on the interpretation. In any case, we can assume that we, and the events described in the Gospels, and even Moses, are all part of one aeon. It's an enormous time period.

CZARNECKA   In this poem, are you comparing the artists of our century to the "demonized" in the Bible?

MILOSZ   Well, if we take today's modern art criticism . . . For example, in *Doctor Faustus* Thomas Mann deals with the issue of the dehumanization of art. The hero, Adrian Leverkuehn, is modeled on Friedrich Nietzsche. Only because of his illness, his pact with the devil, can he create his brilliant compositions—he is a man possessed, demonized.

CZARNECKA   How do you understand the parable about the possessed in the Gospel According to Matthew?

MILOSZ   The Luciferian part of their diabolical nature comes into conflict with their earthbound nature as swine and produces an explosion. The devil's temptations can assume various forms. When they assume their Luciferian form, the predominant aspects are pride and purity, because Lucifer is a pure and haughty spirit. An artist who considers himself a rebellious, Promethean, pure spirit, and is extremely haughty, has been afflicted by Lucifer. And in fact that has also been the case with the majority of those who wanted to improve humanity in our century. They're so pure, they love purity. The revolution is to be in the service of purity. Terror is a kindred phenomenon. It's very clearly connected with modern art, because terror, too, arises from a love of absolute purity.

CZARNECKA   Your poem "Oeconomia Divina" also contains an explicit moral warning.

MILOSZ   The title also means "Divine Pedagogy," because the word "oeconomia" was used for many centuries of Christianity to mean "education" or "edification." "Oeconomia Divina" was understood as the edification of the world by God and a form of education—the meting out of punishments and rewards, God's involvement with the world. For example, all the events of the Old Testament had an educational purpose: they have their own meaning for the history of Israel, but they also demonstrate God's educational intentions in regard to humanity. And in this poem we have God's next educational intention. God decided to withdraw, to become *Deus absconditus*. God is not to be seen. There are no signs that God is intervening, punishing, rewarding. Heidegger is obsessed with that theme—contemporary humanity's loss of contact with the Divinity. God has hidden Himself; no trace of His presence can be found. That's a recurrent motif in the twentieth century: the loss of the life-giving sources. In this case it's clearly through God's own intent, His withdrawal. In one of his poems, Różewicz says that the voice he heard coming from the water, the sky, and the air was only the voice of another man. Or then there's Gombrowicz's concept of the "Interhuman Church." The key lines in this poem are:

> . . . in vain they were longing after horror, pity, and
>   anger.
> Both work and leisure

were not justified enough,
nor the face, nor the hair nor the loins
nor any existence.

The sense that there is no justification. And this is obviously connected with the idea, A million people less, a million people more—what does it matter? Twentieth-century man's susceptibility to totalitarian terror is connected with his feeling that individual existence lacks foundation. In his campaign against that idea, the Pope constantly stresses that each human being is unique. But we're undermined from various sides, even by metaphysical despair. I think I've written something about the performance of *Waiting for Godot* when Roger Blin was first staging the play. I was at one of the first performances, with Lucien Goldmann, a Marxist, a follower of Lukacs. A very select, urbane audience, it roared with laughter throughout the play. After the play, Goldmann and I went for a beer. He was furious. Naturally, he wasn't reacting from a religious point of view, but as a secular humanist. He was seething as he said, "Do you know what this kind of art leads to? The concentration camps." He said this even though Beckett was a thousand miles from any such idea—quite the contrary. But since the play was one of metaphysical despair and clowning, that's how Goldmann interpreted it.

CZARNECKA In the poem "Tidings" you compare earthly civilization to a system of colored spheres. Is this a reference to Leibniz and his theory of monads as the components, the atoms of the world?

MILOSZ No, there is no reference to Leibniz in the poem. It's simply an attempt to speak of a civilization that has vanished. The image of colored liquids is taken from what surrounds us everywhere, like neon light. And skyscrapers or some structures out of a science-fiction film shoot up, while down below a monstrous life goes on. Our civilization undoubtedly exists on two levels. The lower level is the naked struggle for existence, where death is the final sanction, as

Simone Weil said. The final sanction in a society where anyone who won't conform will die of hunger.

CZARNECKA   And what about up above, on the higher level?

MILOSZ   Everything ends in language. Language is our true home. The twitter never stops. In any case, in the last quarter of the twentieth century, I'd be inclined to the view that human language is the essence of civilization. I show myself to be a child of my times in saying that language is probably the essence of civilization. Or maybe something else is, I don't know.

CZARNECKA   "L'Accélération de l'histoire" seems to be a continuation of "A Song on the End of the World," which was written a few decades earlier.

MILOSZ   For all I know, it is. The expression was probably introduced by the French historian Daniel Halévy, at the beginning of the century, I think. He was quite correct in identifying this as a principle of the twentieth century. Events that in other centuries needed sixty or a hundred years to come to fruition do so now in a few years. That acceleration of history is also happening in art, various "isms" multiplying and dying in the space of five years.

CZARNECKA   That's why I brought up "A Song on the End of the World." But in "L'Accélération," the end of the world "draws near on cat's paws." So no one else is aware of the imminent end.

MILOSZ

> It's late for the human race
> Cassandras fall silent one after the other.

There were Cassandras when I was young, but now there are fewer all the time, which is a disturbing sign.

CZARNECKA   Who knows, maybe the Cassandras write science fiction now.

MILOSZ   Yes, that's true. Every novel in that genre ends in catastrophe. There may be some hope for mankind in that. There are so many Cassandras in science fiction!

> Not with flame and cracking walls.
> It draws near on cat's paws.

But then there's a correction:

> O Pessimist! So it's cosmic annihilation again?
> No, not at all.
> I fear the hands that fight for the people
> and which the people itself cuts off.

That's really a very pessimistic, Witkacy-like vision. A total grayness and mediocrity are coming, the long age of the anthill. Marx wanted an end to alienation and demanded a human time devoted to creativity and leisure, but it becomes a parody when that goal is forgotten. That brings us back to a poem I wrote in my youth, "Slow River," with its crematoria of dead wasps, its mandolins or balalaikas, its heaps of food, a purely consumer civilization as a parody of what those who had fought for the people were striving for.

CZARNECKA   "From the Rising of the Sun," the seven-part title poem of this volume, has been termed your *magnum opus* in poetry, a "polyphonic fugue," a new form of the long, digressive poem. It is here that you appear to have found the spacious form that would be free from the claims of poetry and prose, as you put it in "Ars Poetica?" You often address the reader directly here, providing commentaries, footnotes, short introductions to the individual parts or, rather, fragments of the poem. You use extracts from old documents, encyclopedias, you include short discourses and numerous quotes, which are either in plain view or buried in the text. You reconstruct the world from bits and pieces, memories, images, books, all your experience of life; you even reach back to the lives of your ancestors. Two environments—Lithuania and California—often overlap in you, creating a new reality. This poem contains a lot of code, difficult even for a reader familiar with your work. Did you have a larger entity in mind as you began writing "From the Rising"?

MILOSZ   I have to say that this poem might just as well never have come into being. It was written after a period in which I had not been thinking about writing any such thing. By and large, a person's entire literary career and his writing depend on his being able to say: That's it, period, enough. Not a word more. Don't overplay your hand. Besides that, there are frequent barren stretches when you feel impotent. You become skeptical about your own abilities. Then all of a sudden something strange jumps out of you, and there it is. It's very strange for me, because I have a perfect memory of the period when that poem didn't exist yet. And now you're asking me what it is. Very strange . . . All right, then, let's go back to your question. I often think about writing long works in poetry, but when you take a great windup you don't jump very far. Maybe it's better to start by planning just to make a short jump. Many of the things I've written were planned as the beginning of some long work that didn't pan out.

CZARNECKA   Could you give me a specific example?

MILOSZ   There's a poem called "A River," written during the war. A rather tragic description of the Mazovian plain. "O Vistula, so often sung in inspired rhyme . . ." This is a fragment of a long poem that was never written. And there are many others. You have a vision of a large work and the existing poem is a part of it, a little section of the roof or of a column.

CZARNECKA   And it's not necessarily the beginning?

MILOSZ   No. As far as "From the Rising of the Sun" is concerned, I wrote the beginning first, and then it lay around for a long time. I didn't know if anything was going to come of it. There are a lot of poems I've begun but didn't go on with. You can't find a pattern. Painters do a lot of sketches, too. "Once, when returning from far Transylvania . . . ," the beginning of part seven of "From the Rising," was written separately and included later. Actually, it was like this: first I wrote "The Unveiling," but I didn't know how to proceed, and so the poem lay around for a while. Then something started to open up, the result of a summer vacation in Berkeley. It was a fine, sweltering summer, and I went swimming in the pool every day.

CZARNECKA   What year was that?

MILOSZ   I don't remember; I guess it was 1973.

CZARNECKA   How did you come upon those old chronicles, publications, and notes?

MILOSZ   I came across them while writing the poem. They're all in our library at Berkeley, including the Lithuanian encyclopedia.

CZARNECKA   Even the inventory of movable goods you quote?

MILOSZ   Yes, that was in Berkeley, too. I found a book published in Kaunas with a collection of documents.

CZARNECKA   That's astounding—to find your family tree in a library on the Pacific Coast!

MILOSZ   In the map room I even found German ordnance maps from the First World War. The house where I was born was marked on that map.

CZARNECKA   In the first part of the poem, "The Unveiling," you paint a picture of the poet as timeless, beyond time. He writes with a stylus, a reed, a quill, a ballpoint pen. But then you immediately refer to a specific time and place—the present, the Pacific. You divide this section of the poem into monologues and a chorus. The persona thinks in terms of linear time, and the chorus expresses the recurrence in nature, the closed circle. The structure reminds me of your early poem "A Song," from the book *Three Winters*.

MILOSZ That's possible.

CZARNECKA ". . . under a dark-blue cloud with a glint of the red horse." Is the red horse from the Apocalypse of Saint John?

MILOSZ Yes.

CZARNECKA In *Native Realm* you said that Oskar Milosz predicted the outbreak of the Second World War and called it the War of the Red Horse. But since in "The Unveiling" you say, "Now . . . with a glint of the red horse," that would seem to indicate the apocalypse that is always hanging over us, and is not an allusion to the prophecy.

MILOSZ Yes, it refers to the ever-present apocalypse. But at the same time the dark-blue cloud is real. There were clouds like that over the Bay yesterday.

CZARNECKA

Odious rhythmic speech
which grooms itself and, of its own accord, moves on.

You're reluctant to start work.

MILOSZ This is another rebellion against poetry. My relationship to poetry is quite complicated, as you know. I am a medium, but a mistrustful one.

CZARNECKA The second part, "Diary of a Naturalist," is a remembrance of what you read in school, your fascination

with nature, but it has your characteristic ambivalence. A naïve narrator and a narrator burdened with bitter knowledge
are speaking at the same time.

MILOSZ   Of course, if I had re-created the books I'd read as
a child and my feelings for nature, the whole thing would
have been much more positive, sentimental, emotional. After
all, I had wanted to be a naturalist—that was my calling.

CZARNECKA   Your vision of nature in this section is horrifying:

> If the wax in our ears could melt, a moth on pine
>   needles,
> A beetle half-eaten by a bird, a wounded lizard,
> Would all lie at the center of the expanding circles of
>   their vibrating agony. . . .

The "monstrous relationship" of the devouring and the de-
voured. Still, in "Nature—a Threat," a poem you wrote many
years earlier, you say that moral judgments cannot be made
on nature.

MILOSZ   Yes, I was writing about a Dachau of grasshoppers.
I suppose that theoretically one can say that moral judgments
can't be made on nature. But it's difficult to rid your mind of
the pain in nature. Gombrowicz was obsessed with that. He
wanted to write a play about the suffering of a fly, but he
died before he could. It's difficult even to imagine what the
play would have been like.

CZARNECKA   Why do you have such a good memory of the
book *Doctor Catchfly*, which you quote in "Diary of a Naturalist"?

MILOSZ   Because it's the story of a naturalist who miniatur-
izes himself and has adventures in nature, which is shown as
cruel. There's also a certain humanitarian message, since there's

another character who knew the secret of the elixir, an Englishman with whom Catchfly had once gone hunting in India. Apparently in order to attract help in the Tatra Mountains, that Englishman had set fire to an anthill. Catchfly was indignant—how could you!

CZARNECKA   Were you quoting that childhood reading from memory?

MILOSZ   No, someone gave me the book as a present. One of my friends sent it to me, a different edition from the one I'd read as a child. I had a wonderful edition of Catchfly before the First World War, on very good paper, with illustrations. I remember the picture of Catchfly climbing up a spider web and dueling with that Englishman. His revolver had been miniaturized, too.

CZARNECKA   In the final fragment of "Diary of a Naturalist," you describe your pilgrimages. "Stopping perhaps at noon in Sarlat"—where is that?

MILOSZ   It's in central France, the Dordogne, a region with very famous caves, the Lascaux caves, where paintings from the Magdalenian period were discovered. It's east of Bordeaux, where the famous Saint-Émilion wines come from. An area of old Roman colonies.

CZARNECKA   And the Rocamadour, to which you also made a pilgrimage, is there, too?

MILOSZ   Yes. Sarlat is a small town not far from those caves. Les Eyzies is the place where they discovered the oldest caves inhabited by cavemen. It's an excellent area for hunting and has always been liked by man. The Vézère and the Dordogne have wonderful river valleys. To me this is one of the most beautiful places in the world. When I'm there I feel as if I'm in Lithuania.

CZARNECKA   Does that landscape really remind you of Lithuania?

MILOSZ   It certainly does. Lithuania isn't rocky the way it is there, but the landscape is hilly, very varied, with a great many rivers, very beautiful. Rocamadour is east of Sarlat, a sort of French Częstochowa—a pilgrimage site. It's located on a pilgrimage route that runs from the north, from Cluny, which was an important center for pilgrims. It has a church built on very steep rock.

CZARNECKA   In part three of the poem "Over Cities" you insert a quotation that begins with a short prose fragment—"He that leadeth into captivity, shall go into captivity." Where is that from?

MILOSZ   I think it's from the Epistles of Saint Paul. I don't recall at the moment.

CZARNECKA   Then you write about teaching a class at Berkeley, and mentioning Maximus the Confessor.

MILOSZ   He was a very eminent theologian in the Eastern Church, known more in the Orthodox world than in the Catholic. He was one of early Christianity's eminent theologians. To a large extent, the Eastern Church's antirationalistic tendency derives from his thinking. I believe Dostoevsky read him and was influenced by him.

CZARNECKA   Then you say, "Let us formulate it thus: the Universal is devouring the Particular, our fingers are heavy with Chinese and Assyrian rings. . . ."

MILOSZ   The Universal, the undermining of the value of the unique individual in favor of the universal—this is an allusion to the cultural syncretism we're witnessing today. This cultural syncretism stems from the dissemination of knowledge about various cultures by the mass media—photography, television.

CZARNECKA Then why are our fingers "heavy"?

MILOSZ That's a specific image, not a symbol. If you put several rings on your fingers, they make your hand heavy. This is a sensuous image.

CZARNECKA In part four of "Over Cities," you describe a ship covered with an insect-like swarm of people. . . .

MILOSZ That's simply a dream. Swarming humanity, the hippie generation of the sixties, but shifted into the indeterminate future.

CZARNECKA In part six of "Over Cities" you say of your mother:

> And she, who offered me to Our Lady of Ostrabrama,
> How and why was she granted what she asked for in
>   her prayer?

Is this an allusion to the opening lines of *Pan Tadeusz?*

MILOSZ I came down with diphtheria when I was a little boy, and it was then that my mother offered me to Our Lady of Ostrabrama—Our Lady of Wilno. Exactly as in *Pan Tadeusz*. It really happened. I didn't invent it to add an interesting detail to my life story.

CZARNECKA A character named Sir Hieronymus suddenly appears in the last part of "Over Cities." Is he a real person?

MILOSZ I'm not going to comment on Sir Hieronymus. You can tell who he is. He has a snuffbox and that probably places him in the eighteenth century. He speaks about his travels. The atmosphere is that of the eighteenth century, with its cosmopolitan travel.

CZARNECKA But why does Sir Hieronymus mention the Count de Saint-Germain?

MILOSZ   The Count de Saint-Germain supposedly possessed an elixir that gave eternal youth, or at least a very long life. He appears throughout the eighteenth century. He's said to have contacted Marie Antoinette to warn her of what was coming. He was well along in years by then, but he had been seen fifty years earlier at the same age.

CZARNECKA   Sir Hieronymus also speaks about the Book of Hieroglyphic Figures—does that have any connection with the Count de Saint-Germain?

MILOSZ   No, that book is something else entirely. It's an alchemical work. I don't recall the author's name.

CZARNECKA   Several times in this poem you repeat, "Life was impossible, but it was endured." Part four, "A Short Recess," begins that way.

MILOSZ   After all, I did do an anthology of Simone Weil. She speaks several times about the impossibility of life, says that human life is impossible even though a person somehow endures it. If you start thinking that seriously, reflecting on it, it's unbearable. There's too much pain, suffering, danger. But in the poem life is situated historically. And whose life is it? Mine. In the poem Wilno is presented in a slightly mythologized form, unreal, visionary. I am a stranger from some other place and time, a sort of spirit that has materialized and is asked where he comes from. Basically, the situation is a very realistic one, because whenever I'm asked about my home town or my native country, I have that exact same feeling— that I come from another planet, another time, another epoch. I'm writing about my fantasies here—if my early love had come true, if everything had taken a different form, then I'd have lived peacefully in Wilno and been counted among the elders of the city. Had history taken another turn, I would been sent abroad to conclude an alliance with Ferrara, or Padua, or some other such city. But that's not the way things worked out.

CZARNECKA   The last section of this part begins, "And there was a holiday in Megalopolis." Is that an image of America?

MILOSZ   Yes, that's here, California.

CZARNECKA

A service was also being celebrated in Christian
   churches
Where the liturgy consisted of discussion
Under the guidance of a priest in Easter vestment
On whether we should believe in life after death,
Which the president then put to a vote.

Is that really how you see the Church in America?

MILOSZ   It's exactly how it is. The Catholic Church in America was very unhappy when the Pope said that women could not be priests. This is a church experiencing license, under the influence of the Second Vatican Council.

CZARNECKA   Part five, "The Accuser," is, once again, a sort of public confession. Is Satan the accuser?

MILOSZ   We don't know; it's simply a voice. The voice says: Confess, you hated your body, you started on a journey, you remember it all. Only toward the end is there the line "Yet I have learned to live with my grief." The person who is asked the questions defends himself. He would like a ritual of purification. But I, the person who is asked the questions, say, "A ritual of purification? Where? When? For whom?" It's very bitter. The whole section's very harsh.

CZARNECKA   In this part of the poem you also say:

Well, it happened long ago, in Ecbatana,
In Edessa, if you prefer. . . .

I don't understand the allusion here.

MILOSZ   Ecbatana is in Persia, Edessa in Asia Minor. Those are cities where various religious writers worked and various sects arose in the early centuries of Christianity. This is another shift, to invest the poem with a more universal historical dimension.

CZARNECKA   There's a sudden shift of scene and we're in a barber shop—a very strange, unreal barber shop. The hero says to himself:

> O Emperor.
> Franz Josef.
> Nicholas.
> Ego.

And there's a pythoness there, too.

MILOSZ   The pythoness is a fortuneteller. Normally, she's not supposed to dance or shake her hips. But she can. Anything is possible in the crazy world of today's Berkeley. So a person is in a barber chair and receiving the barber's full attention. He feels like Emperor Franz Josef or Tsar Nicholas. And the accuser mocks him: You're so egocentric, you think you're an emperor.

CZARNECKA   The last part of the poem "From the Rising of the Sun" is entitled "Bells in Winter." Is there any connection here with *Three Winters?*

MILOSZ   No, there's no allusion. I'm really describing the bells of Wilno here.

CZARNECKA   You open this section with a description of an imaginary meeting. The hero meets a young man in Greek dress on the way back from Transylvania.

MILOSZ   This is a scene from Saint Paul's Epistles to the Corinthians. Paul orders the young man excluded from the eucharistic feast because he had committed a sin by sleeping with his father's wife. And it's set in Transylvania because that region is connected with the Arians, the Polish Protestants of the sixteenth century. Poland and Transylvania were two of the main centers of radical Protestantism. Poland because of its political system, and Transylvania because it was a principality under the protectorate of Turkey, a Mohammedan power. Polish Protestants would travel to Transylvania. So I could imagine myself traveling there on a mission through the Carpathians.

CZARNECKA   Later on you say, "Yet I belong to those who believe in apokatastasis." Could you explain that term in a bit more detail?

MILOSZ   Apokatastasis is a concept that first appeared in the Epistles. It was developed extensively by Origen, who is not considered a totally authoritative Church Father because he held very heretical views, but let's not go into that here. In any case, he was very much a believer in apokatastasis. In Greek it means more or less the same as "reinstatement," the restoration of the state before original sin, a repetition of history in a purified form. It's a risky concept, very heretical. I'm not saying I'm a great believer in apokatastasis, since the word can have a variety of meanings. In any case, in this poem apokatastasis tends to mean that no detail is ever lost, no moment vanishes entirely. They are all stored somewhere and it's possible to show that film again, to re-create a reality with all those elements restored. We've spoken about telescreens where all our sufferings are shown. Let's hope that memory exists on the other side of the river Lethe but that it has been cleansed. You cross the river Lethe, you forget all your suffering, and your memory itself is cleansed. That's more or less connected with apokatastasis; that's the role of the restoration here.

For me, therefore, everything has a double existence.
Both in time and when time shall be no more.

Or, since it's impossible to imagine the absence of time, there is *aevum*, time redeemed, a completely different kind of time. In other words, apokatastasis is not a formal belief of mine, because those are heretical ideas. Rather, its meaning is that of a restoration of all moments in a purified form. It's hard to pin down the meaning here, but I wouldn't *want* to be overly precise, either.

The Land of Ulro

CZARNECKA   If one were to define *The Land of Ulro* in a single sentence, would it be called a book of prophets? The postulation of a visionary literature?

MILOSZ   No. In a way, *The Land of Ulro* is like Erich Heller's book *The Disinherited Mind*. And I quote Heller in *Ulro*.

CZARNECKA   Yes, I remember. I actually think that reading Heller's book was an important intellectual adventure for you. By coincidence, he published *The Disinherited Mind* in the same year *The Captive Mind* came out—an interesting similarity of titles. Were you already in America when you read Heller's book?

MILOSZ   Yes, and that was quite late, in the sixties.

CZARNECKA   You mention his book back in *Visions from San Francisco Bay*.

MILOSZ   Yes. I mentioned that Heller's approach to everything that Stanisław Brzozowski called the great Romantic crisis of European culture was similar to Brzozowski's, even though Heller had certainly never heard of him. Brzozowski had a great influence on me. In fact, some of the thinking in

249

Ulro follows Brzozowski's analysis of the great crisis at the
turn of the nineteenth century brought on by the impact of
the natural sciences, and the attempt to find a way out of it.
Of course, that could be extended infinitely; you could write
several volumes—the situation of the Romantics in various
countries, the evolution from Romanticism to Baudelaire. *Ulro*
is marked by an awareness of that enormous amount of material. Naturally, like every writer, I'm always interested in
Romanticism. But the traditional approach to Romanticism,
at least the one I was taught in school, meaning faith and
feeling opposed to reason, is insufficient. As I look back now,
I see that *The Land of Ulro* might be an attempt to reflect as
follows: We've been told about feeling and faith as opposed
to the cold reason of the eighteenth- and nineteenth-century
rationalists, but what does that mean? What does that mean
historically? It must be said that a huge amount has been
written on the subject in Poland, but it's entirely superficial.
First there were the classicists, then came the Romantics. They
were against rationalism and in favor of impulse, the passions
of the heart, but the problem was never placed in any wider
context. Brzozowski was constantly involved with the problem of the rise of Romanticism in Europe.

CZARNECKA   I view your interest in Blake, Swedenborg, and
the seventeenth-century English metaphysical poets as an
attempt to go against the mainstream. It's as if you were listening intently to the voices of the past in order to find an explanation for the processes taking place in the twentieth century.

MILOSZ   Do you mean my constant opposition to Western
civilization, which is the product of a scientific *Weltan-
schauung*? We're in a late phase in the development of the
scientific world view, and its influence has led to the permis-
sive society and an emphasis on the individual's right to happiness in defiance of society. You wanted to know what *The
Land of Ulro* was in a nutshell. It's a book about people who
sought a solution to the situation, at the risk of their sanity.
That means that they dreamed of a whole other course. I've

already used this metaphor—a person gets on a subway in New York and discovers he's on the wrong train; he's on the way to Harlem, and he's frightened, but there's nothing he can do about it. It was the same with what was happening at the turn of the nineteenth century—maybe we're on the wrong train? Could there have been a few other options? People like Blake, Swedenborg, Mickiewicz, Oskar Milosz, and Goethe with his color theory were seeking a different system, another possibility. Mickiewicz maybe less, because he's an example of the Romantic solution, but Blake did not want a purely subjective solution. Reading Brzozowski brings similar thoughts to mind.

CZARNECKA   To what extent was Blake an influence on your work?

MILOSZ   Not that great an influence.

CZARNECKA   You said in *Ulro* that your fascination with Blake was so great that one could assume that reasons and considerations apart from literature were involved.

MILOSZ   Yes, of course. It's probably connected with Blake's use of color as a painter. This is difficult to explain. There's the incredibly sensual way he puts colors together. His illuminated manuscripts have a counterpart in the coloration of his poetry, something that runs through his poetry. It can't be put into words. How can I explain a deep emotional attachment? Naturally, I can think of various reasons for being attracted to his work and liking it, but I can't be systematic about them. Why do I like Chardin and all those copper pans— it's some combination that appeals to me. As I've already said, I had read a little Blake during the war. I'm not so sure I understood him then. If I did, it was intuitively. And then for years I had nothing in common with Blake, and it was only in a certain period that I grew interested in him again and started reading him. When I was lecturing on Dostoevsky, I think it was in 1972, I told my students a good deal about

Blake, because there are some astonishing similarities between the two. Some of my students were taking the Blake
course at the university and arranged a Blake poetry event on
Halloween night. They sang his poems to the accompaniment
of a guitar. Very magical. There's a poem of Blake's, "The
Mental Traveller," that is completely incomprehensible and
has been given a host of interpretations. One of the oddest
poems, it requires you to know an entire system of symbols
to understand what it's about. As a result, no one under-
stands it. But it's beautiful, completely magical.

Still, that phase is over now, and I have no intention of
delving into Blake any more. I'm moving on, going somewhere else. I had been very involved with Simone Weil, Shestov, Oskar Milosz, but you have to keep going. I'm not a
specialist in Blake or English literature in general. It would
be an exaggeration to say that *The Land of Ulro* is primarily
about Blake. He simply figures in the book as an important
and interesting phenomenon. I was astounded to learn that
Brzozowski, who died so young, had written a few words
about Blake. And he had understood him: that essential glor-
ification of energy, the rejection of the world of formula, and
the rejection of those three sinister figures—Bacon, Locke,
Newton, the unholy trinity.

CZARNECKA   I didn't say that Blake was the central figure in
Ulro. Oskar Milosz is, in my opinion. Was it he who got you
interested in alchemy?

MILOSZ   Yes, but he didn't conceive of alchemy as a form of
chemistry. Alchemical experiments were also steps in spiritual development. Oskar Milosz attached great significance
to the history of initiation. I don't know how true it is that
Dante was an alchemist and that *The Divine Comedy* contains alchemical ideas in metaphoric form. Dante belonged to
the Order of Templars, which would explain his connections
with the Arab East. *The Divine Comedy* is modeled on the
wanderings of an Arab poet in the next world. The Templars
had ties to the Near East and the mystical current of Islam.

As for alchemy, it was its symbology that interested me: the world as analogies and so forth.

CZARNECKA   Is the title of Oskar Milosz's *Ars Magna* a synonym for alchemy?

MILOSZ   I'm not sure whether it's an exact synonym for alchemy, or whether alchemy is included under the term *Ars Magna*. *Ars Magna* is also the title of a work by Raymond Lully, who was from Majorca, a fantastic and very colorful figure in the Middle Ages. Apparently, he practiced alchemy and attempted a mystical synthesis of Islam and Christianity. Oskar Milosz refers to a Polish alchemist by the name of Sędziwój. But we're between Scylla and Charybdis here. On one side, there's the positivist approach, very prevalent, which considers alchemy a defective form of chemistry. And in a certain sense it was, but it was more than that. On the other side, there's all that esoterica that's so fashionable, especially in California. The history of the Rosicrucians is very interesting, serious, deep. Oskar Milosz was very involved with that. But, translated to the American level, it turns into a Kiwanis Club. There is a Rosicrucian Museum in San Jose. The mysteries of Egypt and all that drivel.

CZARNECKA   Do you consider yourself a Miloszologist, an expert on the works of Oskar Milosz? Do you fully understand his work?

MILOSZ   No, I don't understand it fully. His long philosophical poems are very difficult—you can go back to them ten times, but there's no way to grasp their thinking fully. Though I understand a great deal of it, there's a great deal I don't understand. Certain leaps of thought are beyond me. Something eludes you, as if there were purely poetic and mythological concepts concealed in a guise of iron logic. The logical discourse is developed with great precision. And then at one point there's a leap of thought that can only be a leap of poetry.

CZARNECKA   Did you translate Oskar Milosz's poems in order to understand them better?

MILOSZ   Certainly—that was my principal goal in translating them.

CZARNECKA   It's curious that you translated them into English, not Polish.

MILOSZ   I did it for myself. At the time I wasn't thinking about publishing *Ars Magna* and *Les Arcanes*. I did that translation a few years before writing *The Land of Ulro*. I also wrote that book for myself, without thinking about whether it would ever have readers. That's not been the case. But there was another reason. Some books are terribly difficult to translate into Polish. The Polish language is very bad at sustaining lofty flights of philosophy. Polish just isn't concise enough; it's sensual. All abstractions sound heavy and artificial in Polish. And so I gave it a try in English. I came to the conclusion that English would be good for this, even though French has more of a tendency to personify abstract ideas.

California Poems

CZARNECKA Is your poem "Caesarea" a reference to the city's tradition of philosophical schools in the early stages of Christianity?

MILOSZ No. Caesarea was always a colony. Places were named in honor of Caesar. Here, quite obviously, the name refers to America. The landscape in the poem is American, though it's been transposed, of course. I'm describing a personal experience here, a man approaching the American mainland. I once traveled by ship to America. "Now, when Caesarea is bitterness for us." "How many years were we to learn without understanding"—that's a basic feeling. The longer you live here, the less you understand America.

> We roamed about the markets of Caesarea. . . .
> We are still not sure: were we led astray by the greed of
>   our eyes,
> Or did we so firmly believe that it had come true:
> Our vocation, our very first calling.

In other words, why did we move to America? Were we just seduced, or were we seeking to believe that there was something there? That was the form the initial impulse took. But did we really find anything in that America—this we don't know.

CZARNECKA   Like "Caesarea," the poem "The View" is part
of the volume called Bells in Winter in English. The image of
Wilno, so clear in the original, is effaced in the English translation of "The View." All that remains is some city.

MILOSZ   Naturally. When I say that the students were singing "The Ode to Joy," there's an immediate association with
the song of the Philomaths; the Polish reader immediately has
a point of reference, but none of that comes across in translation.

CZARNECKA   How do you feel about your poems in foreign
languages, French, English? Do they sound alien to you?

MILOSZ   Yes, of course.

CZARNECKA   Even if you co-translated them?

MILOSZ   Yes.

CZARNECKA   Has it ever happened that you preferred a poem
in translation to the original?

MILOSZ   No, I prefer the original.

CZARNECKA   You write rhymed verse rarely now.

MILOSZ   I do sometimes. However, my poems are always
very strongly delineated by their rhythm. The difference between various languages is extremely interesting. A Russian
is completely dumbfounded when he has to translate a poem
without rhyme. For him that's prose—he doesn't feel the del-
icate play of the cadence. Brodsky does, of course, which is
why he can translate me. But, going back to poetry with rhyme,
today it gives the impression of being stylized. This is because
of changes that occur gradually, from one decade to the next.
The sensibility changes. Before the war, it was very difficult
to appreciate unrhymed poems, and very few people had the
ear for it. Let's take the group known as the Polish avant

garde. Peiper devised an entire theory of socialist rhyme, which Przyboś put into practice. If you read Przyboś closely, it turns out that it's all rhymed! He used rhyme and assonance very astutely, so that they wouldn't be noticed. It's concealed. Socialist rhyme is a very deep formal discipline. I was always struck by Przyboś's incredibly subtle rhyme structure. All the rhymes have clockwork precision.

CZARNECKA   Let's go back to your poetry. "The Fall" begins, "The death of a man is like the fall of a mighty nation." Does this have a connection with nineteenth-century philosophical concepts?

MILOSZ   Yes, analogies between the animal or human body and the body politic were used by the English utilitarians, primarily John Stuart Mill and Herbert Spencer. The social classes are coordinated like a body's hands or feet. To a large extent, Bolesław Prus's novel *The Pharaoh* is a study of the state as a body. When some organs hypertrophy and others decay, the body falls ill. In *The Pharaoh* the equilibrium among the priests, the administration, and the people is violated, because the priestly caste has grown enormous and the people are oppressed, the administration is corrupt, and the army is losing its role and is now dependent on the priests. That's one comparison. And another is Plato's comparison of society to a great beast.

CZARNECKA   And Simone Weil took it from Plato. . . .

MILOSZ   I don't know if those things are echoed in my poem. I'm constantly being surprised. Here we are, talking about a poem that was written relatively recently. I should have the feeling that I'm the father of that poem. And I don't remember anything.

CZARNECKA   You don't remember that poem?

MILOSZ   I remember the poem itself, but I have no clear memory of the circumstances in which it was fathered. A person has a twofold vision of himself. On the one hand, he sees himself as an extremely sober, very rational person, always lucid, a rather precise intellectual mechanism, with everything under control. The other vision is the exact opposite: everything seems to be happening in a dream. That poem, for example. As far as I remember, I sat down and wrote it. That's all I can say.

CZARNECKA   In the course of our conversations, you've mentioned that you've developed a special technique for writing poetry—you write a few lines, leave them alone for a time, then go back to them and finish the poem. You've also said that some of your poems seemed to have been dictated to you.

MILOSZ   Yes, there are both kinds. I'd say that everything pre-exists. All that's needed is to work it out. I could make a comparison with the fine arts. As soon as a sculptor makes one cut in a block of stone, he knows what it's going to be, though he couldn't know this from the stone itself. In any case, the next cut is conditioned by the first one. In a certain sense, the structure of the entire poem is already contained in the first line, somehow implied by it.

CZARNECKA   Yes, but on the other hand you've said that some poems were intended to be parts of larger works that never got written. So everything is not known after the first line is written.

MILOSZ   No, not everything. Sometimes there are two lines that I don't know how to develop. And sometimes I write an entire poem that is to be part of a larger whole which I then can't complete. I can more or less sense the poem, intuitively; I just can't find it.

"Notes"

CZARNECKA   If we take as our point of departure here a definition of poetry as distillation, condensation, then your "Notes" consists of nothing except one- and two-line poems.

MILOSZ   I think this is connected with my search for direct forms. In fact, the principle behind these compact poetic notes is very similar to that of certain philosophical texts where I strive to avoid intellectual terminology and intellectual ornament, and instead use my own words to communicate something of philosophical importance. For me this is a form at that boundary.

CZARNECKA   Your "Notes" are reminiscent of Mickiewicz's *Notes and Observations*. You also used a similar form in your "Notes on Exile," though the degree of condensation there is not so great.

MILOSZ   As you correctly observed, there are degrees of condensation. They could be arranged in ascending order.

CZARNECKA   At the upper limits of condensation, the code becomes very complex. The somewhat more extended poetic forms have additional lines that can help the reader build up an image. The very first Note, "On the need to draw boundaries," caused me trouble:

Wretched and dishonest was the sea.

MILOSZ   The sea always appears as elemental, as chaos, primordial chaos, an element fundamentally hostile to man because it is boundless and formless. Man as form, mind, and reason is opposed to it. This is the conflict between nature and man.

CZARNECKA   But why should a symbol of nature be "dishonest"?

MILOSZ   Aha, I wonder. I need to think a minute to answer that. I think the dishonesty is connected with nature's protean quality—that is, you absolutely never know what it is.

CZARNECKA   That reminds me of your poem "Ocean," written in Washington in 1948. First you describe the serene surface of the ocean, a view of the beach, a child swimming, but the ocean's depths contain a "museum of death" and leviathans.

MILOSZ   That's right. The attempt to set boundaries is the opposite of chaos. I wrote that Note without any reference to the Bible, but, as we know, trammeling the leviathan is the same as taming the sea so it doesn't exceed its limits. Supposedly, the trammeling of the leviathan comes from Babylonian myths that are much older than the Bible, like other beliefs that the creation of the world is actually the victory over chaos, over the leviathan or, as the Book of Job has it, the serpent.

CZARNECKA   The second Note is called "Reason to wonder": "The ruler of what elements gave us song to praise birth?" Is this an aversion to procreation like that of the Gnostics?

MILOSZ   If songs in praise of birth come naturally to us, then perhaps people are inclined to accept this as self-evident. Birth is good, joyous.

CZARNECKA   Because we're so careful about separating death from birth.

MILOSZ   Birth is good, death is bad, and here there is reason to wonder. That could be. But in fact who is "the ruler of . . . elements"? That's very much an idea from Schopenhauer. The next Note is directly from Heraclitus. As we know, for the pre-Socratics, poetry and philosophy were inseparable—one and the same. There were attempts at monism, to deduce the entire world from one element. . . .

CZARNECKA   For Heraclitus that element was fire.

MILOSZ   It's interesting that he places fire at the beginning and at the end, as does Christianity. In my work, fire is very much connected with my reading of Oskar Milosz. *Le feu* and *la lumière* played an enormous role in his work. Heraclitean fire, as well as light, is connected with my reading of him.

CZARNECKA   The Note entitled "Landscape" strikes me as very Biblical, sensual. It reminds me of the land of milk and honey.

MILOSZ   I don't know if there were any "unbounded forests" there. The Old Testament uses the word *midvar*, which no one knows how to translate. Some people translate it as "wilderness." The Poles had a tendency to translate it as "forest." *Midvar* means a desolate area. The Note says: "Unbounded forests flowing with the honey of wild bees." This is also the archetype of all bucolic poetry. And I detect here an echo of the translations of Ovid we did in school: "And golden from the green oak seeped the honey."

CZARNECKA   You quote that poem in *Native Realm* when you describe your Latin classes. Let's move on to the next Note, "Language": "Cosmos, i.e., pain raved in me with a diabolic tongue."

MILOSZ   Gombrowicz would have enjoyed that line. Cosmos as mathematical necessity is mostly pain for living creatures. The language of the cosmos, taken to mean the language of blind necessity, is diabolic. It "raved in me"— that is, I, too, am subject to those laws.

CZARNECKA   "Supplication": "From galactic silence protect us." Is this in fact a continuation of the previous thought? A belief in words despite everything?

MILOSZ   A belief in words, of course. But this note is, rather, a refutation of the one that precedes it. The diabolical language is that of nature. And, as a matter of fact, galactic silence is a continuation of that language; it is the voice of the cosmos. To come up against blind necessity is not the best feeling. Many of my poems, such as "Tidings," are in opposition to nature. What do we have to build a world of our own from—the flutter and twitter of language, lipstick, gauze, and muslin, which are to protect us from the galactic silence. As always, it is civilization versus the deadness of the universe.

CZARNECKA   But, as you've said many times, civilization is a very thin protective layer. The next Note, "Just in case," strikes me as inspired by Simone Weil: "When I curse Fate, it's not me, but the earth in me."

MILOSZ   To tell the truth, anyone subject to the laws of earth—meaning the laws of transience, aging, sickness, and death—should curse fate. What else can he do? What is fate— you live a little while, and then suddenly it's goodbye? Why is it like that? This is the anger of earth. I try to find some other, higher law—in religion, in art. An opposing sphere. Because, after all, I should live forever and always be happy.

CZARNECKA   The next Note is entitled "From the store of Pythagorean Principles": "Having left your native land, don't look back, the Erinyes are behind you."

MILOSZ   That's not my invention.

CZARNECKA   Granted, but the placement of that Note in the collection has some meaning. The same is true of the Note "According to Heraclitus."

MILOSZ   Well, what do you think of that?

CZARNECKA   You were always looking back.

MILOSZ   So, then, this Note is based on my own experience. Every time I looked back, the Erinyes were behind me.

CZARNECKA   The warning not to look back appears in many legends, myths, parables.

MILOSZ   It does. Lot's wife looked back. . . .

CZARNECKA   And so did Orpheus.

MILOSZ   It's always the same. But I wonder how correct a dictate that is, because Proust's work, for example, was born out of looking back. I was constantly tempted to look back, either because I sensed the Erinyes behind me or because when I looked back the Erinyes were pursuing me.

CZARNECKA   But can there be any artistic creativity without looking back into the past?

MILOSZ   Well, this Note speaks about one's native land. That's very important to me. "Having left your native land"—that means when I left Wilno, because Poland was the beginning of emigration for me. So this refers to looking back toward Lithuania and Wilno. Of course, I've often thought how different my own looking back is from that mawkish, sentimental looking back that fills whole columns in the émigré press. This is an interesting problem, because the future can cancel out all those illusory differences. For example, *The Issa Valley* is now taken as mawkish, sentimental reminiscences of the land of my childhood. I really did not feel that I wrote *The Issa Valley* out of nostalgia. Other demons were at work there.

CZARNECKA   The poetry you wrote in the sixties has a good many images of California, but lately you seem to be looking back to your native land more and more.

MILOSZ   Could be.

CZARNECKA   Let's return to the "Notes." "Hypothesis": "If, she said, you wrote in Polish to punish yourself for your sins, you will be saved." Do you agree with that verdict? Do you take that opinion seriously?

MILOSZ   Well, in a certain sense, yes, I do. In the first place, my continuing to write in Polish indicates a continuing involvement in the whole Polish mess. In the second place, it's the product of my sense of guilt. In a way, to write in Polish is, of course, to converse with the dead. After all, one does not survive those years with impunity, years when so many people lost their lives. Continuing to write in Polish is closely connected with the sin of survival.

CZARNECKA   Isaac Bashevis Singer takes a similar view: writing in Yiddish means conversing with the dead.

MILOSZ   Singer says: "I believe in resurrection. When millions of Yiddish-speaking people rise from the dead, they'll ask what's there to read in their language." Anyway, for me there's no other way out except to write in Polish. I've said somewhere that there are writers who think more in ideas or images, whereas I think in language itself, so I simply had no other choice.

CZARNECKA   The next Note is called "Portrait," though it might be a self-portrait: "He locked himself in a tower, read ancient authors, fed birds on the terrace. For only in this way could he forget about having to know himself." Is this the fear of knowing one's own nature?

MILOSZ   It's an ironic reversal of the principle "Know thyself." It would appear that an effective way of avoiding self-knowledge is to lock oneself in a cell or tower and contemplate the day in peace, whereas mingling with people forces one to self-knowledge. That's how I see it.

CZARNECKA   The word "sin" has come up many times in our conversations. The consciousness of sin is very strongly present in your work.

MILOSZ   This isn't clear, even to me. Obviously, a Catholic upbringing, if it's a powerful experience, leaves a very deep mark. I assume that's true—a very keen sense of sin. But I have no idea how much of that takes place on the conscious level. I don't know how to probe that. An analysis of my work could certainly show how this works. But I want to point out that in her memoirs Nadezha Mandelstam said that a person should have a sense of sin, and that Osip Mandelstam had a deep sense of his own sinfulness and man's in general. Perhaps a poet should have a sense of sin; perhaps it's not all that stupid.

CZARNECKA   How is the Note "*Do ut des*" to be understood?

MILOSZ   "He felt thankful, so he couldn't not believe in God." Ultimately, one can believe in God out of gratitude for all the gifts He has given us. For the thorns, too. I'm more able to believe out of gratitude. I need many camels, donkeys, and sheep, and I always believe I will get them. Well, and if suffering comes, you endure it. Perhaps this is a little like the Book of Job when Job says: We accepted the good but we won't accept the ill.

CZARNECKA "The perfect republic": "Right from early morning—the sun has barely made it through the dense maples—they walk contemplating the holy word: Is."

MILOSZ That's always a recurrent theme for me, and even in my Nobel lecture I said that the ideal life for a poet is to contemplate the word "is." My nature is not all of a piece, yet in my poetry I frequently display a desire to settle in my native city, spend my life there with a woman I love as my wife, walk to the corner café, and meditate on the word "is." That's utopia, needless to say. There's always something in the way. Either the city burns down or it's taken by the enemy. For me, "is" is the most mysterious word. I once had the idea of forbidding myself to use it, because it's too holy a word. That would have made writing very complicated. The word is used all the time, but in the sentence "The man is a redhead," the word "is" plays a very minor role: it connects the man and the red hair. Can a word so full of meaning be used for such things?

CZARNECKA Reflections on original sin and the Fall are recurrent themes in your work. "The Tempter in the Garden" contains this vision: "A still-looking branch, both cold and living."

MILOSZ Granted, but paradise is also a recurrent theme, the dream of living in what Oskar Milosz called First Nature, instead of where we are now, in Second Nature. That means that one lives the greater part of one's life in the cocoon of civilization—words, expressions, ideas, newspapers, books, everything that is removed from the elementary structure of the world. Those layers protect us, but from time to time they crack open and reveal their horrible interiors. For me at least, to live normally, to function, has always required overcoming a certain fundamental sense of horror, one that does not exclude ecstatic wonder at creation.

We've come to something rather important here. The

blackest humor, gallows humor, is something I can eat for breakfast. It's extremely shocking for Americans, who truly are raised with a sense of the basic goodness of the world. But it doesn't shock me. And, similarly, the most macabre vision of what could happen historically, politically, which was unimaginable for others of my generation, was something I was able to imagine before the fact. And that's one source of my catastrophism, my pessimistic vision. Anything can happen in a world like this. Unquestionably, there is some huge, basic wound here, a complete nonacceptance of the world, the world of Second Nature, beginning with the suffering in nature, the incessant devouring, the transience of individuals and species, and ending with the fundamental cruelty of sex, death, and so forth. I certainly have always considered myself a person who, metaphorically speaking, dons a corset, fastens its clasps, and then goes about the world doing what he does. But there obviously were moments, there were times, when this state of mind verged on madness. I never had any breakdowns, and I consider myself basically mentally healthy, but I know those experiences, and I know what it means to be on the verge and to sit down to write when your guts are wrenched in pain.

CZARNECKA   That reminds me of your poem "A Way": "So sensitive to the smell of hospitals . . ."

MILOSZ   Yes, "that I should spend my whole life in a cork-lined room, my teeth chattering." I have to say that element is very strong in me. And I even admire myself, in the sense that I have always been able to function despite periods of horrible inner quaking.

CZARNECKA   Let's return to the image of the Tempter.

MILOSZ   This may be just an illustration of the Bible. There's something plantlike, branchlike about the serpent. It's as if eyes were looking out from a tree.

CZARNECKA   Is the Note "Strong or weak point" another sketch for a self-portrait?

MILOSZ

> You were always ready to fall to your knees!
> Yes, I was always ready to fall to my knees.

The first line is a reproach, the second a reply, an admission.

CZARNECKA   Is this a poem about submission, subservience?

MILOSZ   Oh no. It's about someone who readily falls to his knees in veneration, who has a need to adore. It can, however, also be expressed as a reproach. In *Transatlantic* Gombrowicz says, "And I fell to my knees"—but that's purely rhetorical; he's making fun of gentry ways. In my Note I'm being serious. I truly consider myself a person by nature inclined to admire. It's definitely a very strong need.

CZARNECKA   Is it connected with your need to have a master?

MILOSZ   Possibly. It's the search for people one can venerate.

CZARNECKA   "Epitaph" seems addressed to passers-by:

> You who think of us: they lived only in delusion,
> Know that we, the People of the Book, will never die.

MILOSZ   You might think this is about the Jews, because they are the people of the Book. But I think that the People of the Book are the people of both the Old Testament and the New Testament, the word in general. Stéphane Mallarmé is no great master of mine. I have many objections to nineteenth-century French aestheticism, but it was Mallarmé's dream to turn the world into a book. To turn the world into a book is man's ultimate dream. This has the same root as the sense that Second Nature is unbearable. There are a number of variations on that tendency. What was Flaubert trying to do? After all, he could not bear life, he was disgusted by the bourgeois, the France of his time, so he tried to turn life into a book. The existence of the Book, the Bible, is man's bulwark against chaos. The People of the Book are against the insidious, immoral sea, against chaos.

CZARNECKA   "A God-fearing man": "So God heard my request after all, and allowed me to sin in his praise." Is this about yourself?

MILOSZ   Yes, this is about my relation to God. I can't help it, it may be pagan. It's connected with the Note where I say that we must be grateful for what God gives us. I'm really not a moralist, as people say I am. They miss the point.

CZARNECKA

> If not for the revulsion at the smell of his skin,
> I could think I was a good man.

Why is this Note entitled "Medicine"?

MILOSZ   It's medicine against having too flattering an opinion of oneself. If I am a moralist, it's in the next Note, which says:

> Not that I wanted to be a god or a hero.
> Just to change into a tree, grow for ages, not hurt anyone.

CZARNECKA   Is the Note called "Mountains" a concise description of a Swiss landscape?

MILOSZ   "Wet grass to the knees, in the clearing, raspberry bushes taller than a man, a cloud on the slope, in the cloud a black forest. And shepherds in medieval buskins were coming down as we walked up." Pretty, isn't it? Yes, it's a description of Switzerland, a bit fanciful.

CZARNECKA   The Note "In reverse" has echoes of your old passionate desire to be a naturalist: "On the ruins of their homes grows a young forest. Wolves are returning and a bear sleeps secure in a raspberry thicket."

MILOSZ   As for the landscape, it could be upstate New York or Connecticut. Places that had once been working farms are now overgrown with forest. I'd go visit my friends on their farm, and more wild animals would be returning to the forest all the time. A cause for optimism in a way—the victory of natural ecology. Yes, this is connected with my childhood dreams of the kingdom of nature, which is described in *The Issa Valley*.

CZARNECKA   The next Note is called "Morning":

> We awoke from a sleep of I don't know how many
> thousand years.
> An eagle flew in the sun again but it didn't mean the
> same.

Is that the eagle from the Apocalypse?

MILOSZ   No, there's a certain reference to Oskar Milosz here. At the end of *Les Arcanes* he speaks about Adam looking at a flying eagle. I'd say that this is a description of original sin. The eagle means one thing, and later it means something else. The same world in the eyes of man before original sin and after the Fall, a changed relationship to the world.

CZARNECKA   Then there's "Abundant catch":

> On the shore fish toss in the stretched nets of Simon,
> James and John.
> High above, swallows. Wings of butterflies. Cathedrals.

Is it the apostles who have that vision of cathedrals?

MILOSZ   This is probably the moment when they become Christ's disciples, but the tossing fish are a part of nature, like

the swallows and butterflies. Everything is happening in nature; then all of a sudden cathedrals appear—they do not yet
exist, but they will. Nature's time and art's time, human time,
the moment when they become disciples. This is a strange
juxtaposition with a tale from the Gospels where there is no
room for such considerations. If fish are mentioned there, it
is not as a reflection on nature's cruelty. Fish are for eating;
the attitude is utilitarian. The whole world is given to man to
serve him for food, clothing, and so on. I don't know why
the monumental outline of a cathedral appears here as another element of the Gospels. It's like the last of the Notes,
"History of the Church":

> For two thousand years I have been trying to under-
> stand what It was.

That's true. And I still haven't understood anything—I don't
understand anything!

The Separate Notebooks

CZARNECKA   Why did you subtitle one section of *The Separate Notebooks* "The Wormwood Star"? Because of the constant threat of Apocalypse?

MILOSZ   The subject of "The Wormwood Star" is apocalyptic, of course. The Wormwood Star also appears in Dostoevsky's work. In *The Idiot*, Lebedev predicts that railroads will be the end of the world. And he's right, too. Dostoevsky treats him somewhat humorously, but Lebedev explains what he means. It's not a question of the railroads themselves but of the technology they symbolize. And so, the Wormwood Star is the fulfillment of one phase of the Apocalypse by twentieth-century civilization.

CZARNECKA   You said that this is a random collection of poems. I had the impression that these were purposely fragmentary images that were often in contrast but had an internal unity. What at first seemed a loose blend of poetry and prose took on a structure.

MILOSZ   Yes, but let's not forget that I have many slips of paper in my hat. I can always pull them out and arrange them so they have a sense of harmony and unity.

CZARNECKA   At the beginning of *The Separate Notebooks* you refer to a "world state" and, at the end, to a "planetary empire." Are those two names for the same thing?

MILOSZ   Yes, more or less. After all, we are now engaged in a battle to see who will control the planet. Ultimately, everything is moving toward that goal. At the moment it's difficult to predict how much of that goal will be achieved and who will do it, but in any case we can see now that the number of states is constantly decreasing. At first, Europe had a multitude of various little states. Charlemagne straightened that out a bit. Now it looks as if the twenty-first century will bring—I don't know—some definitive attempt at unification. Obviously, I don't find this a positive process—on the contrary. A Diocletian Rome, planet-wide.

CZARNECKA   A specific date, 1916, is used in the first prose section. You describe a landscape by a lake, Red Cross tents. Is this Russia?

MILOSZ   I mention Viški there. Geographically, it's located somewhere near the border of Latvia and Russia. I guess it's west of Vitebsk, in those parts.

CZARNECKA   If I remember correctly, weren't you with your parents near the Volga in 1916?

MILOSZ   No, we were there in 1917. Viški was before that. This is a scene of war, not revolution.

CZARNECKA   Are the forces in the third, metrical section of *The Separate Notebooks* the Erinyes, the Fates?

MILOSZ   Forces are forces. There are no references to Greek mythology here.

CZARNECKA   There's a two-line poem:

On all fours they crawled out of the dugout. Dawn.
Far away, under a cold aurora, an armored train.

Is that a harbinger of the revolution?

MILOSZ   No. It's just what I'd call a little scene from life.
Armored trains played a very important role in military
operations at the end of the First World War and in the
Polish-Soviet war in 1920–21. They were a curious military
innovation that disappeared quickly. Very typical of the time,
the epoch.

CZARNECKA   All of a sudden, in the next prose fragment,
bagpipe players in medieval costume are climbing a hillside.
In a minute they'll be playing to the attack. This astounded
me. Bagpipe players at the front in World War I? In Russia?

MILOSZ   The soldiers had rounded up the bagpipe players
and ordered them to play, but this is an image from medieval
times. Maybe it isn't fair to the reader, who'll start wonder-
ing where that band of bagpipe players came from, but these
are images jotted down on the principle of *écriture automatique*. I don't know why I was obsessed with those bagpipe
players when I was writing that section. It must have been
some picture I'd seen and remembered.

CZARNECKA   What about the scene when the boys discover
gravestones with the names Faust and Hildebrand? Is this a
reference to Goethe's *Faust*?

MILOSZ   I don't remember where, but there really was a
cemetery with those gravestones. It's the same in the next
poem, which reconstructs an actual experience, when I
marched with a band playing, and the sidewalks were lined
with women. That was 1922 in Wilno. The women of the
Auxiliary Corps were very energetic; they gave out cocoa to
children, founded the Polish Scholarly Society, the Tomasz
Zan Library in Wilno, and so on.

CZARNECKA   The next problem comes in the following section, when a wagon driver suddenly appears, bringing frock
coats and snuffboxes to a museum.

MILOSZ   That driver is me. Clearly, this is a scene from Warsaw during the war. There was a sense then that all cultural
values were undergoing tremendous destruction, the total end
of everything. We carted books from the University Library
to the National Library, and from the National Library to
the Krasiński Library. An echo of those memories has been
transposed here. And that brings us to the question of com-
position. This fragment is linked with another part of *The
Separate Notebooks*, which describes a trip to the museum in
Maryhill, Washington. I even wrote the two pieces together.
When I was publishing them in *Kultura*, I pulled out various
slips from my hat, made a selection, and sent them in. Maryhill is the museum of Queen Mary of Rumania. It's right at
the Oregon border, on the other side of the Columbia River.
A dreary landscape, gray.

CZARNECKA   In the next poem you describe a woman. Her
image "rises into light." The luminosity and transparence of
bodies is a frequent motif in your work. Even back in *Three
Winters* you said that the most beautiful bodies are transparent.

MILOSZ   Yes, but it seems to me that the motif of light is
different here. Everything changes into light and in that way
is saved. This is a hypothesis used by the cabalists and Oskar
Milosz to answer the question of how the resurrection of the
body is possible. If the entire world is a transmutation of divine, nonphysical light, then, maybe when everything changes
from physical to divine light, everything can be re-created in
full detail. I'll give you a rather remote analogy. The atom
was once believed to be the smallest unit. If everything were
smashed back to atoms, then those same atoms could take
the same form again; a *restitutio* would occur.

CZARNECKA   Light plays various roles in your poetry, and it couldn't have been by chance that you named one volume of your poetry *The Light of Day*.

MILOSZ   Light plays an entirely different role here—there are no images of light as rays, fires, images connected with dreams I had about death. That's the reason the light is cruel in *Three Winters*. The light of day is the same as *la clarté du jour*. I do use the same word, but here light has none of its other symbolic connotations.

CZARNECKA   In the next part of *The Separate Notebooks* you write about a prison train. Is this the same train that appears in "The Spirit of the Laws"? There you spoke of the "sad engineers of prison trains."

MILOSZ   Yes, the train is really quite specific here, but at the same time it's very much a metaphor of the entire situation. I've already spoken about the armored trains that were typical of the end of the First World War. But prison trains are deeply connected with the traumas of World War II. After all, Lwów, Wilno, and the so-called Borderlands were an area of terrible deportations in 1939, 1940. Those prison trains play an enormous traumatic role in people's memories. There's a huge literature on the camps.

CZARNECKA   Trains appear in both your *Separate Notebooks*. In the second part you say, "What am I to do with the conductor of the Trans-Siberian railway . . ."

MILOSZ   It's probably because I was fascinated with technology as a child. But that's an interesting observation: I hadn't even realized the role trains played in my life—it's enormous!

CZARNECKA   In the final prose section of *The Separate Notebooks* you speak of traveling on a passenger train and catching sight of a blood-red star through the window. Are you reproducing an actual experience here?

MILOSZ   Of course. This is the Grodno-Suwałki night train. What's described here is the moment when a person wakes up in his compartment; the forests are receding—the Augustów Forests—and he sees a dark-blue sky pierced by the radiance of one star. There was a bright-red star in the sky in 1939, right before the outbreak of the war. It must have been Mars.

CZARNECKA   I'll ask you a question about craft: why is the poem that ends *The Separate Notebooks* in rhyme, when all the others are in blank verse?

MILOSZ   I don't know why I sometimes write in rhyme; it's a difficult question for me to answer. That was just the way the impulse came. What I don't like about using rhymes is that, once you've started, you have to keep rhyming. The first lines are given, and then you have to keep writing; there's no choice. Like it or not, you have to sit down and finish it.

CZARNECKA   The poem "Page 10" is a description of the mouth of the Sacramento River in California. "Gray winter on the waters and the sky"—is that also a California landscape?

MILOSZ   Yes, it's here, the Bay Area, the Bay in winter. There are gray stretches like that in the winter—and in the summer, too, for that matter: lead-colored water, black ships. The view is from somewhere around Richmond.

CZARNECKA   The prose fragment "Page 12" begins: "He found on dusty shelves the pages of a family chronicle with barely legible writing, and again he visits the murky house on the Dwina where he had been once in his childhood, called The Castle." Which chronicle are you speaking of?

MILOSZ   A few years ago I received some material from an émigré who was living in England, in Birmingham. He had written down what he remembered from the time of his youth and thought it would be of interest to me. He was an old man by the name of Guze, who had been a landowner in the Druja region. Mr. Guze had been the neighbor of Miloszes there and had fallen in love with a young Milosz woman who lost her life as a nurse in World War I; I think she was killed by the Bolsheviks. He sent that material on to me out of reverence for the family, whose last name was the same as mine. There are echoes of that chronicle in *The Separate Notebooks*.

Mr. Guze wrote good Polish. His chronicle concerns the late nineteenth and early twentieth centuries. Among his stories is one about two Milosz brothers whose parents sent them to study with the Jesuits in Metz. All this is about the family in Druja. I have no idea how the Miloszes there acquired such enormous lands. Józef Milosz emigrated to Bielorussia at the turn of the nineteenth century and became an administrator for the princes Sapieha. I was never able to check Mr. Guze's story of how Józef Milosz came to have such large holdings. In any case, he and another nobleman, by the name of Nitosławski, managed the Sapiehas' estates. According to Mr. Guze—and his version may be too romantic—Prince Sapieha would not recognize the Partitions, and so the Russian government ordered him to leave. He was given an ultimatum: either recognize the government or sell his lands and leave Bielorussia. The lands had to be sold by a certain date. In the end, two estates were left unsold—Druja and Czereja. Then, Mr. Guze maintains, Sapieha summoned his administrators and said that he was selling those two estates to them. And they said, "But how? We don't have that kind of money." Sapieha said, "Doesn't matter." He called his secretary and said, "Go to the strongbox and bring me some money." He put a pile of money on the table and said, "Pay me with this money. Otherwise the tsarist government will seize the estates."

CZARNECKA   Did you ever go to The Castle?

MILOSZ   I was there once, as a very small child. At the beginning of the war, maybe 1915. Anyway, they were my relatives, but I never went there again. I knew various things about them, but only from stories. We weren't on good terms with that family.

CZARNECKA So the quotes in "Page 12" come from Mr. Guze's chronicle?

MILOSZ Yes.

CZARNECKA Though the prose fragment entitled "Page 17" is about Schopenhauer, it could also have served as a commentary to *The Issa Valley*:

No one had ever so forcefully opposed the child and the genius to the rest of them, always under the power of blind will, of which the essence is sexual desire: no one has ever so forcefully explained the genius of children: they are onlookers, avid, gluttonous, minds not yet caught by the will of the species, though, I would add, led too by Eros, but an Eros who is still free and dances, knowing nothing of goals and service.

MILOSZ That may be a free interpretation of Schopenhauer, but where's the harm in that?

CZARNECKA "And the gift of the artist or philosopher likewise has its secret in a hidden hostility toward the earth of the adults"—this is an observation that could also apply to *The Issa Valley*. Thomas can't bear the world of adults.

MILOSZ I'm still speaking of Schopenhauer here, but, granted, I am identifying very strongly with him. I even quote him, and the poem "Page 18" is actually an illustration of that quote.

CZARNECKA In the poem "Page 20" I underlined the words "an old dream of a volcanic desert comes true." What does this refer to?

MILOSZ In "Album of Dreams" there's a poem that says:

Our expedition rode into a land of dry lava.
Perhaps under us were armor and crowns
but here there was not a tree,
or even lichens growing on the rocks. . . .

suddenly we saw, standing on a hill,
a pink corset with ribbon floating.

I wrote this description of a dream in 1959. When I visited
Maryhill in 1970, it was total *déjà vu*. I was even a little
ashamed to write this, because it looked as though I was
stealing from myself.

CZARNECKA "Page 25" is a very bitter monologue by a
woman. Is she demanding retribution? She doesn't believe in
the healing power of words, does she?

MILOSZ "You talked, but after your talking all the rest remains"—skepticism about all literary achievement. "After your
talking—poets, philosophers, contrivers of romances . . ."
It's all talk.

Everything else, all the rest deduced inside the flesh
Which lives and knows, not just what is permitted.

The truth of the flesh is located entirely outside the realm of
language, and that also applies to today's language of confession and obscenity. "Birds you killed, fish you tossed into
your boat"—animals have no words; salvation through words
is an illusion. Like the animals, man dies. Really, why should
the animals be excluded from the universal course of things
and only man live after death? This is a philosophical statement, and extremely bitter.

You received gifts from me; they were accepted.
But you don't understand how to think about the dead.

It's very difficult for people to think about the dead. This is a
voice calling someone to order, someone who wants to hit
too high a spiritual note. If we use philosophical terms here,
the woman speaking is an absolute materialist. She's in limbo,

and though she may have been called on to recognize someone, she's not doing that when she speaks. In essence, this
woman deeply identifies with all the dying that occurs in nature and she rejects words—more than that, she rejects culture, civilization. This may not involve an outright rejection
of religion, but it is an ironic, sarcastic rejection of everything
that distinguishes man from nature. If someone were searching for the connection between women and nature in my work,
he would find it very clearly expressed in this poem. Words,
all those constructs—that's the world of men. But women
regard all that with a gentle irony. Their attitude is: Talk all
you want.

CZARNECKA   Does the next section of *The Separate Notebooks*, a prose fragment, illustrate the world of women, their
knowledge of the dark powers?

MILOSZ   Of course.

CZARNECKA   "In reality there is only a sensation of warmth
and glueyness inside, also a sober watchfulness when one ad-
vances to meet that delicious and dangerous thing that has
no name, though people call it *life*."

MILOSZ   Yes, but this is a clearly defined period: La Belle
Époque, before 1914. Women weren't affecting intellectual
airs very much then; it was just beginning then. In this fragment I describe them discovering their own domain. Even the
women who used to frequent the famous Green Balloon literary cabaret in Cracow and put on artistic airs still knew
what was what.

CZARNECKA   While we're on the subject of "Page 27," you
said at one point that this was a description of one of your
earliest experiences—traveling on the Trans-Siberian Railroad. Then the scene of a solar eclipse in the summer of 1914,
in Kovno Gubernia. Who is the woman to whom a "traveler
offered a ring from Mongolia"?

MILOSZ   That's my mother. The man who offered her the ring was an archeologist we'd met on the train. This is not something I remember, and you mustn't think I'm describing my own memories of the Trans-Siberian Railroad here. In any case, that was my first train trip.

CZARNECKA   You end this section with a rhymed poem, as you do in "The Wormwood Star." Here there is a delight in the beauty of the world and a simultaneous sense of its menacing cruelty: "In the hall of pain, what abundance on the table." But I'm not very clear on the "space-age men" who "in thickets, lift bows to fiddles."

MILOSZ   I don't know if this is a good poem. I'm not sure. "Space-age men"—because we live in the space age. "The music endures but not the music-makers." That's the music of the eighteenth century. As my friend Kroński used to say, "What music? A few Germans got together and went *boom, boom.*" This is an allusion to those Germans in their frock coats, velvets, and garters. But the "space-age men" in the "thickets" are an odd combination. And they're "in their villages." Those villages are the great cities of today, interplanetary villages, and in those villages they "drink . . . squabble, let dice rattle." Here we're already in the age of the interplanetary empire.

Part Three

Philosophical Preferences

FIUT Your work prompts a comparison between you and Gombrowicz. Like him, you created yourself as a personality and an artist entirely on your own and in defiance of the prevailing fashions. He, however, formed himself out of what was inferior, low, and shameful; he sought forms that were sclerotic, stunted, compromised, to achieve his independence by parodying them. You, on the other hand, create your self-image from what is venerable, tested by tradition, and part of high culture. Iwaszkiewicz, Eliot, Auden, and Blake are parallel artists, and the ode, the treatise, the longer poem are your genres. Why? What do you see as the basis of that difference?

MILOSZ If it hadn't been for our similar fates—emigration, late fame—no one would have even thought to compare Gombrowicz and me. If the comparison is to be made, the key lies in our different attitudes to our backgrounds—our family home, parents, relatives, and so on.

FIUT I will remind you of an opinion you once expressed about Gombrowicz—that if Gombrowicz looked at an apple, he'd be interested in its form, whereas your interest would be in its essence, its appleness. Could you amplify that distinction?

285

MILOSZ   We're heading toward a great philosophical discussion here. Gombrowicz would immediately steer a conversation in a philosophical direction; he was always asking, "Do you think the world is real, that it really exists?" The problem of the reality of the world truly absorbed Gombrowicz: does the world exist out there or does it exist only in your head?

FIUT   That's the problem in *Cosmos*.

MILOSZ   In any case, Gombrowicz studied both Descartes and Kant. He thought that Descartes had become frightened, whereas Kant had made a new beginning, and so forth. But for Gombrowicz the world always existed in the mind. We cannot judge whether the world exists or not. In other words, his stand was actually very skeptical. I don't know why, but instinctively I always sided with extreme realism. Even the realism of Saint Thomas Aquinas. Horseness exists and so does the horse, as a particularization of horseness. I'm not being entirely serious here. We shouldn't launch into a major philosophical discussion. I'd prefer just to state my preferences. I actually prefer to oppose the nominalists and to believe that horseness exists and the horse is its particularization.

FIUT   What are your philosophical preferences?

MILOSZ   You could say that I've read the whole debate on the reality of the world. That debate began quite early and in some ways determined the direction of modern philosophy. But I frankly admit that I don't find the epistemological side of the question very enticing. I acknowledge the importance of all that, but those are mountains of wisdom that I prefer not to climb. Since, as you know, I've always said that I'm not a philosopher, I'd prefer not to take a position in that quarrel. I think that my orientation is akin to that of the Russian philosophers, I'm very sad to say.

FIUT   Why?

MILOSZ   Because I'm no Russophile. Quite the reverse. I'm very skeptical about all Russian thought. When we speak about beauty, I have the horrible suspicion that I might have something in common with that God-awful Vissarion Belinsky, who thought beauty and truth were one and the same.

FIUT   That's an old Greek tradition, that beauty and truth are one, isn't it?

MILOSZ   It is. But, as we know, the Russians applied it to what's called "realism," even interpreting poor Gogol as a realist. They took him completely differently from the way he wished to be taken. They turned a man who was utterly possessed into a noble social satirist.

Names? Pascal, Shestov, Simone Weil. I love reading writers like them. I love to read theology. But . . . I'm horrified by contemporary Catholic theologians. They write nonsense. They water down things that should not be watered down. The last work of theology that gave me any surprises was a book by Gaston Fessard. What was the name of it? I don't remember. But it's an interpretation of history, the history of Western civilization as a dialectic between Jew and pagan. I'm interested in such theologians as, say, Sergei Bulgakov. He was one of the great figures in the religious renaissance that took place in Russia right before the revolution. He did most of his writing as an émigré in Paris. He was a lecturer at the Russian Orthodox Theological Academy. I've also mentioned people like Louis Lavelle.

FIUT   Solovyov?

MILOSZ   No, I'm very suspicious of Solovyov, as far as his philosophy is concerned. But my book *The Emperor of the Earth* begins with an essay on Solovyov. The essay's on Solovyov's last book, *Three Conversations*, which contains something of a prophecy about the twentieth or twenty-first century. The prophecy, supposedly written by a monk, is read to a group of people involved in a discussion. This is a some-

what different Solovyov, one who departs from his usual op-
timistic view. Here he takes a rather pessimistic stance. It's
actually a polemic, primarily with Tolstoy and Tolstoyanism.
A polemic with the belief in unlimited progress, the lack of
any metaphysical basis, which was very widespread in Russia. But that's all there in my essay.

FIUT   Existentialism is alien to you, isn't it? You even ridi-
culed existentialism, or the popularized version of it, in *Treatise on Poetry*.

MILOSZ   Well, I don't know. If it's a question of writers,
existentialist authors, then Shestov is considered akin to
Kierkegaard. Incidentally, it's quite interesting that Kierkegaard was known in Poland before Russia. A collection
called *The Symposium* published in Lwów in 1907 contained Stanisław Lack's translation of *A Seducer's Diary*.
This is just a digression, but it's interesting that he was known
in Poland at the beginning of the twentieth century. Yet he
was completely unknown in Russia, so Shestov, who spent
his formative years in Russia, hadn't ever heard of him then
and only learned of his predecessor much later on.

Other names? I've read a little Jaspers, if he can be called
an existentialist. But that was all after the war. Sartre. Well,
Sartre, that's another story altogether. I dislike Sartre in-
tensely. Though, when lecturing on Dostoevsky, I did use his
analysis, what might be called existential psychoanalysis, unless there's some other name for that nonsense. But that's the
title of one section of Sartre's *Being and Nothingness*. An
analysis of love, an analysis of relationships—say, the role
played by a waiter—and so forth. In one way it's very similar
to Dostoevsky or to Bakhtin, who of course preceded Sartre
by a few decades.

But here we're mixing various times and various periods in
my life, not a very honest thing to do. You asked me about
the existentialists and I'm mentioning the names that come to
mind. Camus is not even thought of as an existentialist. In
any event, he didn't want to be. But *The Myth of Sisyphus*

was in fact basic to the rise of the existentialist movement in France. Still, I'll say it again, let's just not create any myths here. In other words, you're making a philosopher of me again.

FIUT   But your philosophical erudition is immense and it's reflected in your poetry. One can't just walk away from that. That's a problem we've already discussed, the link between poetry and philosophy. Naturally, you formulate certain problems instinctively, spurred by your own experience, but at the same time they're consistent with your literary and philosophical preferences. There's no question of that, is there?

MILOSZ   No, there isn't. For example, if you're writing a poem and you're aware of the quarrel about universals, then the poem itself takes a different form.

FIUT   In the poem "Magpiety," which is typical of this, you say:

> Who would have guessed that, centuries later,
> I would invent the question of universals?

It's as if poetic experience were the way back to philosophical experience. Through your own experience you rediscover problems that had been formulated in philosophical terms earlier.

MILOSZ   It's more or less what Simone Weil said somewhere, that it's one thing to understand an idea and another thing to experience it with your whole being. That's the difference between what we read in school and what we read much later on. When we're very young, we can understand some things, but to digest them, if they're to penetrate into our core, well, for that certain experience is required. That's why so many things go right past us and so very little takes root.

Simone Weil

CZARNECKA   In the lecture you delivered at the Swedish Academy in December 1980, you mentioned the names of two of your masters—Oskar Milosz and Simone Weil. When did you first encounter the writings of Simone Weil?

MILOSZ   In the early fifties. I guess it was 1952. My friend Józef Czapski told me to read her. Do you have some idea of Simone Weil's story? All she left after her death in 1943 was notes and notebooks. She published practically nothing in her lifetime, just some articles.

CZARNECKA   She didn't want to publish?

MILOSZ   I don't know. She probably didn't have the time. First she was involved with the workers. If she published anything, it was in little trade-union periodicals. Political sociology was her main interest. She wanted to take part in the Spanish Civil War. She was extremely brave and resourceful but terribly impractical and nearsighted. She set out for the front in a detachment of anarchists. She wanted to be useful, to cook in a field kitchen, but she accidentally stepped into a cauldron of hot soup. That was the end of her war adventures. What she wrote in those notebooks was primarily for

290

herself. The first book of hers to appear was *La Pesanteur et la grâce—Gravity and Grace*. It was a collection of her aphorisms selected by Gustave Thibon, sort of an anthology. That was the book Czapski put me on to. Her other writings began gradually appearing in print.

CZARNECKA   Can you recollect your reaction to that book?

MILOSZ   Not very well. I wouldn't be able to recollect it with any precision. But as soon as I had finished reading Simone Weil's first book, I could see that is was very important. The idea of translating her into Polish came to me after I'd read her other books. I worked on Simone Weil between 1952 and 1958, when I published my translation of her, entitled *Writings*.

CZARNECKA   I noticed some of Simone Weil's ideas in *The Issa Valley*.

MILOSZ   That's very possible.

CZARNECKA   One of her aphorisms is quite similar to Thomas's reflections on evil—that perhaps every evil is a hidden good.

MILOSZ   That may be, but it doesn't necessarily indicate her influence. What influenced me greatly wasn't so much French literature as theological literature in French, Catholic philosophy. That was important. And so my knowledge of French came in very handy.

CZARNECKA   Did you visit the house in Paris where Simone Weil had lived?

MILOSZ   Actually, I was on social terms with her mother. That was in the fifties. I'd sometimes go have tea with her. She showed me the room where Simone Weil lived when she was a student.

CZARNECKA   Can some of your work be interpreted in terms of Simone Weil's influence? We've already spoken about the line from the poem "From the Rising of the Sun": "Life was impossible, but it was endured." That's almost a quote from Weil.

MILOSZ   Of course there are affinities—I don't deny it at all. She was a major influence on me. And not just on me; on Albert Camus, too, for example. Simone Weil's mother told me that one day the doorbell rang, and when she opened the door, there was Camus, with his collar turned up. This was after Simone Weil had died, and he had already won the Nobel Prize. He told her that he had to go to Simone's room to do some thinking. He went in and sat at her desk. Simone and Camus had never known each other, of course. But Simone Weil's mother knew Camus personally, because he had consulted with her about the publishing of her daughter's works.

CZARNECKA   Simone Weil's works and your book *The Land of Ulro* frame the question of atheism in a similar manner. Simone Weil had respect for atheists.

MILOSZ   It's very possible that there are certain correspondences, even though this comes out of my own experience. I knew atheists who were very noble and pure.

CZARNECKA   In one of your poems you say, "And only in denial was my house holy." And in Simone Weil it's: "He who denies the existence of God may be the closest to God."

MILOSZ   You shouldn't focus so narrowly on Simone Weil, because she represents a certain broader current. She was not the only one to express that tendency. She was pervaded by it, of course, and that's why it's formulated so sharply in her work.

CZARNECKA   Here's an aphorism of hers: "Necessity is God's camouflage." How do you understand that?

MILOSZ In her view, God had subjected all of creation to Nature's blind determinism and to mathematical law. The universe is ruled by necessity. Simone Weil's determinism was quite extreme, and she was close to being a follower of Spinoza. Her determinism may have been as extreme as that of the geneticist Jacques Monod, who was a very radical materialist, a complete determinist. Monod devoted himself to the study of genes. He received the Nobel Prize for his work on DNA, and he thought all chromosomes stamp out copies like a printing press. Simone Weil, too, always spoke of determinism and absolute necessity. A world bound by necessity and chains of causes has no room for God. God seems to have withdrawn. He has hidden, and that is why necessity exists. Simone Weil even went so far as to say that God had given over power to the prince of this world and that's the reason determinism is, from a human point of view, cruel and merciless. This is what is meant by Second Nature. Perhaps original sin is just the placing of God in the chain of causality. Simone Weil thought nature's determinism was innocent. Nature is neither good nor evil—it is only necessity. Animals do not know sin; they have no sense of guilt or cruelty. Everything operates like a mechanism. We human beings are in the worst situation, because we are part animal and part spirit. Above us, there are beings who are pure spirit. They no longer carry this burden. And so determinism is God's screen. And why does the prince of this world rule over determinism? Well, on the human level, he is the one who instigates all suffering. He draws his power from blind determinism. One could ask what significance God's protection, providence, and grace have in Simone Weil's system. They do have a place, except that she amplifies the contradiction that exists in the very structure of the world and says that blind necessity and providence are not mutually exclusive, even though they contradict each other.

Of course I don't deny the enormous influence Simone Weil had on me. The way she posed the key problem, that of necessity and determinism, is very close to my own. And I am indebted to her for an understanding of contradiction. As a rule, people struggle to unify their ideas, and reproach themselves for being inconsistent. But her definition of contradiction is very beautiful.

CZARNECKA   Are you referring to "Contradiction is to be felt in our very essence; it is a rent, a cross"?

MILOSZ   No, I was thinking of the aphorism where she says that one should use all one's power of intelligence to overcome contradiction. One shouldn't start feeling at home with it too quickly. One should strive to conquer it. But there comes a point when the mind has exhausted all its resources in the attempt to free itself from contradiction, when the mind reaches an extreme where two fundamental assumptions are at odds with each other. And there is no choice except to accept contradiction, but with the awareness that there is a contradiction between blind determinism and free will, between gravity and grace. But how exactly does grace intervene if everything is subject to determinism? That's a very important point.

CZARNECKA   But do you accept her idea of beauty, which is very Platonic?

MILOSZ   Simone Weil's conception of beauty is very important. For her, creation was marked by blind, merciless determinism, but it was also inexpressibly beautiful. The beauty of creation was basic to her, and I take no exception with that—it's just that there are many things I don't understand here. In general, one should not approach Simone Weil like a disciple and accept everything she said without offering it any resistance. There are points of kinship between her and Lev Shestov, but radical differences as well. Simone Weil is completely Greek, and sometimes she is inhuman in a way. I find her extremely Manichean.

CZARNECKA   There is an aphorism of hers that I jotted down in connection with your own eschatological vision: "On

Judgment Day, when creation is laid bare by the light of God which reveals it utterly, it becomes pure light; there is no more evil." This is also a Manichean concept. The devil and the damned suffer for an infinite time, but the coming of eternity puts an end to time.

MILOSZ   That's right: by then it has reached apokatastasis. Origen thought that at the end of the world even the devil would be saved.

The Fall

CZARNECKA   When awarding you the Nobel Prize, the Swedish Academy said that mankind's expulsion from paradise is central to your work.

MILOSZ   Yes, for me the Fall and original sin are the key mysteries. And I think I've always written too little about them. To study and analyze original sin is extraordinary, absorbing. In the Book of Genesis, Adam and Eve make themselves clothing from animal skin. They have lost their innocence. God asks them, "And who told you you were naked?" This is what it means to exist in the eyes of another person. The problem of nakedness did not exist before. Now Adam is conscious that he is not Eve, and Eve is conscious that she is not Adam. Eyes that look and see. There's no question here of any primitive interpretation of this as a punishment for sex. In Milton's *Paradise Lost*, Adam and Eve live together as man and wife before the Fall. What matters here is the consciousness, the realization of duality.

CZARNECKA   In *The Garden of Knowledge*, you compare the way Blake, Milton, and Swedenborg conceive the Fall.

MILOSZ   Yes, but to a great extent the difficulty in writing about people like Swedenborg and Blake is that we always

forget the general mentality of the eighteenth century, in which
they lived. And that was a very rationalistic mentality. If we
look at the philosophy of the Founding Fathers—Jefferson,
for example, had no place for sin or the Fall. Essentially, that
was a very un-Christian and completely deistic approach: man
and the harmony of nature. And Swedenborg is also very much
of the eighteenth century. There is no original sin corrupting
human nature in his work. Swedenborg interprets original sin
symbolically, as the fall of the First Church. For Blake, the
Fall is cosmic in nature and took place before creation. Exactly the same thing is found in certain Jewish cabalists—
Isaac Luria, for example. God's attributes were so strong, the
radiance so strong, that certain channels burst, and then came
the disaster that caused the creation of the world. The problem is that in Blake it's not clear how to connect the cosmic
fall with the essential disruption in the unity of the four elements that make up man. I don't understand that, and I don't
think many people do. Blake looks at man as he is and sees
that those elements have been sundered, and so, since he was
a Gnostic, he connects this with the act of creation. But at the
same time Nobodaddy, the God who created the world, is a
demiurge. It's very unclear. With Blake, psychological analysis and cosmology somehow run together. But they're connected in a way that is symbolic, not strictly discursive.

CZARNECKA   How does contemporary theology interpret the
Fall?

MILOSZ   I'll read you the author's introduction to *Vocabulaire de théologie biblique*, which I translated into Polish. The
author is Xavier-Léon Dufour:

> In the Book of Genesis, Adam's sin appears essentially one
> of disobedience, an act in which man consciously and pur-
> posely opposes God by breaking one of his laws. Further,
> the Scripture uses that outward act of rebellion to make
> clear reference to the inner act from which the outer act
> arose. Adam and Eve were disobedient because, yielding to

the serpent's temptation, they wanted to be "like gods who know good and evil." In other words, according to the most widely accepted interpretation, they think that they are the sole masters of their fate and can do as they see fit. They struggle against their dependency on that which created them, thereby perverting the connection between man and God. According to the the Book of Genesis, chapter two, that connection was not only one of dependence but one of friendship as well. The God of the Bible did not refuse anything to man, who was created in His image and likeness. He did not reserve anything for Himself, not even life, unlike the gods of the old myths. But at the serpent's promptings, Eve and then Adam begin to doubt that infinitely gracious God. The law given for the use of man then becomes a subterfuge used by God to maintain His own privileges, and it is simply a lie that there is a penalty for breaking that law: "No, you will not die."

This is pivotal, very important. How is one to view the fact that, to use today's terminology, the survival of the fittest, the battle of all against all, is a basic law of the world, and is to be applied to God? That is, here we come up against the distinction made by mystics, cabalists, and others, between a First Nature and a Second Nature. First Nature is when man is in paradise; Second Nature is what comes after the Fall. The law of struggle did not apply in First Nature. Second Nature is a world based on the principle of struggle and the so-called iron law, where the struggle for existence is sanctioned. That did not exist in First Nature. But all that was needed was to suspect that God was acting like a monarch and retaining privileges for himself.

But God knows that on the day you taste of that fruit, you will be like the gods who know good and evil. Man does not trust God, who has become his rival. The very concept of God has been distorted. A God who is completely disinterested because He is completely perfect, who has everything and can only give, is replaced by a mean and indifferent being solely concerned with protecting Himself against His own creation. Sin had deranged man's mind before it caused him to sin, and since it overtakes him in his very relationship with God, of whom man is the image, it is difficult to imagine any more thoroughgoing corruption or to be surprised that it entailed such far-reaching consequences.

There is only one mysterious passage, of which Dufour does not speak here—that in the Garden of Eden there were the tree of the knowledge of good and evil and the tree of life. Biblical scholars disagree as to whether this is one tree or two different trees. At one point God says: I must be careful now because they are reaching for the tree of life and want to be as immortal as we are. There's an enormous symbology about the tree of life. In some illuminated medieval manuscripts the apple even appears marked "Mundus," "World." There is also a direct connection between the tree of life and the cabalists' tree, the tree of *sefirot*—that is, of God's attributes.

CZARNECKA   Each branch symbolizing one of God's attributes . . .

MILOSZ   Yes, and those branches are arranged like a tree's. God's attributes of splendor and wrath are grouped on one side, with grace, kindness, and love on the other. In other words, the tree itself could be the tree of God's wrath and the tree of His grace. All right, but how do you interpret what God says, that now they're reaching for the tree of life and they want to be immortal as we are? The interpretations vary greatly. Some people even think that this is ironic, but that seems highly unlikely. In any case, according to the interpretation in the *Vocabulaire de théologie biblique*, God gave Adam and Eve everything in the Garden of Eden, including eternal life. They had no need to reach for the tree of life. But they lost eternal life as soon as they reached for the tree of the knowledge of good and evil—they were no longer immortal. So maybe it was then that they reached for the tree of life.

How this should be interpreted symbolically, well, that's a very interesting question. Suffice it to say that Lev Shestov thought it impossible that the most profound philosophical allegory of all time, the allegory of the Garden of Eden, was, as we're led to believe, composed by illiterate shepherds. Philosophers have been racking their brains over it for centuries, after all. I'll read you some more about the consequences of original sin from that same work:

> Everything had changed between man and God. Even before they were punished in the true sense of the word, Adam and Eve, who had once communicated with God, now hid in the trees from God, Yahweh. The initiative came from man; he did not want God any more and flees Him. The expulsion from the Garden is a confirmation of man's will. Then, however, man understands that the threat was not a false one. He who is distant from God has no access to the tree of life. Now there is only a final death, breaking the link between man and God.
>
> Original sin also breaks the link among the members of the human community, even in Eden, beginning with the first two. Scarcely has the sin been committed when Adam breaks faith and accuses Eve, whom God gave him as a helpmate, "bone of his bone, flesh of his flesh." The punishment sanctions that break. "Your lust will incline you to your husband and he will have dominion over you." Later that break extends to Adam's children. And hence, the murder of Abel, rule by violence, and the law of the stronger, which is exulted in Lamech's strange song in the fourth chapter of the Book of Genesis.
>
> That is not all. The mystery of sin exceeds the limits of the human world. A third person comes between God and man, a person of whom the Old Testament says absolutely nothing, no doubt to avoid making a second God of him, but one whom the Book of Wisdom calls the devil or Satan, and who appears again in the New Testament.

Satan plays a secondary role in the Book of Job.

CZARNECKA   Still, doesn't he challenge God to something of a duel?

MILOSZ   Yes, but he's only a functionary.

"Reality"

CZARNECKA   You raised the issue of art as mimesis in the essay "Reality," which is part of *The Garden of Knowledge.* You returned to that subject in a lecture, "On Ignorance, Learned and Literary," which you delivered in Berkeley. Is this the classical idea of art as the imitation of reality?

MILOSZ   It's a very old idea, of course. However, my concern was not to trace its lineage in the history of aesthetics. Those conflicts go beyond formulations. The formulations codify fundamentally divergent attitudes toward reality. Cézanne was fascinated by nature, the visual world. All his life he tried to paint from models, from nature. At times, that sort of fidelity has a strange way of almost leading to abstract art; it gradually evolves in that direction. Today, there are contradictory tendencies. One is the penchant for form, *écriture*, writing that feeds on itself. This tendency, which is very strong today, moves away from nature; it is antimimesis. There is another and opposite trend: the attempt to describe reality, to depict reality. There are few artists exploring this second path, because reality is so very elusive.

CZARNECKA   And do you represent the latter stance?

MILOSZ   Yes, since art is a minor affair compared with the complexity and richness of the visible world.

CZARNECKA   You declare yourself on the side of describing reality, yet literature that makes reference to the author's literary predecessors and quotes from them is also literature feeding on itself. That would seem to demonstrate antimimetic tendencies. And yet you pursue them.

MILOSZ   Yes, I do, but what matters to me is something I will probably never achieve as a poet because of my advanced age—certain goals cannot be achieved after you are past a certain age. Quotes and references to one's predecessors must not be used as an incrustation of literary jewels. These are references to the historical dimension, which is an essential component of reality. And when I use stylization in my poem "Conversations on Easter 1620," it is, of course, to flesh out that dimension. I present the metaphysical problem against the historical background, the conflict between Protestantism and Polish Post-Tridentine Catholicism. As soon as quotations are used in poetry, a certain continuity is created, an expanded sense of context. When I use quotations from the poetry of the sixteenth, seventeenth, or eighteenth century, I am communicating with the spirits of the poets who wrote those poems. I use style to show that I am continuing a certain literary language. This has various historical aspects. History is extremely real. It may not be to American poets, but for us it is very, very much a part of reality.

CZARNECKA   In your essay dedicated to the memory of Father Józef Sadzik, you said that you began translating the Bible out of despair with twentieth-century literature. Was translating the Bible into Polish by any chance an escape from the impossibility of catching reality in words?

MILOSZ   Of course it was. There's the simple realization that, no matter how hard I try, I cannot get my hands on the world, which keeps eluding my grasp. That's one aspect, and another is, as I said in the introduction to my translation of the Book of Job, that when a person with a certain consciousness lives in America among people who do not share that consciousness, he tends to read the more useful books. As you know, I did not try to adapt in the sense of changing my colors or attempting to impose another consciousness on myself by changing my language. I always have a sense of being at cross-purposes with my American readers, who do not quite get the point. That's how it seems to me. Lastly, you shouldn't forget that in *Bells of Winter*, "Lauda," a part of the poem "From the Rising of the Sun," has been left out because it was untranslatable. In others words, I exist for the American reader in an oddly abridged form; I am someone else to them. Here is a book, an anthology called *The Poets' Work: 29 Masters of XXth Century Poetry on Their Origin and on the Practice of Their Art*. And the entire collection opens with my poem "Ars Poetica?" I find that very surprising. That poem is an example of inspiration. I wrote it in a span of twenty minutes, without having had the slightest intention of writing a poem.

CZARNECKA   At some point you wrote that you felt satisfied with a few of your poems. Would you like to say . . .

MILOSZ   . . . which ones?

CZARNECKA   Well, let's say Publisher X is doing an anthology and asks you to give him the five poems you think most important.

MILOSZ   It depends on who the publisher is.

CZARNECKA   Let's say it's a Polish publisher.

MILOSZ   Well, then I'd have to look through my books. I like "The Song," which was published in *Three Winters*. Then I think there are some poems from *The Voices of Poor People* that I like. Oh, and "The World." I don't know what else, I don't remember.

CZARNECKA   It's odd that you mention very old poems.

MILOSZ   I'm also fond of "From the Rising of the Sun." I am not ashamed of that poem. And I also like "Bobo's Metamorphosis."

CZARNECKA   I'd like to go back to the *The Garden of Knowledge* and the question of reality. In the essay "On Authors" you compare contemporary writers to dogs chasing a mechanical rabbit. You have many grievances with them for lowering the level of literature.

MILOSZ   To be frank, that essay was not entirely fair. If we look at the writers of the past, a great deal of their work was a waste of ink and has to be written off as a loss. Gombrowicz was right in saying that literature is not a factory, not production. There are a few great writers, and that's it. Still, the host of writers practicing the profession have to do something. Yet they're unable to penetrate to the essential matters—that's beyond the poor devils. How many people can there be engaged in creating genuine literature? An enormous social evolution has taken place. Now, to be a poet, a writer, is a profession, it confers status. How many people who a couple of centuries back would have been in business or out hunting with their hounds are now involved in literature? I may be a little unfair, but what always counts for me is catching some of reality. And that's not easy.

Let's take contemporary Polish dissident poetry. It's drawn toward concrete social reality, but there's a dimension that eludes it. It becomes too civic-minded. And so there's the problem in achieving any reality. Perhaps it's so difficult because our heads are so crammed. We can't say: Everyone can see what a horse is. The development of psychology and sociology have made us aware of the infinite complexity of the world. And that's a very heavy burden to bear. Moreover, since we're speaking seriously, this is something of a Heideggerian problem: the question of the flight of Being. The gods have abandoned us, in the sense that all invocation of Being (Heidegger says that man, especially the poet, is the shepherd of Being) eludes us. Let's say there are deep and serious reasons behind the inability to create powerful forms.

CZARNECKA   If a literature student were to ask you how to remedy that situation, what would you advise him as an experienced poet? To read as much as he could? To observe life?

MILOSZ   Fortunately, I don't have to give advice. I don't know—no doubt there is a literature oriented to literature, meaning that everything takes place in purely literary terms.

CZARNECKA   A sort of cloning?

MILOSZ   Yes. It's difficult to free oneself of that entirely, but I do think the best results are achieved by those who relate directly to life, and not to the written word. But then another problem crops up. Let's take a specific example. Contemporary American poetry is full of descriptions of the most common everyday events. American poets aren't sure what to write about, so they describe whatever life hands them. They pack everything into poetry, in forms that have not been refined. They fail to understand that poetry is an act of enormous distillation. This sort of liberation from literature in the name of what is called life also leads nowhere. Moreover, I don't think it's good for a person not to be educated. It's better to be educated. A person knows many things, even though he may forget them. And when he is writing, that knowledge will be ingrained in there somewhere. For an educated person, certain lines of reasoning cannot be followed, because they are crude and hackneyed: they bypass all the knowledge mankind has accumulated in some area.

You plague me with the question of substantiality. What matters is the inexhaustible riches of the reality before our eyes. It's a bit the way a painter feels about the world when he is arranging colors in harmony on canvas. I doubt he does this with a clear conscience, because the world around him is one of such inexhaustible depth and complexity. He evokes that world. Arranging colors harmoniously on canvas is a paltry thing compared with what calls out to be explored. Incidentally, I recently translated an essay by a friend of mine, Jeanne Hersch, a professor of philosophy, an essay on the anemia of reality with an attempt at diagnosis. Except that her subject isn't art but science. Her thesis is that in the last few decades science has lost its sense of reality, its orientation to reality.

CZARNECKA   Is she saying that the scientific world is moving in the same direction as the literary, becoming locked in self-enclosed domains?

MILOSZ   Yes, there's been an incredible proliferation of fields that are self-enclosed circles. Our basic curiosity about the world, which calls out to be studied and understood, is disappearing. In the humanities, structuralism is, of course, one instance of that complete self-enclosure around issues concerning the means of expression. And so there's no longer any question of saying, Fine, but what does the text have to do with reality? The entire question loses its meaning, because there is no reality. Reality disintegrates into the means of expression. Even the idea of truth, or untruth, disappears. All means of depicting reality are equally valid. The means themselves become the subject of study. But there's the basic and utterly simple question: What does that have to do with the cow over there in the meadow? There is no cow—only the word "cow," which enters into combinations with other words. But its relation to that animal with the horns and the hoofs, that we don't know.

Thinking in Poetry

FIUT You said that you were not a thinker but a poet. That distinction does not actually exist in your poetry, for you are a poet-thinker. You use poetry to think about reality: "thinking in poetry," as you put it. Is that close to a tradition you're quite willing to be identified with, the pre-Socratic tradition of philosophers of nature, who did not make that distinction?

MILOSZ That's right. It's just that we've managed to complicate things a little since those days.

FIUT I'm interested in your very approach to language, the fact that the language of poetry can express the problems of philosophy and that you constantly struggle to achieve this.

MILOSZ Yes, but it's not done purposefully, in the sense that I strive to be a poet-philosopher. I find it quite strange that now all of a sudden I'm a poet-philosopher. It's like suddenly feeling you're an alligator. You never wanted to be an alligator, and then suddenly one day you wake up and you're an alligator, or a famous, celebrated poet. Somehow I find all that very strange.

Yes, all right, we can say that my poetry is philosophical. But let's take a simpler look. A young man goes to the university and starts studying. There are mountains of wisdom

to be scaled—philosophy and epistemology, seminars and
proseminars. Philosophy is the first class of the morning, when
it's still dark in Wilno; the lights are on as the students stam-
mer out maxims without understanding one iota of what
they're saying. I studied law, but I also attended a proseminar
in philosophy and lectures on Polish literature. Then later I
took the history of the philosophy of law. I was very good in
that. I met my teacher, Mr. Sukiennicki, not long ago in California. He reminded me of the first-rate job I'd done in
the philosophy-of-law exam. He also mentioned some
eighteenth-century English philosophers that I had spoken
about. I told him: "I've never heard of them." So, you see,
there's that whole huge world of culture. Later on, during the
war, I attended Professor Tatarkiewicz's seminars. We had a
very small philosophy seminar: secret study groups had to be
small. I delivered lectures myself, but I had a great respect for
authority, Tatarkiewicz—that was genuine philosophy. And
I'm an amateur, you understand.

So, I don't know, maybe it's childish, a childish attitude.
I've done extensive reading in philosophy and so on. But the
poetry comes only from pain, only from personal experience.
Not because I wanted to create any philosophical theory. The
philosophy simply grew out of the pain. I can assure you that
recently, at the academic senate at Berkeley, when I heard an
encomium for me on my election as one of the two research
lecturers for the next academic year—a great honor—when
I heard that encomium delivered in the senate, heard that
professor praised, and presented as a thinker, the author of
deep works and so forth, I felt I had turned into an alligator.

FIUT   You are too modest.

MILOSZ   No, it's not a question of modesty. It's a question
of making a certain distinction. We can say that my philosophy is like the case of Molière's Monsieur Jourdain, who hadn't
known he was speaking in prose.

FIUT   But you were educated in philosophy.

MILOSZ   Fine, fine. I did write a book, *The Captive Mind*, that caused a stir and is considered something of a classic. The analysis there is of more than the problems of communism. To a large extent, it is a book of philosophy, but it was also written out of pain and conflict.

FIUT   Of course, but the two are not mutually exclusive. And it seems to me that, as far as your poetry is concerned, it has become increasingly philosophical. Poems appear that are directly bound to philosophical problems, such as "Esse" or "Magpiety."

MILOSZ   Those poems are direct allusions to philosophy.

FIUT   The same is true of "Heraclitus," for example. Your poem "Heraclitus" is your own poetic interpretation of his philosophy.

MILOSZ   My readings in philosophy may well find some expression, and be an influence. But if one believes that philosophy is the admission of one's ignorance, then, yes, of course, my poetry has become increasingly philosophical.

FIUT   The language one uses is a very important problem in philosophy. I mentioned the philosophers of nature and was also thinking a little of Heidegger's interpretation of them. I'm very curious to see if you agree with this juxtaposition. . . . I'm grappling with the entire question of methodology here. Specifically: to speak of what is philosophical in poetry means to reduce poetry only to those propositions that can be deduced from it, a process that is in no way simple or unambiguous. Poetry assumes ambiguity, and, of course, a philosophical statement or a philosophical problem can be interpreted according to several schools at the same time. That can enrich poetry's philosophical meaning. In your work, philosophical problems would seem to be purposefully formulated in such a way that various interpretations could be applied. I am especially struck by the persistent, recurring theme of being, existence. Existence as a riddle, as questions: What does "I am" mean? What decides that something is? Is that only the realm of language? decision? assumption?

MILOSZ   You mentioned Heidegger and his going back to the pre-Socratics. In a sense, that's connected with what I said about the mountains of wisdom, all the centuries of philosophy. All those centuries of philosophy, and a young man comes to the university with a great respect for it all but says to himself: "No, that's not it. That's beside the point. Why sit and pore over books? Those philosophers are so wise, I can't be as wise as they are. What do I need all those Humes and Kants for? It's all terribly complicated. That's not what I'm after." This could be a sort of instinctive return to the pre-Socratics. With no theoretical assumptions.

   And then all of a sudden it turns out that someone's been involved in a parallel enterprise—say Heidegger, whom I don't know because he has to be read in German. I read him in English, and it's terribly hard work, mind-bending. A parallel case of starting over from the beginning. We've already talked about Shestov. Why am I so taken with Shestov? Because, in true Russian fashion, he wants to remake the world from scratch. He says, "Three thousand years of Greek philosophy have come to naught; we have to start over from the beginning." In his work, that means going back to the Bible, the Book of Job. He's also extremely bold when it comes to using the whole tradition of philosophy. Like Simone Weil. But that's a different story. She was called a "Holy Terror," "*la vierge rouge.*" She could do everything, was well versed in everything. She, too, returned to the sources, but by then it was for different reasons.

Between Poetry and Prose

FIUT   What is your attitude toward the relationship of prose and poetry—that is, the language of prose and the language of poetry? For example, when I read "From the Rising of the Sun" I came across prose fragments that one could easily imagine in verse form. What is your sense of the difference?

MILOSZ   The intonation of prose is always different from the intonation of poetry.

FIUT   That's not entirely obvious, because *vers libre* or blank verse brought poetry so close to prose that the difference is purely a matter of notation.

MILOSZ   That's not my feeling.

FIUT   What's the key distinction for you?

MILOSZ   If, for example, you take the entire history of the prose poem . . . The prose poem came into being because a metrical and rhymed poetry already existed. The prose poem came into being to counter it. Had there been no metrical, rhymed poetry, there would have been no prose poem, whose very intonation made it clear that it was rejecting the French Alexandrine.

312

FIUT   Why not? What would the criterion be?

MILOSZ   The specialists have not formulated a criterion. The rhythmic structure would need to be analyzed. That issue emerged in connection with my translation of the Psalms, because, in my opinion, a Biblical verse is more than, let's say, the three or four lines grouped under the same number, the way the translations present them today, possibly influenced even there by modern poetry. In just the same way, of course, a prose poem is a specific intonational whole, different from a Biblical verse and from metrical poetry. I am speaking about the prose poem here partly in answer to your question about prose. I could be wrong, but I don't think that the prose sections of "From the Rising of the Sun" are divisible into "stacks of lines."

FIUT   I could give you an example. In my opinion, a fragment of the passage on Maximus the Confessor could be turned into verse. The question of how the text should be broken up is obviously a separate matter.

MILOSZ   One characteristic of prose is that it's always approaching Stendhal's ideal, which, as you know, was the Napoleonic Code: transparency, continuity from one sentence to the next. Good prose is transparent, and it also moves in a single incantational flow. Naturally, you can take a whole chapter of Flaubert—say, from *Madame Bovary*—and show how the incantation moves in what are supposedly the most realistic passages. I feel this as a definite difference of intonation. For me, the ideal prose has a certain Stendhalian dryness, consistency, transparency, but ultimately those are pseudonyms for intonation, aren't they?

FIUT   But poetry isn't only intonation. There's also a condensation of meaning that doesn't occur in prose.

MILOSZ   Yes, of course. I can give you an example that might amuse you or serve you as an argument one way or the other,

I don't know which. In the spring of 1935, Grasset published a new edition of Oskar Milosz's mystery play *Miguel Mañara*, and he gave me a copy. I opened the book and said: "What's this! Why is it printed as prose? Until now all the editions were in Biblical verses, free verse." And Oskar Milosz's answer was: "I was so irritated by constantly being compared to Claudel that I decided to have it printed without marking verse lines." Paul Fort, I think, did the same for some ballads. At the beginning of the twentieth century in France there was a trend, a movement, to print poetry like that, to erase the outline of verse, to print it as if it were prose while, internally, the work might have a very strong, pulsing rhythm, even rhyme. Astonishingly, Oskar Milosz used that technique when translating Mickiewicz. Take his translation of "The Lillies"—read it aloud. It seems to be a prose translation, pulsating with rhythm but allowing for greater freedom. Naturally, the entire text can easily be written out in lines and "stacked up." But since it's written in prose, the reader has greater freedom.

Let's say that the contrast between a visual perception and an extremely intrusive aural perception has some meaning here. The same is true for Oskar Milosz's *Contes et fabliaux de la vieille Lithuanie*. But it's another situation with his *Miguel Mañara*; the rhythmic pulsation there is different, which is clear in Bronisława Ostrowska's translation of it into Polish. She has the lines set distinctly apart, but when it's printed as prose the entire design simply becomes more discreet. You know, it's a little like the contrast between Polish and Russian poetry. For us, its very rhythmic structure makes Russian poetry insufficiently discreet.

FIUT   Apart from rhythmic structure, is there anything else, any other element of poetry, that determines your choice of form, whether rhymed or in prose?

MILOSZ   It's the simplest thing in the world. I think I am better when I express myself in poetry than when I express myself in prose. That's one thing. And another is that I do

not consider myself a thinker, a philosopher. Those are specialized fields. From time to time I write an essay, but I'm
quite skeptical about philosophizing.

FIUT   The relationship of prose and poetry would seem to
have two aspects: within the text and outside the text. . . .

MILOSZ   All right, but let's point out another aspect that may
be important—that I do not consider myself a novelist. I don't
work in that genre. I don't write novels or short stories, and
I have my reasons for not wanting to. My poems, or the short
prose fragments that are inserted into my poems or function
as commentary, take the place of novels for me.

FIUT   In "From the Rising of the Sun," everything becomes
poetry to some extent, even extracts from the encyclopedia.
So it wasn't form in the sense of how the text was notated or
broken up that made it poetry but, rather, the emotional and
intellectual content. . . .

MILOSZ   Now I'll ask you a question. Yesterday, while giving a reading of my poetry, I wondered how it came to be
that about thirty years ago, say, poetry without rhyme and
distinct meter would not have been accepted by the public,
as it is today. As my poetry was yesterday. There were customs.

FIUT   It seems to me a certain revolution has already taken
place, so that the positions are reversed: nowadays, if you
come across a poem in a traditional form, you take it as stylization.

MILOSZ   Yes, except that I'm asking you a question here. I
may be asking you the question or myself: how is it possible
to wrest verse from a weakly accented language like Polish?
If you listened carefully yesterday, you noticed that, when I'm
reading, I put a strong accent at the end of every line, right?
There is a certain rhythmic structure, which I won't ana-

lyze—after all, I don't count the accents on my finger when I write. To what extent is this possible in Polish, and how does it work? Russians I've spoken with don't sense this as poetry. For them it's strong accents that make poetry.

FIUT   That must derive from the special qualities of the language.

MILOSZ   What interests me is that Polish can have a poetry that uses unrhymed verse, and even a varying number of syllables, and, despite that, a given poem can have a powerful rhythmic structure.

FIUT   You seem instinctively, and a bit unconsciously, to be seeking a form of expression close to your own biological rhythms, your breath.

MILOSZ   Your remarks on breath rhythm are much like what Allen Ginsberg said at a recent poetry festival in Rotterdam. When explaining the revolution in American poetry to the audience, he pointed out that William Carlos Williams was the first to say that poetry should be written in everyday language and use the breath rhythm as its guide, rather than construct metrical units. This is what is known in Poland as the fourth system of versification. My feeling is that my own poetry is a poetry of incantation.

FIUT   What do you mean by incantation?

MILOSZ   A sensitivity to the rhythmic structure of a line even if I'm writing prose. This makes it hard for me—harder, I think, than for others—to write in a foreign language. A philosopher, a thinker, thinks first and then put his thoughts into words. But for me the meaning takes immediate shape in the rhythm of the line. I once asked Kenneth Rexroth, "Why did you praise the translations of my poetry? Ultimately, my work does not belong to the poetry of the English language. I made those translations with my students and never relied on my own knowledge of English syntax and idiom. That's why those translations are just so-so compared with translations done by people who had been speaking English since they were children." He said: "That's not true. Your translations are better, because you have an ear for one language. Anyone who has an ear for one language will have an ear for them all." I don't know if that's true or not; I'm just repeating what he said. All I know is how hard it is for a person so attuned to the incantational quality of the line to imagine writing in a foreign language.

FIUT Let's speak about your interest in English poetry. What form did your relationship to Eliot take?

MILOSZ It went through a long evolution. I discovered Eliot in Warsaw during the occupation. I found him very, very odd, very exotic. I did know about Eliot before the war, because my friend Józef Czechowicz had translated a few of his poems and had told me about the magazine *Criterion* and about Eliot. But I really didn't know his poetry, and so translating "The Waste Land" in occupied Warsaw had, I would say, a certain piquancy to it. The satire in that poem—ultimately it is a satiric poem, deeply ironic, or even sarcastic. Elements of "The Waste Land" are of course close to the catastrophists. To a great extent it's a poem of catastrophe, speaking as it does of the collapsing towers of London, Alexandria, Paris, and so on. The poem strikes the same chord Witkacy did in Poland between the wars. That vision is alien to me. And several other things were alien, too. Eliot is a poet of many allusions, full of cultural references to a variety of texts. "The Waste Land" is a compendium of quotations. All that struck me as very odd and very strange, because I didn't understand the various allusions. Later on, when I was abroad, I visited Eliot in his office in London. He was very nice and gave me a very warm reception. I saw him again in America, and later I translated some of his poems in addition to "The Waste Land": "Gerontion," "Journey of the Magi," "Burnt Norton," "The Hollow Men."

My attitude toward his poetry changed gradually, and to-day I'm not sure. Eliot is in limbo today. Eminent poets often go into a long limbo after they die. The situation now is that, for all his eminence, Eliot doesn't exist on the horizon of English poetry. I don't like Eliot's poetry when I hear recordings of him reading which brings out the poems' monotonous, Protestant structure. His linguistic sensitivity to English phrasing was extraordinary, but I don't know what Eliot's future is.

FIUT   What kindled your interest in English literature? It was not well known at the time. To the best of my knowledge, it was French literature that dominated among those with an interest in literature, and among snobs.

MILOSZ   Let's not overstate the case. American and English literature were very much part of Polish consciousness in the nineteenth century.

FIUT   Yes, in the nineteenth, but here I'm referring to the period between the wars.

MILOSZ   Well, let's skip Conrad, but Jack London was a tremendous presence in Poland at that time. We knew that literature primarily from its fiction.

FIUT   What about the poetry? Czechowicz won renown for being the first Polish translator of Eliot.

MILOSZ   That cannot be isolated from a certain general revolution that was taking place at the time. Czechowicz may have been the first swallow of that spring, but there was a revolution happening then, as we can see today. English is known everywhere now, and is much more widespread than French. That revolution started in the prewar period. And it seems to me that my interest in English poetry in some way coincides with it. My desire to study English coincides with what had started to happen a few years before the war. The last stage play I saw in Warsaw before the war was Thornton Wilder's *Our Town*. That play is deeply embedded in the tradition of American poetry, strongly connected, in my opinion, to Edgar Lee Masters's *Spoon River Anthology*. Curiously enough, I became friends with Thornton Wilder later on in America.

FIUT Were you reading Blake, Edgar Lee Masters, and Browning during the war?

MILOSZ Yes, but Browning was very difficult. I may have read a few poems from the *Spoon River Anthology*. And I had read a few of Blake's poems. Naturally, I have a different perspective on them today. But a shift really had taken place. English literature also infiltrated in ways that were entirely accidental. As I said, Jack London was translated. And now I'm living where Jack London came from. He was born here, and he attended the university where I teach.

The Image of the Poet

MILOSZ   It's possible to detect a single refrain in everything I've said here—namely, the desire not to appear other than I am. I have to admit this has bothered me my whole life, and still does. Naturally, each of us realizes that his own image of himself is one thing, and his image as reflected in the eyes of others is something else again. The two never entirely coincide, because we know more about ourselves than others do. When we use art, when we express ourselves with the written word, we are not completely sincere: that isn't possible. Someone even said that it's only through the lie of the novel, the fabrications of the novel or of poetry, that some truth can be told. To do it directly is impossible, simply because there's always some process of selection involved and we create an image consistent with our persona. Still, it's striking that we're so disturbed each time we're taken for something other than we are.

I think I've had special and ample opportunity in my career to be taken as other than I am. And the Nobel Prize is obviously one of those special circumstances. When I received the Nobel Prize, I lost all control over the situation. It drove me to despair to see how I appeared in other people's eyes. For example, I have always considered myself a rather hermetic poet, a poet for a certain, small audience. What happens when that sort of person becomes famous, celebrated, like a singer or a soccer star? Naturally, some basic misunderstanding occurs. We should be aware of the novelty of the situation. None of the so-called *poètes maudits*, none of the poets who staked out the territory of modern poetry in various languages, none of them probably ever appeared in a tuxedo to speak at a king's reception. Somehow I can't see that happening. None of them were popular, either, in the sense of being known to people who weren't involved with poetry. I use this as an example. But other examples could have been used, to shed different light on the subject.

In our conversations we've spoken a great deal about Polish affairs, different ways of being Polish, and so forth. It makes me extremely uneasy to be turned into a patriot-poet, a bard; somehow I wasn't prepared for that role. It is true, though, that historical circumstances have often wrung literary works out of me in which either I or some persona, usually a persona, spoke as the medium for certain collective feelings. My years in occupied Warsaw produced some poems of that type. I can't say that I like those poems; they show me in a posture that isn't in keeping with my temperament or my main interests. The play *Prologue*, which was commissioned by the Underground Theatre Council, was an idea that Wierciński put into my head. That was a social commission. And of course it's an expression of what underground Warsaw was feeling, more or less. But I realized very quickly that that was not for me. Naturally, if you take some of things I've written or published, you can create the image of an *engagé* poet. Recently, in traveling around America giving readings, I came up against a very difficult problem. When young poets ask me about political commitment—how politically committed should a poet be, and so on, since I have the aura of a poet who wrote anti-Nazi poems, the aura of a poet who fights for something—I don't really know how to deal with their questions. Their concept of political commitment is naïve.

I should also add that I've appeared in a variety of guises. Not many poets appear in such a variety of guises. When I found myself an émigré and wrote *The Captive Mind*, my poetry was completely unknown; no one knew that I was a poet, but I became known to many readers as the author of *The Captive Mind*. Then the fact that not all my poems can be translated—for example, those that use meter and rhyme are practically untranslatable—also distorts my image. Like Proteus, I appear to people in different incarnations. And that of course disturbed me. To a great extent, the course I took as soon as I was in the West, at the beginning of '51, was determined on the one hand by certain necessities—the writing of *The Captive Mind*—and on the other by the need to undo that image. I did not want to be tagged as a specialist in communist affairs, for example, even though I could have become a professor of political science. But I didn't want that. Writing *The Issa Valley* was an attempt to liberate myself from that image in the eyes of others.

FIUT Still, you did write several poems that corroborate that image. I'm thinking of works like "To the Politician" and "On the Death of Tadeusz Borowski."

MILOSZ Of course. The point here is that every so often I get an itch and I write something, a poem not destined for print, a private note. The poem "In Warsaw," written in '45, is an example. I certainly didn't intend that for print; it was a note I made under the influence of emotion. The same is true for "To a Politician" or "He Who Wrongs a Simple Man" or my recent poem "To Lech Wałęsa." I continually write that sort of thing, then afterward worry that it'll ruin my image as a philosophical poet.

FIUT Unquestionably, there's a pattern to all this. The constant changing of masks and roles is a principle detectable in your early poetry. Was that a conscious strategy right from the start, or did you choose that way of speaking intuitively and only later shape it into a purposefully applied poetics?

MILOSZ I just think that various demons or beings inhabit me; they take me over, and I regret it afterward.

FIUT   In that case, did you feel there's a contradiction between the way others see you and the form of poetic expression that prompts that perception?

MILOSZ   Let's be frank here. Certain objective criteria still do exist. I'll give you an example. Recently, when my book *Visions from San Francisco Bay* appeared in English, I received clippings of various reviews, most of which pained me because the book was seen as a collection of essays on California, loosely connected meditations on twentieth-century America, extremely European reflections. But when *The Nation* printed a review entitled "The Devil and Mr. Milosz," I said to myself: "Now, there's an intelligent man; he got the point." He understood that America, California, were actually pretexts, and that other important issues were at stake. He was very good at catching the book's basic drift. In this case there was both a certain false image based on appearances, and a reaching past appearances to some essence. And that, of course, is something that an author wants very much. Because if he is taken superficially, he experiences a form of distress that is difficult to name. Where does that desire for truth come from? It's hard to say. Where does that desire to appear as one truly is come from?

FIUT   What makes this all the more problematic is that your strategy as a writer tends to reveal as much as it conceals.

MILOSZ   Of course. Obviously.

FIUT   Going back to what you said about the role of a bard, I would like to point out that the idea of a national poet is completely out of date now. On the other hand, in Poland you have became a symbol of integrity, a moral authority.

MILOSZ   It's very good that you've raised that point. Me, a moralist—I find that a little humorous. Do you understand? I've never seen any especially moral principles in my work.

Rather, what I see is some miraculous dispensation preventing me from straying as far as some of my colleagues did. But, once again, that did not spring from strength of will or moral sense, and was—to a large extent—just the result of various factors, a set of very fortunate circumstances.

FIUT   I would argue with that. I think that both your entire body of work and your path in life demonstrates a fidelity to certain principles.

MILOSZ   That's false to the extent that it creates an image of me as a moralistic writer. And that, of course, wouldn't be true, because morality is not in fact a great concern of mine. And certainly I am also very far from my own ethical ideal, which both I and my work fall very short of. I see myself as a person who does not measure up to a certain ideal. I am not what I wanted to be. My life did not turn out the way I wanted it to be—lived according to high moral standards.

FIUT   Your work doesn't moralize but, directly and indirectly, it does express a certain moral stance. *Treatise on Morals* alone is evidence of that, not to mention other works.

MILOSZ   Could be. But for me that moral persona of mine is a little suspect. I've asked myself to what degree collective pressure, the temperature of the civilization in which I grew up—meaning Polish civilization—to what degree that imposes certain ethical standards. To what degree the concepts of good and evil are so rooted in it that everyone who writes gives voice to them in some way. Gombrowicz said that ethics are a writer's sex appeal. That may apply especially to the Polish culture in which we grew up, Gombrowicz and I. And that image of me as a heroic figure, especially when I was in Poland in 1981—well, I just happened not to disgrace myself so badly, because I was living abroad the whole time, actually from the end of '45 on. I was crafty, I stayed outside the country. Later I emigrated and did not disgrace myself then, either. But, oh, would I have disgraced myself if I had stayed in Poland! And then all of a sudden, in the Solidarity period, they made me into something of a moral authority. . . . I treat all that as a series of singular coincidences. It's very embarrassing to be held up as an example of integrity.

FIUT   In that case, how would you like to be seen by your readers? What would you think a satisfying image?

MILOSZ   It seems to me that I couldn't be satisfied by any image that was for mass consumption. I'd feel best with the image of a hermetic poet who sits home in his slippers and translates the Bible. That's another reason why I translated parts of the Bible. I had various motives, though, including one that's not to be sneezed at—that the image of the poet-scholar suits me very nicely. But I'm probably not a total bookworm. Certainly I find inspiration in books, but inspiration directly from life and my own ecstatic sense of life also play a very powerful role for me. Of course, the greatest constant is probably a conflict that started early, when I saw my work printed for the first time in *Żagary*, a supplement to the Wilno newspaper. I was horrified to think of regular guys buying that newspaper and finding themselves reading some utter foolishness. That conflict has been with me my whole life: I always wanted a small number of ideal readers, but then all of a sudden everything went topsy-turvy.

FIUT   But to some extent those various images are your own fault. It's paradoxical that you project yourself in various roles, change personas, but at the same time you desire to be seen quite unequivocally.

MILOSZ   No doubt. Books like *The Captive Mind* or *The Seizure of Power* present a completely different image from, let's say, *The Issa Valley* or my poetry. *The History of Polish Literature* gives another image, the philosophical essays yet another. On the one hand, all of a sudden young American poets are asking me what it means to be politically committed and how to write political poetry; on the other, I recently

wrote the introduction to a collection of works by Oskar Milosz in English in which I dealt with more or less the same
subjects as I had in *The Land of Ulro*—Blake, Swedenborg,
and so on. Where's the unifying principle, I ask?

FIUT   Maybe this is unity in variety?

MILOSZ   If we look at the life of someone who writes, we see
him constantly spinning a thread out of himself like a silk-
worm: he makes cocoons that lose their initial softness, becoming hard, almost crystalline structures in which he can no
longer live, and so he has to move out. And again he makes
a cocoon, and again it hardens and becomes alien to him.
This is a paradox worth noting, a general one that may apply
to other people as well. And another thing, going back to
what we said earlier, I can't call myself a Polish-speaking
Lithuanian, because that beast is really extinct now. In an
attempt to remain honest, I accentuate the specific features of
my "dichotomy" in nationality, which makes no sense to the
younger generations in Poland. They don't even know it exists. The textbooks don't say anything about Polish life and
culture in Lithuania, how it arose, what it was, what those
people felt, their sense of nationality. This can serve as a case
in point that certain historical complications do not lend
themselves to modern simplifications. Even to me a great many
things still seem unclear. In any case, the desire to communicate a true image of myself is a constant. I have to say—and
you'll probably agree with me—that some of my books have
that as their goal. If you take *Native Realm*, what else is it
but an attempt to reveal myself as truthfully as possible? *The
Land of Ulro* was another such attempt. If I had set myself
to it, I could have written a few other books like those, each
of which would have caught a somewhat different side
of me.

FIUT   Of all those various roles, the one that seems to irk
you most is the role of Polish bard. Why?

MILOSZ   There are a few points to my answer. First, for example, take the readings I gave in Chicago, or other places
with a lot of Poles, who come to see a famous Pole to lessen
their own feeling of inferiority. All my work is completely
alien to them. I grew up in Poland between the wars, at a
time when a small audience and isolated groups of poets were
the accepted pattern. When the Skamander poets gave readings for the first time in newly independent Poland in 1918,
they may have been availing themselves of a situation a little
like the one Solidarity created. In 1918 there was such a great
demand for the poetry of a free country that the Skamander
poets were carried along by that wave; no other poets achieved
the renown they did between the two wars. Though it's also
true that later on, right before the Second World War, Gał-
czyński did achieve something of the same sort, as the bard
of rightist magazine. That was a very curious cultural phenomenon, indicating a mass readership that was extremely
nationalistic.

Anyway, all the other little groups—the Vanguard and so
on—sat in their little cafés, miserable, penniless, unknown,
scorned. That was the accepted situation. A situation more
or less analogous to that of American poets who humbly accept their isolation. As I said recently at the University of
Virginia, 150,000 copies of my poetry have been printed in
Poland. Absolutely astounding!

So there's a basic sense of discomfort when the Polish-
American community suddenly starts applauding me. This new
situation clashes with the habits of my youth. And there's
also my knowledge of America, my knowledge of those people, and my constant, painful awareness of the cultural crudeness of Polish-Americans, a crudeness that can be explained
in various ways. It's probably that some civilizations do not
shape people so they have enough resilience to be able to stand
on their own two feet outside their ghetto. And then all of a
sudden *The New York Times*, I think it was, calls me "The
leading poet of the Polish diaspora"! That doesn't hold up in
the least! That's a complete travesty of the truth! It just isn't

so. If diaspora means the various Polish ghettos in the West, than I am not the poet of that diaspora.

And there's also the constant problem of my heroic image. Poland's models are romantic, and there is always a tendency to identify literature with life. No one ever says anything to me about *The Issa Valley* except: Thomas is you, of course? It's not read as a novel but as if it were all taken from life, as if all the characters were real, and all the events really happened. And as soon as I'm a bard, they drape me in the romantic, the heroic, and so forth.

FIUT   What was your experience of young audiences in Poland?

MILOSZ   There were moments of tension between me and those audiences of young people—for example, in a student club in Warsaw. The fever of the audience reminded me of Warsaw before the Uprising of '44. I had come there from America and I encountered that fever. . . . Who am I to beat the drum, when I'm aware of the reality of the situation? Who am I to grab the flag and lead people to the barricades?

FIUT   I wonder what image of you has been created by the translations of your poetry into English.

MILOSZ   I think it's quite good. A distinction has to be made here: I don't like it very much when critics seize on the most historical poems, particularly those written during the war, and create an image of me as a survivor of the Holocaust. That's false—the proportions are distorted. But as far as critics or readers go, there are others who have quite a good feeling for the issues in my poetry, and I am very happy that longer poems, like "From the Rising of the Sun" or *The Separate Notebooks*, met with appreciation in their English translations. I think that speaks well of the readers. In those poems my image is that of the meditative poet, which I find more comfortable and suitable. That's a far cry from the poet of action, the poet actively involved in history. I never wanted to be involved in history. Everything we've been talking about may be reduceable to my discomfort when my image is too noble.

FIUT   Or too simplified.

MILOSZ   Could be. Too noble and too simple. And I am neither noble nor simple.

Barańczak on Salee 128

180
America: 1 184, 187, 188, 189, 190, 192 // 207, 208

57-58 (194)

Chronology of writings → 57-58 (194)

Polyphony (Barańczak essay) 107, 114

Dry form : 173-4

Irony 117, 228, 231

Esse vs. existence : 127, 146, 180

Civic-minded poetry/rhetoric, important for Selected Poems, T. o. (witness) 132
also dates & circumstances of a poem important (witness)

Stl. Poems (witness) : art vs. life/reality : 135-139
include "Central Park": 152-3, Treatise on Morals 153
political art. not his calling: 158, Task 231, Tidings 234, L'accélération de l'histoire 235(?)

"brotherhood of the guild" (drawn to other poets) 111